THE POLICE AND
SOCIAL CONFLICT

THE POLICE AND SOCIAL CONFLICT

SECOND EDITION

Nigel G Fielding MA PhD AcSS

London • Sydney • Portland, Oregon

Second edition published 2005 by Glass House Press
Glass House Press is an imprint of Cavendish Puslishing Limited,
The Glass House, Wharton Street, London WC1X 9PX, United Kingdom
Telephone: + 44 (0)20 7278 8000   Facsimile: + 44 (0)20 7278 8080
Email: info@cavendishpublishing.com
Website: www.cavendishpublishing.com

Published in the United States by Cavendish Publishing
c/o International Specialized Book Services,
5824 NE Hassalo Street, Portland,
Oregon 97213-3644, USA

Published in Australia by Cavendish Publishing (Australia) Pty Ltd
45 Beach Street, Coogee, NSW 2034, Australia
Telephone: + 61 (2)9664 0909   Facsimile: + 61 (2)9664 5420
Email: info@cavendishpublishing.com.au
Website: www.cavendishpublishing.com.au

First edition published 1991 by The Athlone Press Ltd

British Library Cataloguing in Publication Data

Nigel Fielding
The police and social conflict
1. Police–Great Britain 2. Police-community relations–Great Britain 3. Social conflict
I. Title
363.2'0941

Library of Congress Cataloguing in Publication Data
Data available

ISBN-10: 1-90438-523-0
ISBN-13: 978-1-904-38523-3

Typeset in Shannon by Compuscript Limited, Shannon, Ireland
Printed and bound in Great Britain

13579108642

For Jessica

Series editors' preface

The *Contemporary Issues in Public Policy* series aims to publish books which provide highly informed and comprehensive analyses of topical policy issues. It has grown out of an earlier project by the same editors, *Conflict and Change in Britain: A New Audit,* which looked set to founder when its publishers, The Athlone Press, ceased to exist on the retirement of its mainstay staff. We have been fortunate in finding, in the GlassHouse Press imprint of Cavendish Publishing, a new publisher keen to relaunch the series with a fresh steer. The main change will be a greater emphasis of the new series on cross-national, comparative perspectives, both in their own right, as crucial for a better understanding of the issues under scrutiny, and for the light they shed on the situation in the UK.

Three developments have given added urgency to a more comparative perspective. First, the past few years have seen the quickening pace of globalisation and the engagement of nation-states in increasingly complex supra-national formations. Without subscribing to the view that this renders a national focus redundant – in some ways national frameworks have been strengthened by, for example, devolution – the shortcomings of a purely national focus are, in most cases, all too apparent. Secondly, the proliferation of international agencies and supra-national political and trade entities have led to data mountains of such variable quality that only the truly expert can make sense of the terrain. Thirdly, and to some extent consequently, a newfound populism and impatience with hard-won expertise have become increasingly evident in most media and political representations of public policy issues. Against the appeal of gut reaction and electoral advantage, academic scholarship is all too often consigned to the margins or dismissed out of hand. The need for measured and dispassionate weighing of the evidence and theoretical clarity is all the greater.

The focus of this, the second book in the new series, has never escaped political and public contention. Police and policing are symbolically and practically at the very core of the State; they represent one of the few institutions charged with the legitimate use of force in the service of the State and, more abstractly, the public; they are highly visible and often contested by those who challenge how that force can and should be deployed; and they are beset by endemic contradictions. Chief amongst those contradictions is the mandate of the police simultaneously to protect, reassure and control the populace, a mandate that cannot but engender abiding dilemmas of policy and practice.

Although there were important forerunners (for example, Westley, 1953, 1956, 1957), the conventional history of police research traces its origins back to the social anthropological work of Banton (1964) which concentrated on the control of police/public relations. The theme of his *The Policeman in the Community* was how conflict was managed so that a potential for trouble was addressed and generally avoided, and it was to be a theme borne into ever more vexed times in which the police/public relation began to show signs of strain. It is a mark of that transformation that the book appeared at the same time as a Royal Commission was established to address the increasingly manifest troubles of policing.

During the next two decades, the police/public relation was not only marked by the substantial disaffiliation of large sections of society but also affected by a polity seriously divided on sectarian lines. It is no wonder that Reiner (2000a) characterised the social science of policing in that period as the conflict stage in the history of police research, a stage marked by radical conceptualisations and a generally hostile perspective on the nature of contemporary policing. But no trend is without its counter, and 'appreciative' studies of the police continued, although they were studies that were necessarily obliged to contend with the weight of structural critiques of the police enterprise and its alleged politicisation.

Banton's achievement had been to make the social science of policing empirical. It could not, of course, have come about without a new willingness of the police to afford researchers access to their working world, itself arguably a consequence of growing concern at the way in which the police went about their work. Yet, whatever the cause, the knowledge base for our analysis of policing has grown dramatically, and it is interesting to consider whether it is this, or the evolution of the polity and the consequent changes in the police organisation, that has been chiefly responsible for a social science of policing that is less strident and more considered than the somewhat starkly divided field of the 1970s and 1980s.

It would be wrong to conclude that internal divisions and conflicts have all subsided and that police research can settle into a more cosy future. That would be a view as narrowly led by the conditions of the times as had been the earlier, more conflictual perspectives that once marked the field. The contemporary world of policing is multiplex and nuanced: there is policing *by* government (the public police), policing *through* government (partnership policing), and police *beyond* government (private policing). The central activity – regulation – and the forms of behaviour that are its object (whether they are branded *hooliganism, anti-social behaviour, riot* or *'public event management situation'*) remain ineluctable features of society. The conflicts that inform and configure policing endure, and the trick is to tease out their pattern despite a natural but misleading urge to believe that the contemporary is always the new.

Compressing all this intricacy into a lucid analysis requires patience, skill and knowledge. Nigel Fielding is one of the most experienced and thoughtful commentators on policing matters, and his radically revised book brings up to date and distils an extraordinary breadth and depth of understanding of the complex, diverse and evolving character and context of policing in Britain in the early 21st century. As much an essay on the progress of conflict in Britain, *The Police and Social Conflict* is firmly anchored in broad social theory and a well-developed comparative and historical sensibility that allows him to qualify what are the sometimes unbalanced (and on occasion apocalyptic) pronouncements of others. Fielding is aware of how very difficult it is to come to simple conclusions about the nature of policing in a diverse and changing society, and he has managed to pick his way fastidiously amongst what are often tendentious and opposing positions. The regulation of conflict, it becomes apparent, must frequently be a matter of compromise, negotiation and discretion, and it can yield paradoxical outcomes where one set of police or political goals must give way to another. In all this, and because it obliges us to consider policing much more thoughtfully, *The Police and Social Conflict* is to be welcomed indeed.

David Downes and Paul Rock
London School of Economics
December 2005

Introduction

The police work at the heart of social conflict, and always will. Themes of endurance and recurrence seem quaint and blinkered in present times, when few days pass without the declared obsolescence of yet another 'eternal reality'; but social institutions do not change as rapidly as versions of computer software. Calling poverty, xenophobia and religious bigotry 'social exclusion' does not make them any less the age-old sites of social conflict that they have always been. The thesis of this book is as obstinate in its new edition as it was in the first: the police are inextricably central, not only to society's response to social conflict, but to the terms in which it is understood. As long as there is society there is conflict, and as long as there is conflict there will be the police.

In the past the police were unsubtle, even violent and crude, in their alignments in respect of the lines of schism, naively and instinctively standing with established interests, although the history of police unionism tells a more complex story, and one that will be sketched in later. However, the police have marched a long way in the last two decades, and the terms, if not the sentiment, in which a former Metropolitan Police commissioner, Sir Robert Mark, depicted the post-1945 trend of social and political relations, already seem to be echoes as if from the roar of a naive and blundering dinosaur. In the foreword to a book on police accountability, Sir Robert claimed that since 1945 'liberty under the law' had been extended to 'the freedom to steal and to misbehave ... with a high degree of immunity from any adverse judicial consequences' (Oliver, 1987: viii). Top-ranking police are these days more apt privately to speak as academics do, and publicly pronounce as do politicians. Where the vantage point of the 1980s offered a view dominated by political and industrial strife, and by the brute force of the police response to it, this second edition is informed by two decades in which the 'enemy within' has become the 'enemy without'. Our compelling threats are international terrorism and international organised crime, not the miners, steel workers and student militants. In recent years, conflict involving the police is as likely to have been with government and other 'partner' agencies as with the public, and was played out in the concealed forum of bureaucratic forms of confrontation rather than on the picket line. Communities protest at receiving too little of the police resource, not too much. Mundane crime has fallen, but serious crime, physical and sexual violence, is up. No one now sees such crime as an inarticulate, but political, act, as the Black Panthers once did in respect of assaults against whites. Industrial and political disputes are muted, and there is a sense that our contemporary ruptures are not with those wanting a bigger share of the cake, but with those who want to ship the cake abroad to manufacture it with lower wage-costs, or dictate its ingredients according to religious strictures.

If the lines of division within our polity and community are increasingly blurred it is not a sign that humankind no longer distinguishes between us and them. The lines are simply being drawn along new fissures. Class as a frame of reference may largely be gone, or at any rate have been obscured by a perceived affluence founded more on borrowing and the ever-decreasing cost of magical technologies rather than on any improvement in the share of national wealth held by the poor. But our gaze has moved off the estates and the dole queue. Ethnic tensions likewise endure, but are confined and local, and seem increasingly archaic set against a kaleidoscopically eclectic popular culture and hearteningly high rate of interracial marriage. We draw together much more than in the past when we 'do social control', because our worst 'enemies' seem unambiguously external: the international gangster, the 'economic migrant', the alien terrorist. These are the targets to whom we increasingly direct our police. When we do focus our gaze on our own divisions, we are as likely to find ourselves on the metaphorical picket line as the outcasts. Our contemporary set-piece confrontations are over the price of vehicle fuel (the 'fuel blockades' of autumn 2000), the juggernaut of multinational capitalism (the annual May Day protests, the demonstrations against the G8 summits), the building of new roads across our diminishing countryside, the banning of hunting with hounds. Indeed the polyglot jumbling of sectional interests is well-represented by any of these; the followers of the Countryside Alliance are as likely to be rural craftspeople and middle-class libertarians as they are toffs wearing scarlet; but a styrofoam cup will still break as conclusively as an old bottle, if in less predictable ways, and the fact that society ruptures on different lines does not mean that our first and last recourse is not to the police, nor does it deny the substantial continuities in the way that they respond.

The statement by Mark, earlier quoted, also declared that, because the courts are 'faced with controversy where there should be unanimity', they cannot effectively deter or punish, so the police have increasingly had to project themselves into the public order arena. Their role in containing disorder has become pre-eminent by default: '

there is no other agency in our society capable of achieving it.' While Mark's claims were ahistorical in the extreme and revealed a daunting ignorance of the complex interweaving of the parts of the criminal justice system, they did lead him to a blunt statement of the boundary over which the conflict between police and dissenters is contested. The containment of wrongdoing is most problematic, he argued, 'in the field of public disorder arising from political dissent, industrial disputes, racial tension and mindless hooliganism'. Leaving aside the definitional complexity of these categories, he makes the important observation that '[p]olice behaviour in dealing with the latter will always provoke strong criticism if applied to those involved in the former. Quite simply, if police are to keep down the level of public objection to their policies and practices, they have to make sure they do not treat the organised working-class and the vocal middle-class in the same way they do the 'mindless hooligan'. It is a most revealing statement of the police perspective on social conflict. It is highly pragmatic, providing a crude typification of groups likely to challenge public order, which no doubt serves police in their need to make rough and ready decisions about how to respond to particular circumstances. Implicit in it is the core belief in a 'professional' police, independent from the quarrels beneath them.

It is a perspective with a lineage. In the 1840s, the early years of provincial police forces, riots came about as attempts to arrest thieves or other miscreants were opposed by people suspicious of efforts to impose order by police from outside the locale. Likewise resisted were the strike-breaking function and political surveillance. Embourgeoisement has heightened acceptance of police practices that do not normally weigh on the working population, but rather on marginal groups, such as the homeless. That the post-Second World War consensus is changing, and old alliances breaking down, is not the object of speculation it was at the time of this book's first edition. There is no longer any doubt that mainstream politics is about the dismantling of the Welfare State. Old certainties have given way to new ambiguities. Today's 'hooligan' may be a stockbroker, and the picket may be self-employed. We cannot settle whether it is the times that are changing, or our perspective, or both at once; but we can look again at our recent history, and the role of our police in the conflicts that have made our society, and wonder if all this is really new. Is crisis really society's steady state?

Mark's concern over a changing and threatening revision of our 'liberty under the law' helps us to recognise how central to these matters the police perspective is. Historians have charted the rise of the police at the expense of the magistracy, but in terms of visibility this could today be extended to their profile relative to the senior judiciary. We might recall the words of a parliamentary committee's report to Home Secretary Sir Robert Peel before the formation of the police:

> It is difficult to reconcile an effective system of police with that perfect freedom of action and exemption from interference which are the great privileges and blessings of society in this country, and your committee think that the forfeiture or curtailment of such advantages would be too great a sacrifice for improvements in police, or facilities in the detection of crime, however desirable in themselves, if abstractedly considered.
> (Quoted in Evans, 1974: 46)

The committee was thinking in absolutes, and pragmatic needs soon predominated, but the period since can readily be seen as a series of battles consistent with that conflict.

However, is 'conflict' an adequate typification of the contacts between police and public? Does our notion of conflict contain only public order, or law enforcement? Is the distinction merely a convenient heuristic without adequate empirical underpinnings? If public order is our chief referent in discussing social conflict, does it include only major disturbances, or the pervasive application of police conceptions of normality at the neighbourhood and town centre level?

These questions are initially pursued here by examining popular notions of crisis and conflict, and their relation to the analysis of conflict in policing. It is argued that we too readily see difference from past times, rather than continuities brought by the rootedness of social institutions. In Chapter 2 this is illustrated by the relation of historical events to the mythology of a 'golden age' of policing. A distinction between public order policing and routine order maintenance informs Chapters 3 and 4. Chapter 3 concentrates on the set-piece major confrontations that provoke paramilitary responses, while Chapter 4 considers conflicts in the everyday policing role that are more pervasive, if less spectacular. Responses distinctive of these two demands are examined in Chapter 5 and their implications for accountability to the public and civil liberties in Chapter 6. The book concludes with a commentary on the future.

Contents

Figures and tables

1. Policing and social conflict

The perception that society is 'in crisis' often features in both journalistic and social scientific discourse. Perceptions of 'crisis' implicitly have at their core some notion of society's normal state. If existing arrangements differ from the presumed normal state, commentators are apt to see a 'crisis'. Since normal society involves a balance of interests, society tends always to be in crisis from the perspective of the ideologically-committed. Narrowly conceived critical perspectives tend to elevate collective values, and narrowly conceived neo-conservative perspectives tend to elevate the value of the individual. The notion of 'crisis' as an endemic feature of society is harder to sustain when political systems are seen as necessarily seeking some reconciliation of values both of categorical equity and individualised justice. This perspective helps us to recognise as inevitable the tensions that arise in pursuing a temperate treatment for all people, as individuals and as instances of collective social categories. If these tensions are inevitable, so is social conflict. Using the language of degree and increment reserves the language of 'crisis' for extreme circumstances – a dictatorial government, a proven conspiracy, a corrupt constabulary.

There are dangers in playing the crisis card for radicals and reformers. To engender public engagement such groups may wish to exaggerate problems. Often the result is more power for the established order, as when the late Lord Scarman's assessment that the Brixton riots had been of a scale that brought Britain to the brink of total collapse was used to justify equipping police with new armaments. The truer vision is that if one comes down too hard on any socio-economically pressured community it takes little to provoke disorder; but power is better prepared for the apocalypse than are the weak, and is always poised to profit from a crisis that can be depicted as resolvable by more repression.

It is worthwhile reminding ourselves how familiar, and conventional, the language of crisis has become. Rather than being endemic, longstanding conflicts and problems of disorder are represented as an alarming contingency, an incipient cataclysm. These alarmist representations are more apparent at a distance. Thus one 1970s commentator claimed that Britain's 'closely woven social fabric' was 'now subject to growing stress ... And the conditions and forces which make for strain, tension and division show every sign of increase throughout the society'. Almost everything was implicated.

> Rapid technological change, ceaselessly modifying the shapes both of our economic and social structures, creates inherent instability; whilst in the foreground are the consequences of our immediate problems: anxiety and insecurity bred of economic decline and monetary inflation, together with a declining faith in our political management that also serves to devalue the political system. In this climate of unease and disaffection, extra-constitutional and extra-legal uses of power become more frequent – tactics all the easier to deploy in a society where both individual values and communal systems of self-regulation lose hold. And usage serves to normalise, if not to legitimise disorder. Yet though political and economic issues take the limelight, there may be more deep-seated, long-term causes of insecurity in the social fabric: losses of meaning in family and community life; traditional values, beliefs and sources of authority all giving ground; a culture of commerce gaining sway, enshrining the anarchic values of individual acquisition, individual gratification; and western man divided – crucified, you might say – across his desires to achieve in the world's terms of success and his growing alienation from them ... In this climate, common purposes and consensus become more difficult to achieve ... The multifarious components of society pursue their own paths, often with intransigence. (Brown, 1975: 95)

This cosmic catalogue of travails moves from topics dimly relevant to Brown's subject (community policing) onward into existential imponderables. It was written in *1975*. Can things truly have developed from there without the apocalypse, or is social conflict society's normal state?

Social conflict has held a central place in social theory since its earliest days. Even in theory preoccupied with social integration, conflict motivates the problematic. For example, Parsons (1952) dealt with what is needed to procure 'shared value orientations' and the 'fulfillment of role expectations'. His work can be regarded as a sustained attempt to determine means by which tendencies to conflict are resolved, obliging him to consider situations where 'value-patterns' are not shared and expectations are unfulfilled. As Rex (1981: 2) noted, because Parsons's theory was based upon the concept of 'action', his methodological individualist position must negotiate what happens when differently motivated actors pursue competing goals, creating conflict. For Weber, too, the term 'conflict' refers to action 'oriented intentionally to carrying out the actor's will against the resistance of the other party or parties' (1968, vol I: 38). Moral or legalistic argument represents conflict's first stage. If ends truly conflict, its purpose will

> not be simply to arrive at *the* moral truth but rather at that interpretation of the relevant morality which allows for the attainment of each party's goals.

It will consist in special pleading and rationalisation by each party on his own behalf coupled with an attempt to expose the dishonest or ideological nature of the other's position. (Rex, 1981: 12)

The first stages of conflict are, then, verbal and ideological. Conflict may be resolved when one party's moral or cognitive definitions of the situation prevail or where the parties agree they have made mistakes; but, if this does not end the conflict, sanctions will escalate, taking passive or active form. Resolution may occur when the cost of engaging in the struggle becomes greater than any foreseeable gain. Relationships between the parties will have changed and power centres relocated. This can be seen in the jockeying for position between police and magistracy, and police and police authorities, which began in the 19th century. An even more risky possibility is where the party that gained what it sought, senses the prospect of further gains and demands wholly new terms. At an individual level this could apply to cases successfully showing police practice to have been unlawful where the complainant goes on to seek damages or compensation, but such an end to conflict is rare in conflicts of collectivities in the law enforcement arena. The acquiescence accompanying conflicts so conclusively resolved that one side has 'won', does not last. A more normatively structured situation comes to pass, in the process Parsons (1952) called the 'twofold binding-in of the social relation'. The process can be seen as recurrent. Viewed as a social relation, social conflict is indeed enduring.

This is not to suggest that dominant and subordinate groups will always maintain their relative position. Those most alarmed by a theory that implies the persistence of conflict, may well be those who stand to lose the most if one of its outcomes, social change, is brought about. Those who profit from the *status quo* may feel that all they want is a quiet life, but, however passive, they are parties to social conflict too. There is a difference between conflict and random disorder. Conflict is seldom 'mindless'.

The history of policing offers many instances of the enduring character of social conflict. Manwaring-White maintains that it is 'a history which all along the line has been modified by parliamentary and police reaction to violent disturbances – just as it is today' (1983: 3). She notes such events as the riots of starving field-hands in 1830 that resulted in three hangings and 400 deportations, the great electoral reform riots of 1831, the 1839 Birmingham riots when the police and army charged the crowd with drawn cutlasses, the baton and mounted cavalry charges against Fabians at Trafalgar Square in 1884, the riots and looting during the 1919 police strike in Liverpool when three warships were diverted to the city, and the confrontations of the Depression years, including the hundred-plus baton charges against demonstrators between August 1931 and December 1932. From that perspective conflict is enduring, and the embrace by police of CS gas, Taser guns and electronic surveillance is consistent with what has gone before.

It has to be emphasised that, if we are to see such historically dramatic events as 'crises', that terminology has to be reserved for them, rather than applied to an endemic condition of society. The divisions or cleavages suggested by dramatic social conflict are mediated by integrating factors that hold at bay the kind of rupture implied by the dictionary sense of 'crisis'. Manwaring-White reminds us that the period leading up to the First World War was known as 'the great Unrest', with over a thousand strikes in 1913 and the formation in Ireland of citizens' militias by Nationalists and Loyalists; but the war changed this. Social conflict is not inexorable, nor does it develop in linear fashion. The relations between its causes are variegated and interactive. During the war, Home Rule for Ireland was shelved. All attention was focused on the external threat. The Home Secretary was able to extend his control over the police and the police also increased their power. The conditions under which the pre-war forms of conflict had proceeded were altered. The Home Secretary became closely involved in policy direction, co-ordinating operations and fixing the distribution of police. Centralisation increased, capacities for managing conflict were extended; but conflict endured. Change was patchy, there was backsliding, resistance, indecision.

In Bittner's (1980) analysis the capacity legitimately to use force is the core of the police role. His argument is not founded in the struggle over equitable distribution of material resources, but in the struggle to achieve a pacific civil society. Arguing that the search for peace by peaceful means is a culture trait of modern civilisation, he contrasts this with the *Pax Romana* that sought to 'subdue the haughty by force'. The modern commitment to abolish 'the traffic of violence' has ultimately been checked by the need to deploy responsive (reactive) force against provocation and illegitimate attacks. Responsive force is thus legitimate, but constrained (Bittner, 1980: 36). Force is authorised in self-defence, provided all else has been tried, including retreat. Coercive power is, in its second form, acceptable when exercised by specifically deputised persons against named others, for example, in respect of prison officers and mental hospital staff. The power is legitimated by court orders and is acceptable only in the degree required to implement the judicial order. The third legitimate use of responsive force is through the police. In contrast to the first two it is essentially unrestricted. Bittner invites us to cease looking at police work as mainly to do with law enforcement and crime control. He argues that 'it makes much more sense to say that the police are nothing else than a mechanism for the distribution of situationally justified force in society' (Bittner, 1980: 39). This mechanism enables the police to play a key role in maintaining the *status quo*.

In practice, police efforts are unlikely to be equal, either between bodies of law, social groups or jurisdictions. The exercise of discretion is inevitable in a society where resources are limited. Even with a police force equal in size to the population policed it would be impossible to prosecute every law. The police have to decide priorities, and that is, of course, a question of politics. Setting action in relation to particular conditions is an exercise of discretion familiar to every officer. Speaking after the Brixton riots, former chief constable John Alderson said 'in order to enforce your law you end up with ... £4 million worth of property burnt to the ground. You may think you're being efficient in enforcing your laws ... but look at it, the place is burning around you ... I mean, do you enforce the Litter Act in the Mile End Road the same way as you would do in Belgravia?' (quoted in Kinsey and Young, 1982: 121). Such judgments are inherently political: '[t]o argue against the prosecution of ganja smoking in Brixton does not mean that demands for racial discrimination in working men's clubs in Leeds are to be met' (Kinsey and Young 1982: 122). Similar police dilemmas were expressed prior to introduction of the ban on hunting with hounds in 2005, with police doubtful they had the resources to control extensive civil disobedience by those determined to continue fox hunting.

A copy of any newspaper will reveal conflicts whose bases lie in class, ethnicity, gender and sexual politics, region, nation, employment status, age and ideology. Conflict is endemic. Technological innovation, environmental pollution, economic uncertainty, fear of international terrorism, and the break-up of customary community norms may all engender conflict. The major problems of any age inevitably direct attention to their most dramatic form of expression.

Yet the danger is that while our attention is naturally drawn to spectacular public order disturbances, intrusive governance, and policing that seems more biased than discretionary, we neglect the more insidious forms of low-level conflict whose effect is more pervasive. In particular we neglect *institutionalised* forms of conflict. The term 'institutionalised' refers to subtle processes that have been distorted in popular usage, to the point where, in its most familiar application, to ethnic and racial relations, the term adds nothing at all to the word 'racism' in the phrase 'institutional racism'. In policing, institutional racism can include the structured inattention the police apply to the demands of blacks in poor inner-city neighbourhoods for more effective crime control. It can speak of the different police deployment figures between adjacent areas with different standards of living. It can refer to the tendency to regard groups of blacks on the street as the problem rather than as the community; but too often it simply means that individual officers are colour-prejudiced. While this is undoubtedly an obnoxious and real problem it is trivial compared to the fact that the police continue to allocate officers to given geographical areas on formulae set at a point in the past when it was accepted that middle-class communities had a greater right to expect that their interests be protected than did poorer communities. One hears little about such institutional discrimination, even following the Metropolitan Police Commissioner's acceptance in 1999 that his force was indeed 'institutionally racist'.

Similarly, institutionalised discrimination can be seen in the balance in law between offences against property and against the person. English law has been keen to protect rights to property, and relatively casual in protecting the safety of the person. These points coalesce in the continuing complaints of ethnic minorities that attacks on them are treated less seriously by the police. Police deployment figures are relevant, as are the legal powers under which the police operate, and their assumptions about the warrant for and character of harassment. The law's perspective, or the intentions of its legislators and judicial interpreters, can frame another element in institutional discrimination. Whether an offence can be prosecuted by police or requires a complainant, and which offences attract a right to jury trial as opposed to summary judgments, have effects that shape the official response to a particular social problem, such as spouse-abuse or being a person 'reasonably suspected' of being about to commit an offence. While some behaviours are regulated, not all are regulated equally.

Institutionalised discrimination, by definition, implicates the system-wide, macro-level of selection and discretion as essentially political choices affecting large social groups. Critics of police institutionalised racism generally do not go far enough. Often such criticism fixes at the level of occupational culture ('canteen culture'); but it is doubtful that the key players can be identified in a personified form. Institutionalised discrimination is a product of decisions taken in several settings, in Parliament, in the courts, in the administrative settings of the state, whose consequences may be unforeseen and unintended. Those decisions are informed by a sense of history, of predilections determined by the inspiration of common law and re-interpreted and re-applied at particular, often non-comparable, historical junctures. Another tack in blaming occupational culture is the idea that the racism that affects the perspective of police officers is part of wider working-class culture. 'The police are not an island of prejudice in a sea of working-class tolerance' (Kinsey and Young, 1982: 125). Notwithstanding the complexity of institutional discrimination, the police do have some power relative to it. The police are not demure in commenting on given laws or policies affecting their interests. If it had been a priority they could have lobbied for law to ameliorate institutional discrimination instead of waiting to be dragged to the issue by the Macpherson Inquiry, during which the Commissioner insisted his force was not 'institutionally racist', accepting the judgment only when it appeared in the Inquiry report, and then only on the definition given in the report. While it would be wrong to imagine that social conflict could be softened by change only at the legal level, it is worthwhile considering how many outbreaks of disorder begin as a result of police action.

It may be that amelioration in the forms of institutional discrimination could prevent riots and disturbances. In any case, contemporary protest has largely taken less dramatic forms in respect of racial tensions and problems of discrimination. The greater willingness of police to acknowledge the problem has had some impact. The extension of civilianisation and the Community Support Officer schemes introduced in 2003 have been marked by substantial increases in the proportion of police employees drawn from ethnic minorities. While figures remain modest relative to other occupations, the trend is the first positive development in a long history of the police missing ethnic minority recruitment targets.

There is longstanding evidence of racial stereotypes in targeting black populations. During the 1970s, reports from the Community Relations Commission, Institute for Race Relations, Runnymede Trust, National Council for Civil Liberties, and West Indian Standing Conference all documented the effects of racism on housing, employment, policing and welfare. Ethnic minorities are in a situation of multiple disadvantage. They are at the bottom of the class structure and are disproportionately affected by unemployment, bad housing and inferior facilities. For many years they suffered the application of the 'sus' (suspected person) procedure contained in the Vagrancy Act 1824. In 1975, over half the 30,000 people arrested on 'sus' were black (Hain, 1979: 5). Those circumstances epitomized, for a generation of minority people, the coincident effect of obsolete law and dubious street-policing practices on promoting institutional discrimination. Police long defended their practices by reference to the crime rate in black communities. For the first time, in 1994, the Home Office published an ethnic breakdown of stops/searches. Nationally, 110,522 out of 441,905 people searched came from ethnic minorities. In 1993/94, 132,565 whites were searched in London, compared with 95,751 black or Asian people. Over 40% of Londoners stopped were black or Asian, while only 20% of London's population was non-white ('Police accused of racism in use of search powers', *Guardian*, 5 December 1994). Earlier statistics suggested black prisoners were worryingly over-represented in a dossier of 163 alleged miscarriages of justice, 23% of which involved black defendants (*Guardian*, 11 November

1992). To those who see the state as a monolith designed to secure ruling-class interests, sectionally biased enforcement is of secondary concern. For them, policing is less concerned with crime than with the extension of surveillance, manipulation and coercion. That approach underplays the reality of 'mundane crime' and over-emphasises the high-profile policing of strikes and public disorder. Such an approach is blind to internal conflict within and between state agencies, and minority experiences of victimisation at the hands of other disprivileged people are of marginal concern. This stance also has difficulty accommodating the emergence of self-help organisations and community initiatives directed at confronting the gun and knife culture amongst minority (and white) urban youth.

Police stereotyping by ethnicity has been at its most manifest in the practice of on-street stop and search, which has periodically been used to exert control in the absence of clear grounds for intervention. In law, the officer must have a 'reasonable suspicion' that the person may be about to commit an offence, but 'reasonableness' is determined by the officer on the spot. One might assume that most stops are for 'going equipped' – having tools to break into property – or 'weapon carrying', but the statistical reality is that most on-street searches ending in arrest are for drugs possession, mostly small amounts of cannabis. More worrying is that most stops and searches do not result in arrest at all. There are also large variations between forces, suggesting stops may be frivolously conducted ('fishing expeditions').

A main reason for the Police and Criminal Evidence Act 1984 was the finding of the Scarman Inquiry that a major factor in riots was hostility and resentment in the black community at the excessive rate of stops, particularly of young black males. Initially, researchers related simple numbers of stops to simple population percentages of different ethnic groups, giving a clear picture of disproportionality, with blacks being stopped more often than their share of population would suggest; but there are methodological problems. For example, the proportion of population from particular ethnic groups is usually measured by census data. The longer it is from the last census the more out of date that information will be. To get round that, Young's research in Islington (Young, 1989) interviewed residents about their experience of stop and search and recorded their ethnic group, which gave black males aged 16–24 a factor of 40 times the average likelihood of being stopped by police; same age-group white males had a factor of 33 times the average, and black males aged 25–34 a factor of 29 times the average. However, this assumes all residents are equally mobile and go out in public at the same rate, so are equally available to be stopped; but young people tend to be out in public more than the elderly. If most of the elderly in an area are white, but the age groups are more evenly distributed in the black population, this will depress the availability of whites to be stopped, relative to that of blacks. Also, some boroughs are primarily residential and others have more mixed uses, giving more locations where people may be stopped, and pulling in people from other areas whose ethnicity may not match the information available about the proportion of the different ethnicities actually living in the area.

We have noted the police justification of on-street practices by reference to ostensibly higher crime rates amongst minority ethnic groups. Research arising from the Macpherson Inquiry tested the racial dimension of on-street stops and offered an answer to the propensity issue. Although the research was a national study, two things mean that the prime interest is the situation in London. First, the great majority of the country's black population lives there – some 62% (the next largest concentration is in the West Midlands, with 9%). Secondly, while the national figure for the rate of stop and search was 22 per thousand population (1998 figures, all racial groups), the London rate was 51 per thousand. Thus, stops involving black people in London have a major effect on the figures for the country as a whole. The research (FitzGerald *et al*, 2002) established that the comparison of crime rates with the ethnic mix of the local population, long the basis of claims both of criminal propensity on the part of minorities and of bias in street stops, was misleading for several reasons, not least because of the non-resident population represented in the street stop figures. In some areas people from outside the area accounted for most of those searched.

The two main influences on the ethnic patterns in the figures turned out not to be ethnicity *per se*, but age, and the extent to which different groups featured among the suspects described in crime reports – see Figures 1a, 1b, 1c, 1d. The figures compare the pattern of searches on different ethnic groups in London with overall population (Figures 1a and 1b), the secondary school population (Figure 1c) and crime suspect ethnicities (Figure 1d). Comparing Figures 1a and 1b shows the basis on which disproportionality has usually been calculated. It confirms the extent to which, measured in this way, black people are over-represented in search figures in relation to their presence in the population. Yet Figure 1c shows that this over-representation reduces considerably when age is taken into account, since there are variations in the age structures of different ethnic groups. In many areas white people will constitute a much higher than average proportion of the older population, while ethnic minorities constitute a very much higher than average proportion of the youth population than is apparent from figures for the population as a whole. In over half of the 32 London boroughs, ethnic minorities account for 45% or more of the school age population, and in some boroughs they constitute a majority of the young people in the area. The

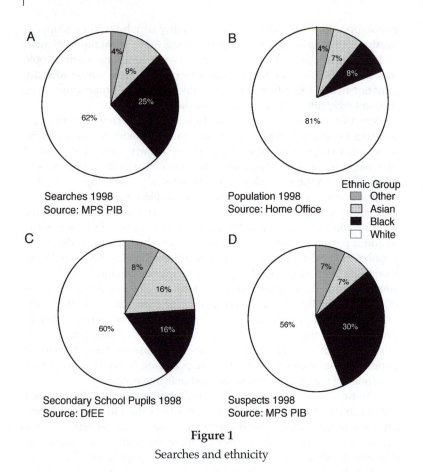

Figure 1

Searches and ethnicity

picture is very different when we control for age than the impression we get from crude ethnic statistics. In fact the closest match for the ethnic composition of the search figures is with descriptions given to the police of suspects of crime (Figure 1d). Here, significantly more black people were being reported as suspects than the police were actually stopping.

FitzGerald *et al* (2002) also showed that when officers acted entirely on their own discretion blacks were no more likely than whites to be stopped and that blacks were arrested at the same rate as whites following searches. In other words, the data on suspects suggests that the police were actually using their discretion *to avoid* stopping black people. This, of course, does not say anything about the situation that may have prevailed in the past, nor make the practice any more welcome in minority communities. However, one last finding from the study is very important. It found that all population groups, including young ethnic minority people who had been stopped frequently, actually supported the need for on-street stop and search in the pursuit of crime. Their complaint was about the manner in which the police conducted the stop. Many feel that the best way of achieving more sensitive treatment, and other improvements in police/ethnic minority relations, would be by boosting the numbers of ethnic minority police, and by seeing them promoted into senior roles in the force. In 1998, the year of the research, there were 124,798 police in England and Wales, some 2,483 (2%) of whom were from ethnic minorities, well under half the ethnic minority percentage of the country's population. On 31 March 2001 there were 125,519 police officers in England and Wales, of whom 2,975 were from an ethnic minority (2.4% of the total).

A more empirically sound perspective than theories representing police as part of an integrated, monolithic state interest would emphasise relative police autonomy, an autonomy necessary to advance reforms to ameliorate social conflict. For cultural, organisational and ideological reasons the police have a substantial degree of autonomy both from power elites and from the public. From a civil liberties perspective this more sophisticated understanding of police autonomy makes police potentially dangerous political actors. Prominent miscarriages of justice, from that of Hanratty, wrongly executed in 1962 for the A6 murder, to the 1970s cases of the Birmingham Six and Guildford Four and 1990s cases such as the M25 Three, prompt concern that where the case is of less national importance, doubt over malpractice must be sharper. After the 1976 Devlin Report failed to bar prosecutions solely on identity evidence, a case was reported where a 15-year-old boy was easily distinguishable when he was charged with attempted rape and put in an identity parade – he was the only black in the line-up. In a previous incarnation as a critic of the police, Peter Hain, sometime New Labour minister, commented that, post-Devlin, 'some restraint has certainly been shown in major, Old Bailey-type trials [but] it is highly doubtful whether much has changed at the ground level of the legal system' (Hain, 1979: 10). That is surely borne out by the case that served to symbolise the problem most sharply in the public mind, the bungled investigation into the murder in 1993 of the black teenager Stephen Lawrence.

There is evidence that the public remain exercised about routine and pervasive forms of malpractice, even compared with major public disorder. In Liverpool, at the height of the 1981 Toxteth riots, a police committee working party considered means to improve police/public relations. Problems of police harassment dominated the report, including 'the indiscriminate and extensive use of formal "stop and search" procedures', 'verbal abuse and physical violence on the part of the police', and complaints of 'over-policing' and 'aggressive policing'. Testimony spoke of a police tendency to see large elements of the Toxteth population as second-class citizens and criminals, and of a lack of understanding for the way of life of ethnic minority people; verbal abuse, particularly of youths, was widespread. The police responded that verbal abuse was the result of police being abused themselves and that it was the customs and practices of ethnic minorities that put them outside the law (Scraton, 1982). While this line can still be heard, it is muted. There is more subtlety in police impression-management, and undoubted change as a result of higher graduate recruitment, 'diversity training', and the spread of tolerant attitudes more generally in public culture, but the key remains practice at the level of mundane, routine work, particularly when under pressure. Police still defend racism by saying forces represent a cross-section of the community and the community contains racists, a tolerance never expressed in regard to the criminal cross-section of the community.

There is little doubt that the most entrenched forms of social conflict with the police involve those people near the bottom of the heap; but a focus on public order necessarily widens our view to take in dissent that exercises sections of the middle-class. Were we to focus on crime and on law enforcement, the confrontation of police and working-class would be stark indeed. Crime is a major problem for the working-class in ways that it seldom is for the middle-class. Street crime is committed by the marginalized, but largely within working-class areas. The working-class suffer most, both from working-class crime, and at the hands of the powerful (as in evasion of safety at work legislation). Enforcement initiatives, such as the Anti-Social Behaviour Order and the extension of Community Support Officer schemes, remain focused on public housing estates, 'problem families', and the new outsiders, the refugees and asylum-seekers. The assertion by Sir Robert Mark, with which we began, that the only real distinction between 'mindful' and 'mindless' hooligans is that the former protest louder about police brutality, is a greater insult to the disprivileged, who daily experience the conflicts inherent in an unequal society, than to the middle-class, who can generally stand aside from, if not above, social conflict.

Journalistic meanings of crisis and conflict

Policing is news. A substantial proportion of routine media content relates to crime, policing or police. Like the media, the police are there every day, reliably producing output, be it direct action, court cases and testimony, dealings with government, or press releases. It pays journalists to attend closely to every aspect of police business. Despite the many contacts between them, the two sides are wary of each other. The police know much about bias and distortion, if only because they know how police/public interaction is transformed when converted into official accounts of police action for the files. The journalists are aware that at least some of their readership does not like the police. Police malpractice sells papers just as well as police heroism.

Journalists operate according to what they call 'news values'. They value the superficially new, the shocking and surprising. The irony is that the news is seldom ultimately new. The urban riots of the 1980s were a major issue for police, and the media, but within two years of the last the preoccupation with inner-city riots and violent industrial unrest had given way to concern about hooliganism in small towns and resorts. Faced with public disorder in unlikely places, like Berwick-upon-Tweed, the press proclaimed that 'the era of the lager lout' had begun (*Guardian,* 6 April 1989). A more sensible appraisal was that the brawling, which had forever been familiar in towns, had followed the population shift to the 'semi-rural, semi-urban areas so characteristic of the prosperous Southeast' (Tuck, 1989). Events proved Tuck right, but she did not foresee the extension of the trend in the following 15 years as relaxation in licensing laws, leisure preferences and a commercial move to immense super-pubs and clubs fueled a new 'night-time economy'. The press duly discovered the phenomenon of 'binge drinking' (Hobbs *et al,* 2003), a 'new' social problem that has troubled society for over 6,000 years. Most news is 'eternal recurrence', the same category of story endlessly repackaged. It is a ritual, different in detail, but the same in form (Rock, 1973). The apparently ephemeral is, in fact, the eternal; but to say this in print is to negate 'news values'. It is to confront the audience with the gloomy prospect that change is illusion, that each day is the same, that there is no magic, only mortality.

The human condition does not sell papers. Its representation must be exaggerated. If it is good it must offer radical new hope (such as the periodic discovery of a 'major breakthrough' that will ultimately cure cancer). The journalist's problem is the escalation required by overuse of sensational language. The terminology of crisis and conflict becomes devalued. A classic instance was the press reporting as a 'riot' the disturbances in Watts, Los Angeles, which left 45 dead and caused $45 million of property damage, while also describing as a 'riot' a disturbance in which three people broke a shop window (Knopf, 1970). In 1855 Karl Marx watched a London crowd angrily occupy Hyde Park in protest at plans to close all places of public amusement on Sundays, including pubs. Marx wrote, 'We witnessed the event from beginning to end, and believe we can state without exaggeration that yesterday in Hyde Park the English revolution began.' Dull as it may be, the point is that we seldom encounter the extreme of any social phenomenon. A truth lies between.

That perspective can be applied to the journalistic treatment of crime and policing in Northern Ireland. Our perception of crime there is formed by the media representation of the 'troubles'. Despite the peace process and the Good Friday Agreement, such is the cast put on the Orange Order parades every summer, and that was applied to the £26 million bank robbery in late 2004, attributed by police to the IRA. The prevailing image is of a society at the brink of crisis, on a course of self-destruction, where lawlessness is endemic. In fact, during the 1980s and 1990s it was more hazardous to live in most American cities than in Belfast. The risk of serious injury or death as a result of the 'troubles' was under half that from a traffic accident (Boyle and Hadden, 1985). In a league table of serious crime in 11 countries, Northern Ireland was sixth, with less crime per 100,000 citizens than the USA, France, Germany, England and Wales, and Denmark (Northern Ireland Office, 1986). The province had the lowest overall crime rate compared to seven regions of England and Wales with equal populations. For most of the period since then, the rate of increase in crime has been less than that in England and Wales or the Republic of Ireland. Some account for this on grounds that Northern Ireland is, in essence, a stable environment with particularly strong religious and family affiliations, but it is not an argument that registers with the media.

Continuing anti-social behaviour was predicted because the 'troubles' disrupted young people's lives, and would continue as long as those who grew up during them were active. Crime in the province would continually escalate as each generation was replaced by another tainted by the disruption. The 'troubles' are still with us, and so are Northern Ireland's low crime rates. The case of 'ordinary crime' in Northern Ireland indicates the complexity that journalists face in making sense of crime and policing issues. Ambiguous cases do not make good news stories. The vocabulary of extremes helps audiences digest the news smoothly by making it clear how they are to receive each item. Journalists' efforts to depict events in clear terms are helped by the mesh between their world view and that of the police. The police have both a physical and a symbolic role as defenders of the established consensus. The symbolic role is implicit even in routine patrol, but highlighted in major crimes, such as murder (Innes, 2003), or when the police suffer dramatic loss, as in a classic *Daily Mail* editorial after three police where shot dead in Shepherd's Bush.

> In Britain the policeman is still the walking sign which says that a society has reached and takes for granted a certain stable normality of public order and decency ... That is why the death of a policeman by violence is so deeply felt by us all ... A dazed incredulity is followed by the realisation that

> order is not to be taken for granted. The jungle is still there. There are still wild beasts in it to be controlled. (Quoted in Chibnall 1975: 70)

Such sentiments are expressed after each such loss, as in the reporting of the 2003 murder of a police constable where the perpetrator's status as a formerly wealthy American led into depravity by steroid addiction gave rich material for tabloid sensationalising. An extension of this merging of police with cherished 'British' qualities is the idea that their/our sense of fair play obliges them to fight crime with 'one hand tied behind their back'. This idea is often deployed after evidence is found of malpractice. Further, while police deviance is itself newsworthy, the journalist's tendency is generally to affirm the integrity of the force, if necessary at the expense of vilifying officers whose failings have become public. Like the news story, the spectrum of police officers is reduced to two extremes – heroes and villains. At the level of collective action and institutional *processes*, the need to fragment reality into more or less isolated *events* plainly militates against a coherent overview (the paper that often wins award for its 'depth' of coverage, the *Guardian*, is also regularly judged as the worst for being late with the news). This fragmentation favours the same interpretations that have served in the past. Shifts and trends in policy and methods are obscured. Instead, the media rest with the topical, dramatic and sloganistic. Both world view and 'news values' demand immediate intelligibility.

There are other important reasons why the media are drawn to simplistic treatments and sensational language. One is simple bias, more apparent from the perspective of distance. In 1955 mounted police dispersed a protest at Westminster against German rearmament, and the road outside Parliament was closed. The *Daily Sketch* headline was 'Crowds of Reds attack police at Commons' and the next day it used a version of the old 'he attacked my fist with his head' joke in its headline 'Commons Mob attacked PC's horse'. There is also the process of information-gathering itself, as when Fleet Street sought to overcome police suspicion of journalists by designating a very small number as crime reporters.

During the 1990s and first decade of the 21st century it was technological affordances rather than significant social progress or development that dictated the pace of change. The mobile telephone grew from fashion accessory of the urban affluent to near universal ownership and increasingly offered capacities to receive news on the move. The internet grew from a quirky assemblage of disparate information resources to an increasingly prominent retail site and backbone to virtually every other aspect of human enterprise, including a point of access to 'print' media news and as relayer of television and radio broadcasts. Satellite and digital television secured for a growing share of the audience a vastly increased choice of viewing options, and home cinema systems added to the trend to regard 'staying home as the new going out'. Email and text messaging challenged all forms of letter except junk mail. By 2004, one could receive news headlines by looking at one's refrigerator.

Yet, as widely remarked as the new technical capacities was the sameness of the 'information' that was increasingly quickly being fired around. With the collapse of the Eastern bloc, and China's ruthless adoption of the profit motive, the principal alternatives to Western capitalism disappeared, leaving only the implausible and retrograde vision of the Koranic state to threaten the 'world's only superpower' and its global free market project. Venom appeared to drain from the social divisions that long marked the Western polity. Vague suspicions that the veneer of change and progress obscured enduring lack of progress in addressing the problems that gave class and other social divisions their heat found occasional expression, as when figures were periodically published showing more people living in poverty after two terms of New Labour than before, but the compelling fissures in society were increasingly those of ethnicity and of refugee status, of religion rather than class, and of 'lifestyle'.

If the faces of conflict changed, so did the police. Their act became sharper, with better planned public order routines, greater incorporation of 'corporate sensitivities' motivated by human rights legislation, and a newly professional eye to the media. Police and journalism came to inhabit closer worlds. The threat of international terrorism reinforced the journalist's long-established pro-police default position, with a proliferation of pro-police 'infotainment' opening to public gaze ever more obscure nooks of the police world. For their part, the police came to appreciate that their work is as much the craft of impression management as it is that of pounding the beat, a key episode in the trend being the 'reassurance gap' as crime surveys showed the incidence of much crime declining with no apparent effect on public perceptions of risk and safety, leading to the roll-out of a national programme of 'reassurance policing'.

The police/media relation came to inhabit a world very different from that marked by the long history of class conflict, but as before, when it came to it they almost always sat on the same bench. The news in our society is commercial, competitive, explicitly and implicitly political. It competes for our attention with a bewildering panoply of other stimuli. We can seldom look to the mass media for anything more accurate than the boldest stroke with the broadest brush.

Social science and conflict in policing

The language of crisis is not confined to the media. Social science routinely depicts the police/public relationship in such terms. Stuart Hall *et al*'s book, *Policing the Crisis* (1978), is an enduringly influential example. The tension between the application of the language of crisis to relations with the police and the reality of policing as it is routinely experienced is apparent in the focus of the book. Empirically it concerned robbery from the person in a public place. Analytically it concerned deviancy amplification, whereby police, judiciary and media progressively settled on the emotive term 'mugging' to characterise an offence that was ostensibly increasing drastically. Ideologically it argued that such deviancy-mongering was part of the crisis of late capitalism, and largely directed against the black underclass. Hall *et al* argued that they were charting the end of the post-war consensus. They used the debate over 'mugging' to examine what they saw as the growing polarisation of society consequent on that collapse. That race was central to the panic was apparent in the late 1980s outbreak of 'steaming', where groups of youths threatened bus and rail passengers with knives to demand cash (the contemporary target is as often mobile phones). There were steep rises in these robberies, but this crime was not confined to black perpetrators and social science failed to analyse it in the portentous terms applied to mugging.

The attribution of very broad terms, like 'consensus', to typify a society over a long period, such as 'post-war', suffers from any sustained analysis. As we shall see, social conflict has marked every period since the formation of the police, including the years between 1945 and the publication of Hall *et al*'s book. Hall *et al* suggested, via the case of mugging, that British tolerance for minorities was breaking down and that this was new; but ethnic minorities should not be cast only in the role of victim. Liberal analysis tends to the view that heterogeneous ethnic subcultures are uniformly possessed of unproblematic norms and values, and are capable of harmonious coexistence were it not for harassment by police and racist groups; but this is as over-generalised as the racist view.

Street criminals are not 'inner-city Robin Hoods' and their victims are usually poor and defenceless. From the 1980s to the present, the Lambeth police district has accounted for a large share of London's robberies and snatch thefts, and Brixton for up to a third of all crime in Lambeth and half of all robbery and violent theft. Between 1976 and 1980, the increase in robbery in London was 38%, but in Brixton it was 138% (Lea and Young, 1982: 9), and the Scarman Inquiry heard that 80% of 'footpad robbery' was by young black males. The FitzGerald analysis may indicate why this element of the population was disproportionately represented in that kind of crime at the time, but even without FitzGerald we might note that the idea that police generally suspect black youths is contradicted by the fact that they do not make such claims regarding burglary, which they see as committed equally by blacks and whites. Hall *et al* saw the involvement of young blacks as a consequence of social conflict occasioned by the end of consensus, and others saw it as a result of disprivilege, but there is in FitzGerald a plausible argument for demographics. The problem for those interested in manufacturing a political crisis from friction between police and underclass is not only that the long view tells us that it has always been present, but that the constituents of the underclass have regularly changed. FitzGerald demonstrated the interaction between the immigrant generation, the proportion of ethnic group comprising young males, and areal residence, factors that concatenate to provide a complex mechanism for the cyclical replacement by its successor of each ethnic group purportedly having a propensity to commit crime. Once the proportion of the black population falling in the high-crime 16–24 age group subsides to the average for the general population, more recent immigrant groups may occupy their place simply as a by-product of the trend for high birth rates amongst first-generation immigrants.

The point is not to belittle the experience of racism, but to analyse it in empirically and theoretically adequate terms. The ideal of 'consensus policing' presupposes a stable working-class community opposed to crime, which would tolerate police activity and act as a source of information. An alternative view is that even in routine policing co-operation is problematic and information is less easily gained. Be this as it may, most academic analysis sees confrontational policing as having consequences in the alienation of the community and a denial of co-operation. The notorious 'Swamp 81' operation was widely held to have provoked the 1981 riots, while signally failing to achieve its aim to crack down on burglars and robbers. 'The deterioration in police/community relations leads to a drying up of information which in turn forms the background to the development of aggressive "military" policing' (Lea and Young, 1982: 12). The police strategy put 'riot on the agenda'; but there are several points with which issue may be taken. It is questionable whether 'consensus policing' in the most disprivileged areas was ever any better founded than in 1980s Brixton. The impression the general tenor of academic analyses of the riots create is of inexorable progress toward riot, 'consensus policing' having been abandoned. Such movements are neither inexorable nor universal. Since the 1980s the police have tried many ways of avoiding such confrontation while moving against street crime. It cannot be said that tensions are now absent, but police efforts to inform local publics of what specific operations are aiming to achieve have been reflected in greater public acceptance. A contributing factor may well be the perceived threat of super-violent international terrorism; certainly constraints on civil liberties that would have elicited resistance in the 1980s are now largely accepted.

Without a more informed historical perspective it is easy to exaggerate the extent of public disorder and crime compared with the past. Indexed by crime figures, the period 1945–70 was one of unusually peaceable change, but indices of political and industrial disturbance also suggest that the longer-term trend was to greater order. Moreover, apparent rises in crime rates are often artefacts of reporting variables. For example, burglaries and violent crimes actually increased more slowly in the 1980s than police statistics suggest because the proportion of crimes reported to police rose (Home Office, 1989). Increases in burglary figures were partly caused by more widespread home insurance, especially the switch from replacement valuation to new-for-old policies, and increased reporting of rape and other sexual offences in the 1990s partly reflected greater victim confidence that police would investigate sensitively, using female officers where victims were female, and conducting the proceedings in rape crisis suites. Systematic comparison of crime survey data with police statistics shows that crime, particularly property crime, began a significant, sustained decline from historically high figures, starting in the second half of the 1990s.

Crime statistics seldom provide an unambiguous picture. Criminal statistics released in 2005 showed violent crime to be up, but the large majority of 'violent' offences involved no injury and the murder rate was its lowest in 19 years. Burglary and robbery declined and despite two years of anxious commentary on gun crime, the general tenor of which was that urban youths were increasingly armed to the teeth, gun crime fell. There *was* an increase in gun offences – in the use of replica guns. It passed unremarked that youths may have been exploiting the general anxiety by using fake weapons as 'frighteners'. The first large-scale self-report study conducted under official auspices, the Home Office Crime and Justice Survey, received much attention. The 2005 edition 'revealed' that a third of teenage boys were active offenders, and that, if extrapolated to the population, some 3.8 million people age ten to 65 were guilty of at least one of twenty 'core offences' (Home Office, 2005). Self-report surveys have been subject to savage methodological criticism for half a century, though, and commentators identified some rather obvious problems. One of the 'core offences' was theft from work, and respondents were told this could involve taking a pen home; if this was done several times in a year, they entered the figures as an 'active offender' (Channel 4 Evening News, 25 January 2005). For several years government had highlighted the problem of 'prolific offenders' who accounted for much crime; a figure of 85,000 who performed 60% of criminal offences was often given. As commentators pointed out, if the survey was to be believed, some 3.8 million needed to be added to that figure, and if all were caught, the whole national budget would be required for new prisons. Hearteningly, the conclusion of several commentaries was that a convincing alternative reading of the figures was that society was becoming intolerant of even trivial misdemeanours.

According to Schwarz and Hall (1985), the whole period of 1880–1920 was one of profound crisis in the British polity, as a collectivist social organisation and interventionist mode of social regulation emerged from the *laissez-faire* of the mid-19th century. 'From the 1880s there occurred a succession of crises of the State, each only incompletely and partially resolved before new antagonism arose, which in their combinations, amounted to a crisis of the social order'. Here crisis is the inability of the social formation to reproduce itself on previous social relations; but 'crises' that are as slow to emerge as the difficulties of the liberal state in reproducing its ideology and policies are unlikely to be perceived as such by historical actors. Such long-term processes, only perceptible *post hoc*, cannot account for the sense of crisis that periodically afflicts society, or for social groups who see their interests threatened. Rather than attempting to depict periods decades long as a 'crisis', we would better regard sudden and explosive incidents as crises, and where they arise from enduring problems, see them as signs of a social conflict. This is to do little more than to return to the dictionary from sociology's more dramatic lexicon, where one suspects the identification of protracted crises of capital and the polity may have had more to do with wishful thinking than stringent and convincing analysis.

Any observer would discern much change in recent years, but the point is to track what changes this may have brought in the delivery of informal and formal social control, and the police role in it. Social theorists tell us that we have entered a post-industrial or 'late modern risk society', where less permanency of employment, less engagement with the work process ('de-skilling') and declining respect for the authorities, are all characteristic. Leishman *et al* (1996) and Johnston (2000) observe that, as globalisation developed by means of increased communication and information, the government responded with new ideas of public service management. Globalisation has generally resulted in the re-structuring of state institutions and a transition from welfare state to 'competition state' (Cerny, 1990). These are trends that both Conservatives and New Labour have embraced, and the police have been a key institution in the new arrangements. The 'Right realist' agenda of the Thatcherite Conservatives saw the police supported while other public services were cut. The police gained extra central government funding, with better pay and increased numbers. However, the Conservatives became disillusioned as crime rates continued to rise despite the investment, and the focus shifted to the 'Financial Management Initiative' (FMI). 'The FMI was generally designed to encourage effectiveness, efficiency and cost savings in the public sector services by applying private sector management methods and imposing market disciplines' (Morgan and Newburn, 1997: 47). The FMI represented a hollowing out of the state, as 'peripheral functions are shed to focus upon the core competencies of the state that enhance its competitive function' (Leishman *et al*, 1996: 10). The mantra was 'private good, public bad'.

The application of private sector business principles to the police began with Home Office Circular 114/83 (Home Office, 1983). It presented new management strategies, including 'policing by objectives', giving 'value for money'. Police support for the government began to wane (Morgan and Newburn, 1997). The Conservative government began to advance their reform agenda by legislation, where previously they had used guidance via Circulars. Bottoms (1995) maintains that the hard-line legislation represented a 'penal populism' that enabled the Conservatives to 'govern through crime' (Simon, 1997). The 1992 White Paper on 'Police Reform' resulted in the Police and Magistrates Court Act 1994, which created the biggest changes to policing for thirty years, and which some saw as resulting in a *de facto* national police force (Reiner, 2000b). The police were to receive three-quarters of their funding from central government and the Home Office would set national policing objectives. Police authorities were obliged to produce a policing plan and set performance targets for achieving the Home Office objectives. The 1994 law also reduced the membership and composition of police authorities, with fewer democratically elected members. The authority's role changed from the requirement to maintain an 'adequate and efficient' force to an 'efficient and effective' force, a terminology better attuned to performance measurement.

Both the Sheehy Inquiry into the future role and responsibilities of the police, and the Core and Ancillary Tasks Review, further applied private sector principles to policing. Neither initiative was fully implemented and the changes which were made little affected the crime rate. 'As crime rates continued to rise ... the causes of crime were said to be more complex and the responsibility for preventing it more diffuse' (Morgan and Newburn, 1997: 58). Policy development came to favour 'responsibilisation' (Garland, 2001), where public and private organisations, and the citizenry themselves, were to take responsibility for managing their own risk, alongside the police. Crime prevention, long a criminal justice backwater, was suddenly prominent (Gilling, 1997) and could capitalise on the expert view that 'order and security ultimately depend not on formal agencies of criminal justice, but on informal social controls exercised within civil society' (Loader and Sparks, 2002: 89). Less attention was paid the fact that it is the better-off who are able to cover their own risk (Shearing, 1996).

In tandem with the crime prevention emphasis, an increased focus on local consultation and inter-agency working developed. This further diffused the responsibility for managing crime. Home Office Circular 8/84 had encouraged all agencies to be involved in crime prevention and, in 1990, Circular 44/90 profiled successful partnership examples. The Morgan Report (Home Office, 1991a) promoted partnership, but was largely ignored by the government on cost grounds (Wright, 2002). New Labour, elected in 1997, took up the same agenda though. The Crime and Disorder Act 1998 followed the Morgan Report's recommendations for various means by which partnership policing could be achieved and incorporated a requirement for 'Best Value' practice. These were not policies entirely without difficulty for police. There are tensions between 'joined up' working, viewing crime as a social problem, and unimaginative performance measures narrowly focused on crime detection rates and a 'fire brigade' policing style. Nevertheless the Police Reform Act 2002 maintained that policing is a function carried out by many agencies, of which police are but one (Newburn, 2003). Overall, these policies and legislation represent a change in our conception from 'the police' to 'policing'.

During this period a new player on the policing scene emerged, the Audit Commission, the remit of which is to ensure that 'public money is spent economically, efficiently and effectively in the areas of local government, housing, health and criminal justice services' (Audit Commission, 2003: 1). It has been a significant force in promoting private sector principles, and produced a number of influential reports on policing. In 1993 it promoted a proactive, intelligence-led approach that would improve effectiveness by providing well-collated information and analysis. That 'intelligence-led policing' has not delivered all that was expected (Fielding *et al*, 2002; Innes *et al*, 2004) is indicative of much longer-term realities of police work than are captured in shallow, motivated research of the sort the Commission provides, and will be a major theme of Chapter 5.

Changes as substantial as these could neither be enacted without opposition from the police, nor be implemented without gaps between policy and the calibre and consistency of actual practice; but now, much more than in the 1980s, we must regard the police as one organisation amongst a number required to conduct the policing function. Nor is it only the reform agenda of central government that has played a part, for the changes are bound up with the wider social conditions of 'late modernity' or, less sloganistically and more tangibly, with contemporary constructions of risk, public safety, and protection. We need to examine the implications of change for the dominant modes of social conflict. We must assess the consequences of what has been a significant shift in civic culture, involving a move from 'government' to 'governance', from something imposed by the state and allied with its interests to a more consent-oriented participatory orientation attuned to citizens as 'customers'. We must trace, as well, the effects of much new research-based thinking on the form and delivery of police services, particularly that associated with a concern to 'manage' risk (or at least be seen to be managing it), to 'design out' crime by situational preventive measures, and to work alongside other agencies and institutions on the premise that most enduring social problems are multi-causal and multi-dimensional. Our task is not to be lulled by the swish of new appearances, but to persist in our effort to test whether they mask the endurance and extension of underlying and fundamental divisions.

For while there have been innovations in the delivery of policing services, it has also to be accepted that the greater part of police work is still delivered by means recognisable to our predecessors, and that we might indeed read our new times as having substantially extended the police armoury while lowering the threshold of civil liberties that provide our essential legal protections. *In extremis*, the public police retain enough of their monopoly over the legal use of force to remain at the heart of our understanding of social conflict.

2. A golden age of policing? |

The social history of policing from 1829

It is natural to assume that the problems we face are both unique and pressing. We tend not to take the long view. This is amplified by the tendency to nostalgia, a belief that, for example, our present problems are out of step with some earlier golden age of policing. The drama of the 1980s riots, the trauma of the Stephen Lawrence case, the inept police handling of the May Day protests, and the steady encroachment on civil liberties under the banner of protecting society from terrorism, obscure the fact that 'the development of the police force in Britain has always been ... inextricably linked with the story of civil disturbance, protest and demonstration' (Manwaring-White, 1983: 1). The modern police institution emerged at a time of rapid social change. The population, which doubled in the 18th century, doubled again by 1871. There was a great migration from rural to urban areas. Severe overcrowding and public health problems resulted, and an over-supply of unskilled labour fuelled discontent at low wages and bad conditions. Marches, protests and riots long pre-dated the emergence of organised labour. The maintenance of public order has always been contested. There was never a 'golden age' of police/public relations, and disorder invariably raised doubts over police even-handedness.

Celebrants of the 'golden age', with its supposed 'police advantage' in the form of public support, obviating the need for more forceful methods, forget that before the French Revolutionary Wars the English were seen by themselves and their rulers as an 'ungovernable people' (Townsend, 1993). Things only began to change after the petering out of Chartism in 1848, which ushered in what Townsend called an 'age of equipoise', where both officials and populace shared a spirit of compromise in times of social conflict. However, by 1970, establishment histories, such as Critchley's *The Conquest of Violence* (1978), lauding British 'softly softly' tactics in response to the social uprisings of 1968, seemed distinctly unrealistic. Police repression and political/industrial militancy became mutually reinforcing, with the collapse of the Heath government in the face of the miners' militancy a key event, but one that police mythology took long to accept.

Townsend (1993) shows how two world wars and the Cold War engendered expansion of the formal security apparatus, reflecting a slow transition between two conservative conceptions of order. The organic conception emphasised a balanced arrangement of institutions and values constituting authority. This allowed for substantial political tolerance, but relied on a fiction of a 'British way' involving cross-class consensus around reasonableness. This was finally dispatched by the second form, the monetarist neo-conservatism represented by the administrations of Margaret Thatcher.

Townsend's analysis may over-emphasise the harmony of the post-Chartist period, but his impression of the period prior to it is apt. Peel's 'new police' were born into times of widespread disorder. In 1780, protesting at the Catholic Relief Act, Lord George Gordon and a mass of followers marched to petition Parliament; rioting lasted a week, with widespread property damage, several deaths and the mobilisation of the army. Parliamentary reaction was heated, but it took five years for the Solicitor General to table a bill to provide London with a strong police force. Following intense protest it was dropped. Weavers, incensed at mechanisation, provoked the Luddite riots of 1811, and troops were deployed. The government deployed troops again at St Peter's Fields in Manchester in 1819. Some 60,000 had gathered to hear Hunt, the radical orator, and when the mounted yeomanry were sent to arrest him and disperse the crowd their charges left 11 dead and 400 wounded. However, public condemnation of 'French-style' policing, with a network of spies and 'agents provocateur' of the sort run by Napoleon's deputy Fouche, Duc d'Otranto, prevented attempts to introduce a further police bill. A decade later one was passed, but the riots continued. In the 40 years before the Metropolitan Police were established in 1829 there were 17 parliamentary committees that examined the problem of law and order. While the issue was always on the agenda, the obstacles were concrete: hostility to establishment of an organised, salaried, full-time police force, voiced as loudly by the wealthy middle-classes as any group (Lambert, 1986: 24). In 1822 a Parliamentary Select Committee recorded its famously obstinate belief that:

> [i]t is difficult to reconcile an effective system of police, with that perfect freedom of action and exemption from interference, which are the great privileges and blessings of society in this country; the forfeiture or curtailment of such advantages would be too great a sacrifice for improvements in police or facilities in detection of crime. (Cited in Lambert 1986: 24)

The ambivalence of the British establishment is good reason to take the historical perspective. In 1833 only 29 people staffed the Home Office, described in *The Times* in 1812 as 'the sink of all the imbecility attached to every ministry for the last 30 years'. The administration of justice was almost wholly ritualistic and revolved around the written record. The Ministry was a receptacle for correspondence from provincial magistrates, and made decisions on calling out the militia and yeomanry, but mechanisms were vague. Most decisions were left to justices of the peace (JPs) and magistrates; co-operation varied. The Home Office had no agents in the provinces. In this 'very loosely coordinated "system"' (Manning, 1977: 69) it was assumed that the Crown and associated gentry/mercantile elites would and did control the police. They were competing with Colquhoun's private dock police, private police elsewhere, and the JPs, but the public system gradually prevailed. 'Thus, although the English police were forged in conflict their survival was a question of organisational competition rather than of the source or degree of their mandate' (Manning, 1977: 69). While the new police began to appeal by comparison to the alternatives, another element that moulded police/public relations was recruitment policy. 'Rioters and controllers were bound by shared class, ethnicity and religion in virtually every disturbance. The explosive combination, so common in later American riots and disorders, of controllers drawn from different classes, races and cultures from rioters was not present' (Manning 1977: 69). Perhaps this is why police/working class relations are better characterised by ambivalence than loathing. History complicates any rigid 'class war' thesis.

The historical inheritance of 19th century police was the local character of the office of constable, the common law origin of police powers ('an office relatively indistinct from the citizenry' (Jefferson and Grimshaw, 1984)), and the constables' subordination to the judiciary (originally the JPs). Legislation in the 19th century added the organisation of constables into police forces and the subjection of the forces to a degree of democratic supervision. The office of constable always had a local basis in that each community had to deal with its own law enforcement, with severe penalties for failure. Moreover, constables were answerable to justices for a ragbag of other local duties: they were a 'general factotum of community administration, assuming responsibility for the maintenance of highways and bridges, drainage and other ancillary matters, as well as maintaining the King's Peace' (Oliver, 1987: 13).

The latter half of the 18th century had finally seen abandonment of the ancient duty of obligatory personal service in the office of constable. It was a substantial step toward a police organisation with a unified command. The Metropolitan Police Act 1829 cemented this movement. It established a Police Office for the Metropolitan Police District which was the responsibility of two justices (later commissioners), accountable to the

Home Secretary for appointments, direction and control; but opposition was multifarious, including:

> the immediate threat posed by an organised police force to the fledgling organisations of the working class, the more long-term challenge posed by the idea of professional policing to the near monopoly on peace-keeping powers enjoyed by the county gentry in their role as justices, and the drain on capital a paid force represented to an emergent and thrusting industrial bourgeoisie. (Jefferson and Grimshaw, 1984: 29)

The rallying cries were obvious and emotive: 'freedom from state interference' and 'individual liberty', with the old system exemplifying local priorities and common law powers. Thus, the Act was confined to the metropolis and maintained the common law office of constable with the justice of the peace as the apex. Parliamentary intentions were apparent in the constitutional context in which the Home Secretary was given responsibility over the police. Lodging responsibility there was essential to ensure a degree of democratic supervision. In 1829 there were no elected local government institutions and the electorate amounted to a tiny fraction of the male population. 'Since monolithic party government and the whip system also did not exist, individual ministerial responsibility to the House of Commons was a meaningful concept' (Lustgarten, 1986: 94). In the context of the early 19th century, the 1829 Act was designed to ensure the 'maximum accountability that the political system was capable of constructing at that time' (Lustgarten, 1986: 94). Parliament's preoccupation with democratic control of police establishes a continuity of conflict over police accountability.

The Home Secretary received lesser powers over county forces in the 1839 Act and awaited the County and Borough Police Act 1856 before gaining a role with regard to the whole system; but the relationship of watch committee and borough force, and the judicial role regarding county forces, established in 1839, were untouched. The Home Office gained power to appoint three inspectors of constabulary to assess the 'efficiency' of forces. To encourage consolidation, forces certified as efficient got one-quarter of the cost of pay and clothing unless they served a population of fewer than 5,000. The conflict over police organisation was far from over.

> The municipal corporations and the borough MPs were united during the passage of the Bills ... in their hostility to ... central inspection ... [L]iberty reposed in that most English of institutions, 'local government', and was to be contrasted with tyranny, which resided in that most un-English of government institutions, the 'continental spy system'. (Jefferson and Grimshaw, 1984: 32)

County magistrates were the immediate losers under the 1856 Act. While they still appointed county chief constables 'once in post ... [he] was an autocrat over whom the justices had no power other than the ultimate sanction of dismissal ... he fulfilled many of the duties which in the borough were assigned by the watch committee' (Critchley, 1978: 124). As early as 1833 the Home Secretary publicly voiced an established departmental belief that 'chief constables were a dangerous set of men', due to their statutory autonomy, which disturbed the structure of relationships between Home Office and county magistracy. In the boroughs, force control and administration remained with watch committees, and Home Office authority was confined to the power to withhold grant. These borough and county differences essentially remained until 1964.

There were also debates over ordinary constables' conduct of patrol and legal accountability. Game-preservers wanted police to have wide legal powers to stop and search people on suspicion of them being poachers; but government officials and the press believed it would be 'monstrous' to leave legal matters to a policeman's judgment; policemen were 'taken from a class not very competent to judge what are reasonable grounds for a charge of felony' (quoted in Steedman, 1984: 31). While this argument served to block the game-preservers' lobby it did not resolve the constable's individual accountability at law. Cases, such as one successfully brought in 1858 against a constable by a butcher on grounds of false imprisonment, were used to promote a bill exempting police from liability for actions performed on duty, but the Home Office resisted this and positively strengthened the individual constable's subordination to law.

Borough watch committees continued to exercise authority over chief constables, and to provoke conflict. Birmingham's Chief Constable decided in 1880 to proceed against all drunks regardless of whether they were disorderly, but public and judicial criticism obliged him to withdraw the policy. A year later he unsuccessfully prosecuted a music hall manager for 'improper performances'. He claimed an independent right to institute prosecutions as 'the guardian of public morality and order'. The Committee resolved that 'he should not institute special proceedings "likely to affect a number of ratepayers or to provoke public comment" without first reporting to them his intentions' (Jefferson and Grimshaw, 1984: 39). He refused unless ordered by the Home Secretary and magistrates. The Home Secretary would not intervene, but reminded him of watch committee powers to make regulations and dismiss constables. The magistrates also refused to intervene. The Chief Constable, threatened with dismissal, backed down (Critchley, 1978: 131–32). The shoe was on the other foot in a dispute in Liverpool in 1890 over action against brothels known to police; there had been a general policy of non-prosecution. Anti-vice campaigners complained to the justices, who passed it to the watch committee. The Chief Constable defended the policy on the grounds that indiscriminate prosecution would spread prostitution randomly across Liverpool; but he agreed to implement whatever decision the committee made. Instructed to prosecute all known brothels he immediately did so against 443. Later the committee complained about the dispersal of prostitution to respectable neighbourhoods; the Chief Constable responded that police were merely carrying out their orders (in 2005, the Liverpool council enacted a 'managed zone' for prostitution in the city).

These disputes did not put paid to constabulary independence. For example, the outcome in Birmingham did 'not mean that [the chief] succumbed to the *idea* that he had no independent powers of law enforcement in general' (Jefferson and Grimshaw, 1984: 41). The watch committee had not claimed the right to instruct him directly in these matters, but to have him inform it of his intentions regarding certain kinds of prosecution. The Liverpool dispute's significance was in affirming the police duty to uphold the law rather than bearing on police independence or discretion. These and other police authority/chief officer disputes suggest it is 'politics' and not 'the law' that decided locally prevailing interpretations of the relationship of watch committees, chiefs and Home Office. Legal ambiguity meant 'a variety of practices from a virtual free-hand for chief constables to daily supervision by the watch committees were equally lawful' (Jefferson and Grimshaw, 1984: 44).

Relations were no smoother in London: the late 1880s were particularly trying. The Metropolitan Police were strongly criticised for their handling of the Trafalgar Square riots, in which a demonstrator was killed, but more widespread was condemnation for being unable to catch 'Jack the Ripper'. On this their critics included the Queen. When the Commissioner, Sir Charles Warren, sought the Home Secretary's support for any action 'however illegal' it was refused, and he was denied authority to offer a reward for information relating to the murders. He resigned. As Lustgarten remarks, 'it is startling to realise that an "operational" matter like offering a reward was one that even a notoriously high-handed commissioner understood to require approval from his political superior' (1986: 35). This was hardly 'constabulary independence', but neither was it central direction.

Electoral reform eased conflict over voting rights, but industrial strife was a growing order maintenance problem. In 1908 a Select Committee on 'The Employment of the Military in Cases of Disturbances' reported that between 1878 and 1908 troops had been mobilised to aid the police on 24 occasions, firing on demonstrators on two. In the following 40 years they were called out less often, notably at Tonypandy (1910), Liverpool (the 1919 police strike), in the 1921 miners' strike, the 1926 General Strike and, after the Second World War, nine times by the Attlee Government (Bunyan, 1976: 69). When the Rhondda Valley miners took to the streets in 1910, the ability of the police to handle major disorder was amply demonstrated. Magistrates requested troops, and Home Secretary Churchill sent 500, along with 700 London police and 100 mounted police, with orders for the police to employ 'vigorous baton charges' before using the army. In 1919, following demobilisation, there was serious rioting in South Wales, the East End and Liverpool. The July 'Peace Day' celebrations witnessed riots in Wolverhampton, Salisbury, Epsom, Luton (Luton's Town Hall was destroyed), Essex, Coventry and Swindon, and in seven London boroughs. In 1920 and 1921, police and the unemployed clashed in Sheffield, Bristol, Birmingham, London, Liverpool, Leicester, Cardiff, Dundee, Glasgow and elsewhere. There was a battle between 1,000 miners and the police in the 1926 General Strike, and in 1931 the police in Glasgow were fought by 80,000 unemployed.

In the 1950s and 1960s the chief calls on public order policing were not industrial, but political. During the Cuban crisis of 1962, over 125 demonstrators were arrested near the US Embassy. Some 600 police attended this demonstration of 400 people; demonstrators were knocked to the ground and kicked (Bowes, 1966: 95). In a 'Hands off Cuba' rally at Trafalgar Square police arrested 150 demonstrators; at a sit-down protest in Whitehall demonstrators were dragged away by the hair, kicked and punched. Demonstrators who attempted to march from Trafalgar Square to Grosvenor Square were 'ridden into in the roads and on pavements by motorcycle police who, if they could not injure them in this way, dismounted and used their booted feet and gloved fists' (Bowes, 1966: 96). These events were covered by television.

The next major public order disturbances were the urban riots of the 1980s. Their predisposing elements are enduring: poor housing, high unemployment, inferior social facilities, racial tension. Police chiefs depicted these problems as representing social disintegration, contrasting with supposedly happier times of good order and minimal crime. The golden age was marked by popular respect and obedience. The guiding image was that:

> working class districts ... were also areas of domestic peace and neighbourly trust of a standard which we do not know today. People never thought of locking their houses if they went out during the day, and theft would have been a cause for amazement. (Halsey, quoted in Alderson, 1979: 46–47)

Its demise represented the collapse of a community spirit that bonded people, in favour of individual self-interest.

Such an analysis has a surprising echo in contemporary postmodern theory, which also locates current angst and conflicts in a decline of the old certainties (Beck, 1994); but the idea that the police/community relation has been largely unproblematic is easily challenged. In certain strata, relations have always been strained, violent confrontation frequent. Popular consent was at best passive acquiescence (Brogden, 1981). The 1980s riots confronted police and public with lessons about the myth of policing by consent. 'They signified not so much the breakdown of consent but rather the physical manifestation of a consent that had long since been withdrawn – if, indeed, it had ever existed' (Brogden, 1981: 228); but could the conflict of police and public that was patently manifest in the 1980s riots be reducible simply to a problem of policing? Attributing riots to changes in policing alone, say to militaristic methods, would be mistaken. Lea and Young argue that there has been a 'progressive institutionalisation of conflict' (1982: 13) since the late 18th century. The riots of the 18th and early 19th century expressed resistance to urbanisation and the capitalist mode of production. A disenfranchised workforce had to adjust to new work discipline and pressures on family life.

> The gradual enfranchisement of the working class, its reconciliation to urban capitalist life patterns and the development of a strong trade union and Labour Party organisation steered class conflict into the peaceful channels of political compromise. Class organisation and class politics became a strong instrument of social stabilisation. (Lea and Young, 1982: 13–14)

However the path to institutionalisation (and taming) of conflict was broken in the 1980s by the turbulence of the urban riots and the coal and steel disputes. 'The return of violence as a characteristic of late capitalism is beginning to reproduce some of the social and political features of early capitalism, particularly the economic and political marginalization of whole communities from the political process' (Lea and Young, 1982: 14). Lea and Young's argument relied on two assertions. First, that access to the political process is chiefly through institutions based on the process of production. Without access to 'big business' or 'big unions' participation was marginalised. High unemployment in the 1980s denied the working-class the calming hand of trade union branches, trades councils and Labour Party branches. Patterns of life that come with the experience of work were thus undermined. In previous times of high unemployment the energy of radical discontent was diverted into reformist working-class politics; but what labouring work there was in the inner city employed 'a high percentage of female and ethnic minority workers [who] were effectively resistant to trade unionism' (Lea and Young, 1982: 15). The 1980s and subsequent generations were also denied the motivating power of a belief in socialism: for them the Welfare State did not represent the promised land, but 'an anonymous and coercive bureaucracy'. Lea and Young's second assertion was simply that all this was new.

Both assertions are problematic. The first subscribes to an implausibly generalised image of the appeal of trade union and Labour Party branches. These were never the province of the young. The 1930s equivalent of the disco was the dance hall, not the miners' club. The popular culture of the 1930s was enriched not only by the inheritance of British folk culture, but by a coming awareness of American music and style. Lea and Young's image of working-class life was unconvincingly cloth-capped, in its own way as romanticised as '*Auf Wiedersehn, Pet*'. Also remarkably conservative is their notion of the civilising effect of work, whereas much employment is grim, monotonous, or both, and as apt to fuel bitter resentment and a 'get away with whatever you can' attitude.

As to the second assertion that all this was new and represented a crisis of formerly sound political institutions, our historical awareness of statutory ambiguity, constabulary independence, public disorder, police strikes and the rest surely suggests a society with a turbulent political culture. The multiple fringe organisations around the Labour Party, the appeal of Mosley's fascist New Party to many Labour supporters, and the long opposition of the left to female emancipation readily support an argument that working-class solidarity and political engagement are as mythological as the golden age the police fondly recall. The only really 'new' element of the turbulence of the 1980s was the rising significance of ethnic minority experiences of British culture. Lea and Young's image of black culture as lacking access to politics is as overdrawn as their image of working-class culture. Black culture is vibrant and various, and even in the 1980s there was significant ethnic minority participation in politics. Ethnic minorities play an increasingly vigorous part in politics, whether around the banner of Islam or of anti-discrimination; the last decade has seen the National Black Police Association firmly established (and despite its title, aim to represent all police officers of colour). Minority religious movements and community groups are active. Cultural identity is also formed around less positive things. In 1995 the Met Commissioner preceded a crackdown on street crime by publicising that 80% of those robbed in London identified young black males as responsible (*Guardian*, 8 July 1995). The matter was presented as a race issue, not a poverty issue. It was widely noted that in cities where the poor were mostly whites, most street crime was by whites, and street robberies did not account for a large proportion of London crime; but the damage was done.

Theses of ethnic alienation might better consider a culture of conflict than 'a culture of despair'. Some minority people define their sense of self from their dissimilarity to mainstream culture, and it is the start of realism to recognise that minority cultures are themselves as richly divided as the mainstream. We need not subscribe to the argument that access to the political process is only through economic production, or that we are lately in crisis, to argue that social conflict has reached a new stage and that the police are part of it. Social conflict has always reached a new stage because it is always with us. Police/public relations provide a ready index of conflict, but are neither its chief nor only form.

Policing with consent

Critics of the police argue that the concept of constabulary independence is a fiction designed to obscure movement away from the democratic control prevalent in the mid-19th century watch committee system; but 'democratic control' was often subject to dispute and struggle. The disputes between watch committee and police, which we noted, were principled affairs, but malpractice and collusion also gave rise to conflicts of interest. While the power of watch committees in large cities was not generally a problem as 'reasonable, public-spirited men' controlled the council, 'malpractices were rife' in towns (Critchley, 1978). A particular problem was the coalition of brewers' and publicans' interests. Where this predominated, watch committees barred proceedings against licensees without their express authority. The Chief Constable of Norwich was dismissed for defying this. 'It suited the purposes of many small boroughs ... to appoint as Chief Constable a local man of a quiet and tractable disposition, and as the appointment was not subject to the approval of the Home Secretary, no-one could prevent a mischievous town council from exercising improper pressure on its police' (Critchley, 1978: 124–25). Local control was no panacea. With numerous small forces the status of chief constables was low, being proportionate to size of command. They were easily cowed by watch committees. There was conflict between the high-minded morals of lowly constables and the venal self-interest of their superiors.

There is an obvious contrast between this and the assertion that the problem of contemporary policing stems from the long erosion of local democratic control under a system where all knew where they stood. The public, including rising urban elites, were highly critical of police in the 19th century. Often cited is the occasion four years after the Metropolitan Police were formed when the police broke up a public meeting in Cold Bath Fields with baton charges. A policeman died, but the inquest jury returned a verdict of 'justifiable homicide'.

Securing the consent and support of parliamentary and new urban elites was a large undertaking. The relationship of police and the working-class was central to it. Marshall sketched a typical vision of the 'golden age', leavened by a 'realistic' awareness of a measure of roughness.

For all the problems he faced, the policeman of the 1920s and 30s was serving what appeared to be a collection of deep-rooted, class-based communities reinforced by seemingly unassailable values ... Our policeman of those years would have known a relationship, based not on love and respect certainly, but upon an understanding of the mores of the community he served ... Collectively, policemen might have been referred to as 'our bobbies' or 'the bleeding law', depending on the area in which they served, but they related to the public as individuals and not as an anonymous group. (Marshall, 1975: 17)

The limits on a 'golden age' that began as early as 1920 and lasted until the 1960s can be addressed by a historical analysis that considers what the police did in the community. To do this we must consider the transitional period of the mid-19th century. Police then actually did very little in the public eye beyond walking around and watching.

Action against the respectable was proscribed, but so was a great deal of action against working class people ... [U]nsupervised action could put isolated men in physical danger ... Metropolitan policemen had more need of a formula like discretion than did provincial forces ... for Metropolitan policemen possessed, through various police acts of the 1830s and 1840s, a much greater ability to act without reference to a hierarchy. In the provinces ... it is clear that no policeman could act individually. (Steedman, 1984: 6)

If we are to accept the 'golden age' at all we must qualify it. It was not in the provinces, where relations could be aloof and guided by class. Provincial local government had interests to satisfy other than service to the working-class, and its relations with the middle-class were marked by the status dominance of the elite and the constraint they consequently imposed on the scope for police action. It was thought that 'the policeman on the beat was a drinking, working-class man, and these facts placed as much limitation on his activity against drunkenness as did the licensing laws or the presence of brewers on a watch committee' (Steedman, 1984: 149). The question of drink apart, the nature of the police little concerned the middle class. Their lives were scarcely touched by them. Between 1856 and 1880 only 10 questions concerning provincial police were asked in the Commons. Between Decker's treatment of the Metropolitan Police in the 1840s and Flora Thompson's reminiscences of village life in the 1880s there is no popular literature on the police. Those few illustrations, which included the police, tend to show them as a silhouette concealed in the shadows or as wooden-faced icons grasping a culprit's collar (Steedman, 1984: 7). This invisibility represented the gulf between police and middle-class. A policeman was seen as a servant, a view resting on 'what he had been before he turned policeman: ex-craft shoemakers and rural labourers were poor and unimportant men, only fools dressed in blue' (Steedman, 1984: 7). Such attitudes provide a neglected context for the antipathy of the Victorian middle-class to police. Police were either an irrelevance or a nuisance.

For the poor, sources of hostility to police were more obvious as the century drew to an end. The impact of police on working-class life was more direct than on the middle-class. The Summary Jurisdiction Act permitted police to whip juvenile offenders older than seven, at a magistrate's discretion. After 1856 the police were not only watching and apprehending, but important in trial and punishment. Police increasingly symbolised fear and authority, with birch rod in hand. 'Working class literature became more explicit about the relationship ... towards the end of the nineteenth century. Being beaten by a policeman counted as a common memory' (Steedman, 1984: 160), as it did among older people right into the 1990s.

Both the structural organisation of police and the socio-economic condition and culture of the urban community render dubious any 'golden age of community policing'. In 1933 in London 80% of the force were uniformed constables working a system of beats, fixed points and traffic points. Beats were worked for about three months and then changed. Recruitment problems often left PCs patrolling two, three or more beats each shift. Recruitment to the Met had traditionally been of brawny provincials rather than locals. When White sought former Islington officers from the 1930s he found an ex-miner from Yorkshire, a Luton shop boy, a Leytonstone shop boy, another from East London and one local. Mobility was compulsory on promotion and if a PC made an enemy of his inspector he was swiftly transferred (White, 1983).

White obtained oral evidence in a working-class community that had large numbers of street-sellers, traditionally at odds with police, and of scrap dealers operating on the fringes of legality. The area was also a centre of street-gaming and had a long tradition of street theatre and raucous, drunken nightlife. Antagonistic attitudes would not be surprising here, but White emphasises the 'ambient character of those antagonisms and contradictory social relations between police and people'. There was also in the 1930s a middle-class lack of confidence in police, provoked by corruption in the Met, scandals over the 'sus' laws and political partiality, and by resentment at the enforcement of traffic laws. As for the working-class, in 1930s London the poor needed the police to arbitrate neighbourhood disputes, protect the weak, and help in crises such as accidents. 'The poor were as fiercely litigious as cheap police court justice would allow. They would think twice before involving the police in their private and public lives but this didn't stop them doing so on a massive scale' (White, 1983: 35).

Yet, between such moments, police were generally characterised as the enemy, avoided where possible, feared and hated in equal measure.

People who had too much contact with them were known as 'narks' or 'coppers' boys'. White's respondents remembered two main reasons for avoidance: a class-conscious desire not to fraternise with the enemy, and fear that the police could not be trusted. There was acute awareness of their power and little of procedural safeguards. People expected a 'normal' level of violence from police – hitting troublesome youths with a fist, a rolled-up cape or a glove with coins in the fingers. The general fear of arbitrary use of power crystallised in the idea that police had to make a certain number of arrests a week and it mattered little whom, and was made worse by awareness of bribery and corruption. Along with this, their good wages, pensions, subsidised housing and travel set them apart from the community. The fact that the police were needed did not make them loved. The police role in defending sectional property, production and political relations – 'makes "policing by consent" in working class communities no more than a rhetorical figment of the liberal imagination' (White, 1983: 39).

Ambivalence endures: five years before the riots of the early 1980s, a Merseyside survey found that, even among slum dwellers, 70% thought positively about the police, compared with only 3% who considered them 'enemies', and that 86% of the poorest inhabitants wanted more police in their area, compared with 2% who wanted fewer (Davies, 1978), figures similar to those regularly obtained in subsequent surveys. Surveys regularly report both broad public satisfaction with the police and a substantially different view amongst minorities. For example, 19 in 20 respondents thought they were treated politely by police, eight in 10 were satisfied with the speed of police response, eight in 10 evaluated their local police as doing a good job, and the police were generally thought to be doing well in dealing with public order and accidents (Home Office News Release 8/95, 13 January 1995), but dissatisfaction was higher among young people and ethnic minorities, both in how they were treated when stopped and when they requested police help. The early days of policing were no golden age of rural community and an understanding clip round the ear for city kids. Nor were they easy and uncomplicated times for the police. The plight of mid-Victorian police is nicely shown in a chief constable's testimony of the means used to control late ale-houses. Constables on night duty were to watch for drunkards through the open doors. They were ordered not to go in, nor to speak to the drinkers. It cannot have been only the middle-class who were exercised at the police 'all the time watching'; but what we should not ignore is the effect of such a regime on the constables too. Here was an early sign of the social isolation of police.

In the second half of the 19th century, the police increasingly discharged administrative 'control functions', such as inspecting lodging houses and surveying cellar dwellings. Police took up powers of surveillance inherent in the policing functions of local authorities (Steedman, 1984: 16). The burden of controlling disturbances transferred from those whose interests were being protected to the police. New bourgeois groups were less enthusiastic than the aristocracy and local gentry to respond to calls to arms and there was growing awareness that militias led by landowners and yeomanry exacerbated disorder (Silver, 1967). The period 1870–1920 saw obvious class conflict replaced by the ambivalent confrontation of sections of the same class. Similarly with routine law enforcement, the way police

> came to act as a legitimate instrument of coercion was by no means a peaceful one. Policemen were individually attacked by outraged groups attempting to frustrate an arrest ... But by patrolling working class communities the police also came to act on behalf of individual working people. For the first time working class people gained some protection from attack, robbery on the streets, and burglary. (Bunyan, 1976: 66)

The ambivalence thesis runs through the period of the police strikes to the present and is apparent in contemporary survey data. In 2003, 80% rated police as doing a good job, but satisfaction was lower amongst minorities (British Crime Survey, 2003). This had long been so. The Met's 1983 survey found 72% had confidence in police, but among 16–34-year-olds it was 65% and among non-whites only 54%. Smith and Gray (1983) found 79% of Londoners regarded police as 'fair and reasonable', but 10% completely lacked confidence, and nearly half seriously doubted standards of police conduct. The Met's first 'customer survey' reported that 75% of those polled were satisfied with their visit to the police station, but only 62% of blacks were, and 55% overall reported the police failed to keep them informed of their case's progress (*Guardian*, 13 February 1990). Consent to policing may be widespread, but public attitudes to police are complex and not uni-directional.

The ambivalence thesis implies that, while there may have been no 'golden age', it is also overstated to typify police/public relations as purely conflictual. In routine policing overt conflict is rare. If control is seen simply as restraining people from doing things the officer forbids, under 4% of encounters are resolved by arrest, under 1% by threat of arrest or physical force and in only 5% of encounters do officers raise their voices (Fielding *et al*, 1992; Fielding, 1995). Reasoning and persuasion are much the most common means of exerting control.

Emergence of constabulary independence

The tendency to see our problems as unique rather than historically rooted is only one problem of historical interpretation. We also need to avoid seeing previous times through the perspective of our own. Lustgarten (1986) suggests that such a distortion has happened in the debate over constabulary independence. An example is the case earlier noted of the Liverpool chief constable ordered to proceed against brothels by his watch committee. The action was consistent with the fact that a subcommittee met daily to supervise police operations, issuing an average of one order a week in response to requests from property owners concerning the disposition of officers. As policing became routinised, such direct involvement was reduced, but this was no concession of constabulary independence, simply a sign that procedures satisfactory to the politicians were established. A politically contentious issue, like the brothel case, still provoked explicit direction and constabulary compliance (Lustgarten, 1986: 38). To Lustgarten, [t]he subordination of the police to elected representatives in the boroughs was part of common understanding.'

Complaints that pressure unduly influenced police, particularly brewing interests, did not mean that policing was often contentious in the sense we understand.

> Nineteenth century England was a political oligarchy. Not only did approximately 200 families dominate the national political life of a country they also largely owned, but the franchise was astonishingly restrictive ... In the first decade of the twentieth century, of those states which had established representative institutions, the British electorate was smaller than anywhere except Hungary. (Lustgarten, 1986: 39)

Even with universal male, and limited female, suffrage after the First World War, about half the industrial working-class was excluded by the £10 lodger and occupation franchises, along with paupers, most of the military, the homeless and live-in servants. Until 1888 there was no democratic element in county government, with executive power lying in the hands of justices. The County Police Act 1839 gave them power to vest authority in a chief constable because geography and the lifestyle of the 'land-owning leisure class' precluded their meeting regularly. Chiefs were still subject to the justices, who initially exerted their power. After 1856 'scions of gentry families' often got the job, and the justices assumed that these appointees shared their perspective. Here was the basis of 'constabulary independence' as it applied to chiefs. By 1914, they had clear dominance over their police authorities (Lustgarten, 1986: 42). Direct contact between Home Office and chief constables began immediately, with the justices obliged to the latter for information about the policy of the former.

The county system thus facilitated the police independence doctrine and rise of the chiefs and central government interest; but the real action was not in the 19th century, but the decade from 1919, and related to the wartime co-ordination of chiefs and the aftermath of the police strikes. The Desborough Committee Report recommended high pay and a federation instead of unionisation, but also suggested extending the Home Secretary's power to making regulations for all forces and the inception of a permanent Police Department of the Home Office.

Important developments occurred in Wales, where several chief constables took a tough anti-union line. Despite harmonious local demonstrations during the General Strike they demanded extra police. The Monmouthshire Standing Joint Committee, supported by the County Council, called for the resignation of their chief constable. Both he and his colleague in Carmarthenshire refused. The Home Office withheld Monmouthshire's central grant until the resignation demand was withdrawn. 'In political conflicts over policing, the existence of the chief constable as intermediary was a godsend to the Home Office. It did not need to usurp traditional local government powers to ensure that important policies were carried out' (Lustgarten, 1986: 45). Henceforth chief constables were genuinely in command of their forces and not subject to central government direction, provided government could count on them carrying out policing in ways it found broadly acceptable.

The unwritten compact by which constables achieved independence from local control benefited from the established legal view that the constable was responsible to the law, so that 'the legality of any individual action could be the basis of an action for damages in the courts' (Lustgarten, 1986: 47). Any difference between ordinary and chief constable was simply ignored. Changes in local government, increasing identification with crime fighting, and increasing administrative powers independent of local authority and magistrates tended to make constables 'servants of the Crown'. A further boost was the 1930 High Court decision in *Fisher v Oldham Corporation*, the servant and master case (of which more below). Constabulary independence was enshrined as orthodoxy in the following two decades.

Handling disorder

Under the old common law system, when there was major public disorder the military supplemented the constabulary. However, by 1700 the brutality and ill-discipline of the military had made them highly unpopular. Colonial experience informed early thinking on the management of disorder. Sir Robert Peel's determination to achieve effective policing against dissent was based on his experience as Chief Secretary for Ireland. Once the eponymous 'Peelers' or 'bobbies' emerged, they were pressed to serve against disorder. 'The early 1830s saw the Reform Bill riots in London and the growth of subversive activities which provided endless opportunities for the police to perfect techniques of crowd control and practise the newly acquired art of baton charges' (Critchley, 1978: 80). In 1837 the Met sent 38 police to suppress anti-Poor Law riots in Yorkshire, Essex and the West Country. Detachments were sent to Loughborough, Mansfield and four other towns during Chartist disturbances in 1839. In reckonings of the state of national defence, the police were customarily listed with the army and militia. The Royal Irish Constabulary was used as a model. Several English counties adopted its system of horse patrol around a central station housing strategically dispersed detachments of police (Steedman, 1984: 23).

In 1856, the posting of small troop detachments around the country ceased and from the early 1860s local authorities facing disturbance turned to the Home Office. Its advice was to 'swear in as many respectable citizens as special constables as possible, call on the county constabulary, then the yeomanry (but if possible swear the yeomen in as special constables), then finally, if necessary make application to the military' (Steedman, 1984: 33). The Murphy Riots and Fenian disturbances of the late 1860s led to the distinction between insurrection and rebellion, in which the use of arms was justified, and 'mere riot', where it was not and local police were primarily responsible for maintaining order. William Murphy, an anti-Catholic agitator, provoked 25 riots from 1866 to 1871, mainly in urban areas. In 10 disturbances troops were deployed. On 11 occasions police from outside the area in question were called in, and the militia and yeomen called on one occasion each. Special constables, usually tradesmen in defence of their own property, were sworn on 11 occasions. Failure of containment permitted 'mob rule' and general riot, as in Birmingham in 1867, where 400 borough police, 180 county police, 93 cavalry, 300 infantry and 500 special constables were deployed. The only predictable end to the disturbances was Murphy's departure for another town, and the experience hastened public enthusiasm for preventative policing. For the county force, public order was an accustomed role, but not for the boroughs, for whom it was a departure from the defence of particular, purely local, interests.

During the 19th century, conflict was intermittent and largely confined to workplace issues for the industrial working-class, but a feature of daily life for participants in the street economy. Mass resistance might spring from sectarian or ethnic conflicts, but the economically marginal engaged in a stream of run-ins with police. From 1860 to 1930, one in 20 of Liverpool's population appeared in court every year. There was thus a distinction between respectable and street working-class, particularly with the extension of suffrage. However the 1920s and 1930s Depression years pushed many down the class ladder and provoked widespread industrial conflict. Violent confrontations occurred between police and the National Unemployed Workers Union. From August 1931 to December 1932, police made over 100 baton charges against mass demonstrations. Over Christmas 1931 there were riots in Liverpool, London, Leeds, Glasgow and Stoke; in 1932 martial law was declared in Belfast after demands for higher unemployment benefit were unmet. During the state of emergency of the 1926 General Strike, any form of strike action was construed as illegal. Strike bulletins were deemed 'calculated to cause disaffection' and mere possession could result in three months' imprisonment. In Doncaster a mass picket of 1,000 miners was repeatedly charged by police, and 80 arrests made. In the East Fife coalfield the police were met by a 'Workers Defence Corps' armed with pick-shafts, and prevented from interfering with the pickets. After the strike, a protest by dockers occurred outside Poplar Town Hall. Police made baton charges, struck down a clergyman bearing a crucifix and, at the nearby National Union of Railwaymen headquarters batoned everyone present including the mayor (Bowes, 1966: 27).

Workers were more antagonistic to the Specials than ordinary police in the General Strike (Brogden, 1982: 184). In the Liverpool police strike, Specials were particular targets for the contempt of the mob. The permanent force of 250 Specials was increased to 2,000, 'made up almost entirely of clerks from the corporation, the banks and the business houses' (Reynolds and Judge, 1968: 170). Resentment of the Specials recurred in the General Strike. Brighton Town Council had been preparing for the General Strike for six months by enrolling special constables (Minutes, General Purposes Committee, January 1926). Trade unionists had agreed to co-operate with the authorities (Minutes, Watch Committee, 19 May 1926) and the crowd at Lewes Road was good-humoured and fairly orderly until mounted Specials charged into them. There was little complaint about the regular police during the 'Battle of Lewes Road' or the rest of the strike, but much about the politically motivated Specials (*Evening Argus*, 17 May 1926). The Specials and the police were given a silver cup by the mayor at a victory dinner, where the dessert was 'Ice bricks à la Lewes Road' and the menu aped the design of a police charge sheet (*Southern Weekly News*, 22 May 1926).

Like the militia and yeomanry, the Specials expressed naked class interest, while ordinary police were seen as just doing a job by those who themselves craved secure employment. By now the middle-class no longer subscribed to an organic model of society with the police an exemplar of sober behaviour, but to a class model in which police were the servants of their interest. The 1900–39 period saw the first large-scale confrontations of state and unions (Morgan, 1988). In 1911 Sir Edward Troup, at the Home Office, expressed concern over the consequences of national strikes for an urbanised society vulnerable to interruption of its food supply. Troup concluded that emergency powers and administrative centralisation were necessary to counter the threat, noting the Home Office experience during the 1893–94 Yorkshire coal strike that soldiers and police could be deployed by administrative action without public debate. A centralised system to suppress strike-related disorder operated in the wave of unrest after the First World War and during the General Strike. Local forces were increasingly part of a nationally co-ordinated apparatus when policing major strikes and the 'Hunger Marches'.

During the 19th century and first half of the 20th century, police sometimes served as little more than a private strike-breaking agency. After 1945 there was increasing police appreciation of the legitimacy of peaceful picketing and the establishment of norms of co-operation, informed by their own labour market experience.

Police strikes

Full weight has long been denied to the lengthy history of police strikes. The first well-documented one was during the Manchester cotton trades dispute of 1853. The men had petitioned the Watch Committee for a wage increase on grounds of equality with Liverpool. The Watch Committee deemed it incompatible with their duty to ratepayers and refused. Within hours, 168 out of 435 men in the force handed in their month's notice; over the weekend 250 more did so; but superintendents and the Watch Committee foresaw no trouble filling 400 vacancies with poor farm-workers; most men withdrew their notice. The local press celebrated victory over 'extensive combination'; but a garment trades dispute elicited more police resignations a month later, the police claiming their respectability warranted a living wage aligned with other artisans. There was no march, but an 'ostentatiously dignified assembly' of 170 striking constables (Brogden, 1982: 133). This led to a rapid breakdown of social discipline in Manchester. Blackleg police were attacked and non-striking officers assaulted. The watch committee conceded the increase and all but 15 strikers returned. They were soon at work breaking up meetings of the garment workers.

Increased rents and food prices often led to agitation among police. In 1853, at Hull, 30 men resigned and 50 refused either to work or to resign after a long-disputed claim. The men knew the watch committee had not had one applicant all year. Over the next 20 years, wage claims were generally based on comparison with rates in other forces, helped by the thorough reports of the Inspectorate. The 1871 Birmingham dispute was noteworthy. It was over holiday provision as well as pay, the comparator being London. The men used a sophisticated ploy by making application to the Watch Committee through the Head Constable. Their petition succeeded. This is regarded as the first skirmish in a 'police wages movement' that established the distinct skills and virtues of police in the mind of public paymasters (Steedman, 1984: 135). Gradually watch committees came to see the men as employees, not servants. The police were in fact the first in the public sector to organise a union.

In 1918, the London police struck for better conditions and marched on Downing Street under the banners of their union. Initially, the action seemed successful: more pay was granted and Lloyd George hinted that the union might be recognised after the war; but a year later a Police Bill outlawing the union was before Parliament. Men tried to organise a nationwide strike. It went unsupported by organised labour and was marked by ineffective strikes in London and Birmingham, where there were brutal clashes between pickets and blacklegs, and by mob violence, looting and arson in Liverpool and Birkenhead. The strike spelled the end of the union. Its demise featured indolent civil servants, uncaring and ruthless politicians and reactionary chief constables. Twice before the 1918 and 1919 strikes the word 'mutiny' was used to describe the actions of police, in 1872 and 1890. The warnings of discontent were plain and long-established.

When the 1918 strike began, Scots Guards occupied New Scotland Yard, a loaded machine gun faced Downing Street, and troops with fixed bayonets guarded Whitehall. Lloyd George, the Home Secretary and Police Commissioner, met the strike leaders. As the meeting started Lloyd George was told that the Grenadier Guards outside were fraternising with the strikers and openly saying they would refuse orders to clear them from the street (Reynolds and Judge, 1968: 4). The context for the government was one of a likely continuance of the war for a further year, industrial unrest throughout Britain, a police mutiny and effective control of Whitehall, as the troops aiding the civil power were young, and sympathetic to the strikers. Years later Lloyd George told a policeman 'this country was nearer to Bolshevism that day than at any time since' (quoted in Reynolds and Judge, 1968: 5). He conceded the union's demands, but with a crucial exception.

When Parliament adjourned, the Home Secretary, the Commissioner, and the Permanent Under-Secretary of State all left London. When a police union organiser was disciplined for undermining the Manchester force's loyalty, the union threatened to revoke the no-strike rule on which Lloyd George had insisted. It rapidly became clear there was mass support for an immediate strike. A few days after Parliament had broken up, virtually all the Met were refusing duty. The Trade Union Congress (TUC) was ready to demand recognition of the union and authorise sympathy strikes. The government agreed it must get the strike finished quickly, but avoid recognising the union. They thought this could be done by a generous pay rise and floating a mechanism to deal with grievances. Lloyd George insisted that while the men could have an organisation, it had yet to be settled if it would be a union or an 'internal body' (Reynolds and Judge, 1968: 61–62). There was concern that recognising a union would lead to it being demanded in the army. Lloyd George stuck to the ambiguous line that a union could not be recognised in wartime, leaving the union to infer that the post-war climate would be different. No one involved could have known that the Armistice was only 10 weeks away. Soon after the strike the union was claiming 40,000 members. The government line on membership helped recruitment: if not expressly forbidden to join, men proved only too willing to support the union, and local branches began to grow.

The 1919 strike was very different. The context was the government proposal to ban the union and proceed via an internal body to hear grievances, inspired by a new Commissioner's determination to break the union. The executive was divided, provincial branches were withdrawing, so there could be no national response. The major unions lent no support. 'For the most part the workers felt the troubles in the police were none of their business' (Reynolds and Judge, 1968: 150). The most tangible support was rioting on the Mersey after half the Liverpool police 'went wrong' in August 1919. The worst outbreak of mob violence in Liverpool's history resulted in a battleship and two destroyers training searchlights on the banks of the Mersey. Every shop window in the roads bordering the docks was broken. More than 300 people were imprisoned, and one rioter was shot dead by troops. Some 2,400 police, out of a total union membership of 50,000, went on strike. Only a few who obeyed the watch committee's ultimatum to return to duty continued in the police service; 2,364 never wore police uniform again. In London and Birmingham the police shrugged off the effects of the strike in a few days, but troops stayed in Liverpool for a month until new recruits were ready.

The union leaders expressed defiance in meeting after meeting, but police unionism in Britain was dead. A pay rise (from £1.50 to £3.50 a week) undermined the strike. In such dubious circumstances the Police Federation was born, to be despised by the ranks and ignored by authority for many years. Only after 1945 did it progress. It is unlikely that the role it plays could ever have fallen on the union; but the attitudes of the political masters of the London police made rather obvious the answer to Reynolds and Judge's telling question: if there had never been a police union, would the authorities ever have allowed a federation?

The 1919 Police Act raised the socio-economic status of police and laid the ground for standardisation and centralisation of policing. The strike was broken, its leaders dismissed, and heavy penalties established for inciting disaffection in the ranks. The Home Office gained substantial regulatory powers over forces. The central grant would be paid only where the Home Secretary was satisfied the force was properly administered, and he was empowered to withhold it indefinitely. He could set regulations on organisation, pay, allowances, clothing and conditions of service. Compliance was secured by making it a condition of award of the grant (Lambert, 1986: 27–28). The Act set up the Police Advisory Council and the Police Federation. The latter was expressly forbidden to join the TUC. It was illegal for police to join any union having the object of influencing pay, pensions or conditions of any force. Every policeman below superintendent rank automatically belonged to the Federation. It became an offence to call or attend any unauthorised meeting about matters concerning the force. Meetings are called officially, during official time and at official expense.

It would be as mistaken to believe that the capacity of police employees to act collectively against their employer is now extinguished as it would be to imagine that social conflict is confined to relations between police and public. Conflict within police forces has a mundane reality in everyday cases of sexual harassment, discrimination on grounds of ethnicity, and divisions between the ranks, now augmented by extensive civilianisation that is no longer confined to back-office functions, but includes station counter staff, and the addition of Police Community Support Officers to the cosily-named 'extended police family'. While these are the quiet regularities of social conflict within the police, collective action can still flare when joint interests are threatened. The Sheehy Inquiry into the Role and Responsibilities of the Police Service, remarkable for a change agenda that has been partly implemented in dribs and drabs over the years since it reported, is now mostly remembered for the bitter waves of protest it inspired across the country, culminating in a spectacular police rally that more than filled Wembley stadium. Senior police embrace of managerialism in the 1990s can be read partly as an attempt to break such raw power. An alternative to the 'extended police family' metaphor is the phrase 'divide and rule', but simply because some employees are civilians and some frontline staff have limited legal powers it does not mean the incumbents cannot form the view that their interests are best-served on occasions by standing in unison with the regular ranks against management caprice or ministerial imposition.

Orthodox police histories obscure several points important to an understanding of the police and social conflict. First, there was much more physical conflict between police forces and lower class-groups during the first century of the 'new police' than is usually acknowledged. Secondly, where overt conflict was absent, there was not so much consent as a 'grumbling dissent' (Brogden, 1982). The police as an institution was accepted by lower-class people not because it became any more popular, but because of its power. Thirdly, and crucially, lower-class and 'respectable' working-class attitudes were not unified. Working-class encounters with the police differed from the experience of those outside the primary economy. This can be added to what we know of middle-class scepticism and parsimony, and to the history of police unionism. These dimensions reflect the complex Victorian class structure. The sides had squared off by Edwardian times. Merchants, business proprietors, professionals, shopkeepers and clerical workers increasingly gave assent and support at time of crisis. Industrial workers conceded a grudging acceptance disrupted on occasion by industrial confrontations. Only the lower working-class participants in the secondary or 'street' economy remained in essentially the same relation of opposition as had always marked their relations with the 'new' police.

3. Paramilitary policing and public order

The mediating role

Public order incidents represent a prime form of social conflict and the challenges they pose are aggravated by their extreme diversity. They range from *ad hoc* disturbances and disputes policed by tactical support in small numbers under local command to major set-piece confrontations between organised groups controlled by paramilitary policing. The demands of public order policing have customarily been divided analytically into two broad classes: routine order maintenance, which is practised daily in town centres and other areas where relatively minor public order infractions are apt to occur, and the policing of major disturbances of public order occasioned by industrial disputes and political demonstrations. However, to the latter it is now necessary to add what may be regarded as a hybrid category, the policing of large community-based public events that take place on a regular (usually annual) basis, such as London's Notting Hill Carnival, the Gay Pride events in London, Leeds, Brighton and elsewhere, music events, such as the Reading Rock Festival and the Glastonbury Festival, and religious gatherings associated with New Age religions (for example, the solstice commemorations at Stonehenge) or with adherents mainly drawn from minority ethnic communities (for example, Eid). It is not that such events have only lately occurred. Fairs, carnivals, and associated disorder and rioting have endured for centuries, although media attention gives a new dimension. However, the main consideration is that the police regard these events as ones that require a full police response.

Community-based events are distinct from the other main forms of the major disturbance class of public order policing because (i) they are organised and enthusiastically supported by significant minority interests in the community, (ii) they are regular events, taking place at predictable and publicly announced times and (iii) they attract significant demands for police service both in routine marshalling, response to crime that takes place in and around the event, and in responding to the serious disorder that is always potential when large numbers of people are present, particularly where the group organising and/or associated with the event is one that attracts condemnation from other significant interests in the community. That such events are not, at least overtly, founded in conflict of the kind associated with the industrial and political disputes that largely inform the conventional analysis of major public order policing, suggests that the best frame of reference is in the post-Macpherson Inquiry approach of the police to dealing with minority interests in the community. The specifics of the policing of such events will be considered after that of the legitimation of the police role in public order generally.

Ultimately, whatever the nature of the public order demand, the police claim their authority from the law, not as direct agents of the state. Resort to military support is now extremely rare, but not unknown, as in terrorist alerts, particularly in Northern Ireland. Police control has always been reasserted and its separation from politics reaffirmed. It is also the case with industrial disputes. As long as distance from sectional interests can be maintained and industrial disputes are controllable by police, they pose no political threat. The historical effort to de-politicise policing, and the desire to rely on a criminal law construed as non-partisan, leads police to resist broader political overtones in industrial disputes. Disputes are regarded as political if they do not directly concern conditions of work or if outsiders try to politicise them. Outsiders threaten because non-employees are not part of the dispute and their motive must be to create disorder.

In the context of public order the 'mediating' function is another dimension of the concept of discretion. Discretion, or selective en-forcement, is bound to create controversy. Mixed feelings over the police role in connection with protest have a long lineage, as do formal restrictions placed on the expression of police views on political matters. While police could not vote in parliamentary elections before 1887 or local ones until 1893, and are barred from any active part in politics, the police collectively have found ways of influencing matters they construe as relevant to policing. Nowadays that construction is wide indeed. In some analyses the police play the main role in escalating tension, worsening conflicts being played out peacefully. Bowes charged that:

> [t]he post-1829 history of political movements shows clearly that when the police cooperate, or at least do not interfere with political demonstrations, these remain almost without exception disciplined and peaceful; but when the police seek to enforce bans, discipline is often violently destroyed and sometimes police violence is returned in kind. (1966: 77)

Even in such a jaded analysis reference is made to police discretion to enforce or not to enforce 'bans'. It would be wrong to say that police are just following orders; in a post-Nuremburg era we all recognise that delegated authority is not free of responsibility. From the 1980s onwards the police have become adept at anticipating controversy over public order and have increasingly entered situations with a version of events in hand that accounts for their action in reasonable, consensual terms. The 'mediating' role is a very important tool.

Yet there are occasions when the mediating role is also an unconvincing rationale for action taken. Mass public order disturbances are relatively infrequent and in the 19th century many police conducted their role with a brutality born of the confusion and panic of the moment. During 'Bloody Sunday' in 1887, the Commissioner refused London radicals permission to use Trafalgar Square for a meeting. They went ahead, with William Morris and George Bernard Shaw among the participants. Shaw later described a Scottish MP, Robert Graham, being 'personally and bodily assailed by the concerted military and constabulary forces'. Graham and another Fabian, John Burns, chained themselves to the railings of a hotel where Burns, waving a red flag, was also battered by police. After police baton charges came the foot and horse guards. Graham was truncheoned about the head, he and Burns were arrested, two men died and over 200 were injured. 'Henry Salt, a prominent early Fabian and a master at Eton College, had his watch stolen and later wrote sadly "I couldn't protest the conduct of the police in the square and invoke them against the pickpockets"' (Evans, 1974: 49). Historians of the period suggest such events led eventually to the formation of the Labour Party, to close the gap between government and unrepresented sections of the public.

Protest here is an equilibrating mechanism that restores order to the parts the *status quo* has not reached. This begs the question whether the police necessarily act in the government interest or on their own construction of mediation. It also begs the empirical question of how we are to measure when protest is sufficiently general to indicate a crisis of democratic representation. The police may sometimes feel they are 'holding the lid on the pressure cooker' over social problems the government should address, but this does not make their role neutral. Governments do not act with barometric sensitivity, nor are the police merely 'piggy in the middle'.

It has long been debated whether riots are rational, instrumental political actions pursuing goal-oriented considerations, or impulsive, violent events, products of a herd mentality run amok in the context of anomie and disadvantage. Both are overstated. Riots are the radical end of a continuum of aggressive social behaviours (including collective bargaining and demonstrations) best understood in the context of local cultural dynamics, moulded by historical experience and the impact of government on forms of resistance and protest. The primary sources of grievance in the American riots of the 1960s were police practice, unemployment and housing conditions – in that order (Kerner *et al*, 1968) – the same issues cited most frequently by analysts of Britain's riots of the 1980s and that have featured in disturbances on housing estates and in poor inner city neighbourhoods since. Typically, the American riots were triggered by minor police action leading to confrontation with blacks. Looting, arson and attacks on police followed, but without general attacks on whites. Apart from the mixed ethnic composition of British rioters, this was also the pattern in Britain.

Relative deprivation provides some explanatory purchase in both countries. Despite civil rights advances, US ghetto blacks were excluded from the general prosperity of the 1960s. In Britain, monetarist policy, industrial decline, and the labour market practices associated with multinational corporations and globalisation, created unemployment that fell hard on inner city youths. New Labour administrations subsequent to the monetarist Conservative administrations may have ameliorated some underclass conditions through welfare policy and improvements in public services, but the share of national wealth held by the poor has declined, and the resentment of those in conditions of poverty when surrounded by widespread affluence are classic conditions for relative deprivation; but there are other explanations. 'Fun and profit' are important motives (Banfield, 1968). Thompson (1980) ridiculed the view that crime is displaced revolutionary activity, and Rock the tendency to impute symbolic meaning to riots to the neglect of the desire for violence and excitement, and greed. '[I]t is as if riots cannot be innocent of profound meaning ... very few have proposed that riots are not invariably intended to convey sober meaning and political lessons' (Rock, 1981: 19–20).

The 'pleasures' of riot have their analogue in playing fields and superstores. However, it is the breakdown of social control that is distinctive relative to other 'fun and profit' activities (Field, 1982: 16). Riots may not be 'political' but do symbolise something beyond the urge for hedonism. Riot sites may be high crime areas, but there is a difference between 'widespread cynicism and opportunism regarding the rule of law' and subjecting the police to collective assault (Foster, 2002). Intentionally or not, rioting challenges the state, for the claim to accommodate criticism of institutions within a consensual acceptance of their ultimate legitimacy is central to its survival. At a personal level, too, rioting means more than a free TV; '[i]t can become a reply to the experience of oneself as an object moved around by external forces' (Rock, 1981).

Research in Handsworth after the 1981 riot found significantly greater disapproval of the police, and feelings of fun and excitement among those involved than among witnesses, but fear and disgust were common reactions among witnesses, counter-rioters *and* rioters (Field and Southgate, 1982). Approval was commonest among those who were young, single, black, unemployed, poorer, and not living with parents or a partner. Each factor is an index of marginal social status. Involvement in civil disorder is a rare experience: even in the early 80s only 13% of respondents in London had witnessed any 'crowd trouble' in the two years up to the survey, a period which included the Brixton riots, compared to 27% who had been crime victims in the previous year (Smith and Gray, 1983). Even among blacks in high ethnic minority areas, experience of crowd trouble was rare (14% in the six months, including the Brixton riots). However, rioting accounted for only 10% of 'crowd trouble' witnessed by respondents overall. Sport accounted for 39%, demonstrations 10%, carnival crowds 3%. If we add to sport the 12% that was 'other crowds', the 12% that was crowd trouble with adolescents and the 7% that was trouble with drunks, most public disorder is accounted for by routine order maintenance.

Conflict with police as a pastime may appear to appeal largely to youths in bleak, rundown estates. Young joyriders on a Leeds housing estate nicknamed 'the Zoo' (Halton Moor) made seven ramming attacks on police cars in a four month period as part of a campaign to make part of the estate a 'no go area' for police (*Guardian*, 9 January 1993). The July 1992 riots in Bristol's Hartcliffe estate were blamed on outside troublemakers; police were attacked and buildings destroyed. Only 16 of the 65 arrested were from the estate, where tension was high over the deaths of two local men on a stolen police motorcycle during a police chase. Gangs of young men had converged on the estate from neighbouring suburbs, citing motives such as 'I'm here to see the fun' ('Estate clears debris as police blame lawless outsiders', *Guardian*, 20 July 1992). Sentiments on notes left with wreaths at the crash spot on the second night of rioting included a dedication stating 'You would have been proud to have been there last night. I know you watched it. What a send-off, eh! That's the way you would have wanted it'. The note was signed by four people. Describing the initial riot as 'bloody brilliant' an 18-year-old female, who had been throwing rocks at fire crews, said of police 'they deserved everything they got and there's more to come'. There were divisions within the rundown community; the mother of one of the dead denounced the riot, the other mother the police. Earlier that summer, rioting in Stockton-on-Tees was instigated by youths involved in drug-dealing from two terraces of shops and old flats in an estate otherwise comprising three-bedroom family houses and having a reputation for practical self-help. The trouble was so localised that within 100 yards other residents tended gardens oblivious to the petrol-bombing and gang attacks on police. A heavy-handed arrest of suspected joyriders carrying a shotgun was seen as trigger ('Riot hotspot angers estate', *Guardian*, 19 June 1992). Here there was again testimony to the flashpoint drawing in outsiders 'looking for a rumble' with police. Locals disputed whether it was the 65% unemployment rate, drug-dealing, or the grievance over the arrests that prompted the riot. Gang culture may encourage participation motivated by youthful hedonism as well as disaffection. It is said that 70% of gang members are under 25, 30% under 18, and most join at age 12–14 (James, 2003). The riot dynamic appears to be one where, if police are engaged in an ongoing confrontational relation with local youths and this escalates, other similarly alienated individuals are drawn to the area and are joined by a much larger number of relatively neutral onlookers, some of whom may be tempted to join in.

The idea of a police 'buffer role' implies temporary intervention in social conflict. Historians have argued that the buffer role became insignificant when government recognised the 'political necessity' of keeping down unemployment. It became difficult to entertain such a 'political necessity' after the Conservative administrations of Thatcher and Major. No accommodation of competing sectional interests is ever permanent. Just before the 1980s riots, Whitaker, who documented ongoing resentment of the police in parts of London and South Wales where police were still booed on the cinema screen, suggested that it was diminishing (old songs like 'We'll kill all the coppers who come down our way' had disappeared; Whitaker, 1979: 17). However, such bitterness is readily revived. Songs with exactly these sentiments became common during the 1984–85 coal dispute; police complained of abuse from tiny children, and similar *animus* has periodically been recorded on public housing estates up to the present time. It must be accepted both that social conflict is enduring *and* that the nature of social conflict is not static.

Police warrant their practice in the mediating role on the basis that demonstrators must be handled in such a way that those who are not involved can go about their 'lawful occasions' with minimum inconvenience. When police protect groups with whom they are suspected of having an affinity, or that are identified with sectional interests, the argument about protecting the uninvolved is doubted. In 1937, police protected Hornsey Town Hall in the name of free speech while a British Union of Fascists meeting took place. Although the Public Order Act stipulated that police proceed against those behaving offensively at public meetings, they remained aloof while protestors were beaten up and ejected. An inspector witnessed several assaults, including a man being thrown face down on the steps, and was repeatedly asked to intervene. He refused to do so or to allow police to accompany the injured into the hall to identify their assailants (Bowes, 1966: 54). Such actions seem blatant by comparison with modern, more image-conscious policing.

It is a key part of police ideology that police must protect the freedom of all, as well as those liberties recognised by law. Without a written constitution there is no absolute requirement to uphold freedom of peaceful assembly or association or to strike, but police have a duty to safeguard fundamental freedoms guaranteed in international conventions. However, police still enjoy considerable discretion in setting priorities. During the 1984–85 coal dispute, much police action was based on the view that working miners sought to exercise an important freedom to go to work, and needed protection from violence and intimidation; but police commonly neglect essential demands, for example protection against racial attacks. Further, police have 'a duty to prevent disorder but a discretion as to the methods chosen' (McCabe and Wallington, 1988: 131). Throughout the coal dispute police used their restraining powers to stop strikers getting to picket lines. Working miners were dealt with differently from the normal operational approach to conflicts between preserving order and protecting rights. The release of official papers after the dispute confirmed that it was government pressure rather than exceptional commitment to the rights of working miners that accounted for chiefs' interpretation of the mediating role.

We hear less about the 'mediating role' as a corrective to institutional racism. Police efforts to protect the freedom of racist groups to demonstrate have only latterly been matched by similar determination to act against racist attacks. In Notting Hill in 1958, racists threw petrol bombs at 'coloureds', stabbed, coshed and marauded as lynch gangs. The police had proved reluctant to deploy in greater numbers, which, in light of the quality of Special Branch information, suggested something more than ignorance of the problem. During the Notting Hill disturbances blacks' premises were damaged and blacks were assaulted while local police exhibited hostility and tolerated racist meetings and gangs prowling the streets taunting blacks. A West Indian was stabbed to death by youths shouting 'Hey Jim Crow'. The Home Secretary was pressed in the Commons to draft in extra police in light of the violence and circulation of leaflets titled 'Coloured immigrants go home', but stated, 'I am satisfied that the Commissioner of Police has made adequate dispositions' (Hansard, quoted in Bowes, 1966: 67). Although Special Branch officers attended Mosleyite and British National Party (BNP) meetings throughout the period, no incitement charges arose, whereas such charges were brought against trade unionists and peace campaigners. A group of Mosleyites shouting, 'we've no need for half-castes here' at the entertainer Sammy Davis and who pursued him shouting abuse through a loudspeaker, suffered no police action, while an anti-fascist who shouted, 'you Blackshirt bastard' at Mosley himself as he left Old Street Court was fined for insulting words and behaviour and bound over for 12 months. A man who booed Colin Jordan, a noted fascist, as he arrived at Bow Street Court was arrested for 'insulting behaviour', while Jordan occasioned no police action the same day when directing a Nazi salute at a crowd of 200 as he left the court having been committed for trial (Hansard, quoted in Bowes, 1966: 70).

Few mothers and children have been prosecuted for disrupting traffic while demanding pedestrian crossings, a recurrent form of protest since the 1970s. Obstruction and even conspiracy charges could have applied, if the group was not one to whom the police judged most people to be sympathetic. For police to claim that such decisions, and those to prosecute anti-racist activists, pickets, and fathers disrupting traffic while protesting at the workings of the Child Support Agency, are 'non-political', presupposes a broad social consensus. Such consensus is rare in a highly diverse society where even local politics are now 'party political', threatening the consensual fiction on which the police mediating role ideology rests.

It is important to recognise that the police ideology is no mere public relations device. Ideology is not rhetoric. There is genuine subscription to the idea that the law represents a consensus of the public that the police serve. The consensus contrasts fundamentally with partisan, 'political' law enforcement. The latter sustains 'sectional' interests. The legitimacy of police action is founded on consensual laws impartially enforced. The mediating role involves balancing sectional demands in the interests of broad consensus. Demands seen as uncontentious, such as homely protests at the need for pedestrian crossings, are regarded as compatible with the public interest; but in communities stratified along many dimensions a purely uncontested demand is unusual. The police feel they must ever take into account potential or theoretical opposition, so the default position is to regard *most* democratic demands as sectional. If the 'mediating role' is to have any substance, police require a more sophisticated understanding of partisanship and sectional interests. Political science analyses of policing argue that *uncorrupted* coercive power can improve conditions the free market and established politics neglect (Muir, 1977: 278). Power can be an agent of positive social change; but to do this the allocation of the police resource has to be selective in precisely the way likely to excite charges of sectionalism, for example by designating extra resources to tackle problems disproportionately affecting the weak; the mediating function, which plays a key part in police ideology, is hostile to positive discrimination. Yet it would be wrong to see the police simply as a repressive arm of the state. The notions of consent, and law as expression of consensus, are more than a legitimating dogma.

Major public order events and community-based events

Police involvement in the control of events that may disrupt public order puts them in contact with citizens who are politically active and articulate. Such citizens are inclined to take an international perspective, to be concerned with a range of issues and critical of government. The importance of demonstrations may, paradoxically, be heightened by globalisation and the US having become the world's sole superpower. The reduced power of the individual state affords Britain less prospect on its own of influencing the international causes of the day. At the same time these issues are more thoroughly and immediately reported than ever before. If the nation-state's declining influence, and the increasing need for states to act through large collective power blocs and multinational treaties, frustrates people aspiring to influence action on the world stage, the frustration can only increase as Westminster's direct influence falls relative to US, EU and corporate dominion. The relevance of Martin Luther King's remark that 'riots are the voice of the unheard' is not confined to black Americans.

The police may have no direct influence over the causes that exercise protestors, but they have major influence over the course of protest. Like other chiefs, the Commissioners of the Met and the City Police can make a banning order if, like other chiefs, they feel their power to impose conditions on marches is insufficient to prevent disorder. Conditions can be imposed on route, numbers, types of banner, duration, and entry to public places. Commanders on the ground can impose conditions without notice once 'processions' begin. Orders last up to three months and are indiscriminate. The power is to ban all or a 'class' of processions in a given area. Notice must be given of any procession if it is intended to demonstrate support for or opposition to the views or actions of any group, publicise a cause or campaign, or mark or commemorate an event. The Public Order Act 1986, still in force, redefined and collated the common law offences of riot, rout, unlawful assembly and affray, making them statutory, and added a new offence, disorderly conduct. It does not involve breach of the peace or a threat of violence, and even the government declared it 'not easy to define'. The Act heightened police discretion. A week's notice of a march was required and a banning order could be made on three new criteria as well as risk of serious disorder: 'serious disruption to the life of the community', preventing serious property damage, and 'intimidation of others'. Blanket bans are often imposed even though the orders were designed to prevent single events.

An obscure effect of the development of the capacity to more systematically control large-scale protest was that the new tasks and capacities gave uniformed officers *esprit de corps*.

[I]n most police training establishments, practice in the 'trudge and wedge' which is intended to separate elements in a riotous demonstration gave both recruits and observers some impression of the strength, cohesion, and power of a large, uniformed police presence moving forward together. (McCabe and Wallington, 1988: 43)

There is inevitably a transfer of experience gained in major public order incidents to other incidents similar in certain characteristics. The 1989 Hillsborough football stadium disaster, in which over 90 football supporters died, informed policing of other large sporting events, even ones that were rather dissimilar, such as Derby Day at Epsom ('Hillsborough lessons will help policing of Derby Day crowds', *Surrey Advertiser*, 10 February 2000). After disturbances involving England fans at European football matches, police commentators suggested that forces, such as the Belgian police, had wrongly had no obvious visible uniformed presence, but relied on plainclothes officers intercepting troublemakers when fighting began. Then riot squads appeared. In contrast, on major match days in England there is a large visible presence of uniformed officers from the outset and bars are closed along routes to grounds ('We can deal with football thugs, claims police chief', *Surrey Advertiser*, 23 June 2000). Undercover units are used for longer-term tracking, but hardcore thugs can be stopped from inflaming boisterous fans if a large police presence is apparent. Such targeted police operations result in 'high quality football banning orders'; such bans are the most numerous form of police ban. They are applied to individuals and are rapidly increasing, from 1,794 in 2003 to 2,596 in 2004 (Home Office, 2004d).

It is arguable that fiscal initiatives exert as much influence on the policing of public order, and its balance with community policing, as does the law. Police capacity varies by an area's resources and the complexity of the funding system. The historically-based formulaic determination of establishment figures and the local cost of living, chiefly housing, combine to make any relation between capacity and demand extremely indirect and slow to change. Surrey provides an example. The county is prosperous and regularly claims the status of the 'safest county' in England in terms of crime (*Surrey Advertiser*, 15 October 1999, 2 November 2001, 7 May 2004). The Home Office formula is consequently low. In the 1990s, the county council exploited government policy that permitted it to depress council tax by not investing sufficiently in pension funds for council staff. Attempts to correct this situation starved resources for police and other services. As the cost of housing is high, the county is unattractive for those, such as police, who are on national payscales. This results in high turnover, a 'young' force, and commuter constables. An inspector for an area covering a large part of Guildford, including two high crime areas and an adjacent 'target' area, told a community meeting '"I only have fifty officers to cover this area for a 24 hour period ... Fifty percent of my constables have under two years' service and are relatively inexperienced and some youngsters put on a uniform and have an arrogance about themselves"' ('Inspector is keeping tabs on new recruits', *Surrey Advertiser*, 17 September 1999). Because '"my officers do do some things that are wrong"' the inspector sometimes followed them in an unmarked car to monitor their work. This removed an experienced (and candid) command officer from other duties.

Changes in police funding formulae thus exert an obscure, but substantial, influence on routine civil order and the capacity to respond to major public order events. The 'disorder index' reduces the budget of some forces despite their high crime and disorder rates. The index counts numbers of lone parents, people on council estates and the unemployed. The system reduced Met funding by 6% and Surrey's by 18% when introduced, with Northumbria, Sussex and Hampshire seeing double digit rises ('Police chiefs fret over "disorder index" funding', *Guardian*, 19 September 1994). The Association of Chief Police Officers (ACPO) forecast 'dramatic effects' on policing style. It could indeed be argued that the early-21st century's extra investment in 'reassurance policing' was necessitated by the effects the index had in cutting back capacity to mount regular patrols; the two biggest losers, the Met (in volume terms) and Surrey (in percentage terms) were the two initial test sites for 'reassurance policing'.

Whatever the Treasury's influence, the changing face of major public order events reflects changes in the polity and the composition of British society. These include events signalling ethnic and religious ruptures, including 'white backlash'; the set piece May Day demonstrations focusing anti-capitalist feelings; the phenomenon of consumer, middle-class and rural civil disobedience (expressed in forms such as the fuel blockades and the welding of a pro-hunt Countryside Alliance); arrangements for dealing with large outdoor leisure events (whose nadir was the 'Fatboy Slim' disaster at Brighton, when police failed to anticipate the crowds who would attend, with a participant dying after a fall onto the beach in darkness); and events involving 'new age' and non-mainstream religions (for example, solstice) and more confident expressions of religious practice by adherents chiefly drawn from ethnic minorities (for example, Eid).

Community-based public order events pose some challenges common to other major public order events and some challenges of their own. Standard procedures for dealing with such events, including the 'metallic hierarchy' (Gold, Silver and Bronze commanders), still form the core of the police response, but the 'incorporation' aspect is reinforced.

Positive relations with organisers are perhaps more readily achieved than with respect to strikes and protests where organisers may regard the police as one of the institutions against which they are protesting. 'Incorporation' is also important because community-based events may be more *ad hoc* and involve people less familiar with organising such events, so that fundamentals such as safety measures may need to be explained afresh. This also heightens the importance of advance planning. This is not to say that community-based events are necessarily innocuous or do not pose policing challenges. Logistical arrangements may predominate, but conflict and the need for politicking can also feature, as was made clear in televised coverage of the preparations for the summer solstice proceedings at Stonehenge in 2004. Such events pose all the problems set by major protests and demonstrations, with the complication that in the case of Stonehenge the setting is a world heritage site and the responsibility of two large organisations – a powerful national charity and a government agency – to which rival New Age religious groups also lay claim. That it also has a place in the annals of disastrous public order policing following the dramas at the time of the 'Battle of the Beanfield' was, in 2004, aggravated by an arcane astronomical/religious dispute over whether the commemoration should take place on the Saturday or Sunday. For the police it was not so much a matter of keeping order during the event as keeping their patience with a myriad of competing organisations, groups and perspectives in the months of negotiations leading up to the weekend; ultimately the most serious problem proved to be finding somewhere to park. With events that happen annually, such as the summer solstice and others in the religious calendar, advance preparation is effectively a permanent obligation on police; research suggests the great advantage that accrues is if continuity can be achieved in the officers with key responsibility, as they can build relationships with organisers over time (Pike, 2005).

Mandate and techniques

During the late 1980s and the 1990s, public order policing was greatly influenced by former Commissioner Newman's philosophy that the main threats to order were terrorism and 'the growth of multi-ethnic communities'. The latter produced a deprived underclass likely to turn to crime and disorder. Rejecting saturation policing, Newman developed the idea of 'symbolic locations', multi-ethnic areas involving dealing in drugs and stolen goods. After the Broadwater Farm riot in 1985 police designated 11 such locations in London. There was a contingency plan for each in the event that police, councils and education services failed to regenerate such areas (*Guardian*, 30 August 1989). At the 1989 Notting Hill Carnival, mounted police and 28 groups of 20 riot police each, directed through headphones inside their helmets, cleared the streets by pushing, shouting, and waving (and sometimes using) truncheons. A large area was sealed off and anyone seeking entry, including residents, faced arrest by one of 5,000 officers at dozens of roadblocks. Police action to control the bottle-throwing, which injured 30 officers and a few bystanders, was approved, but the long exclusion was not. Such criticisms have recurred periodically since, featuring, for example, in complaints about the length of time bystanders were confined by police during the 2001 May Day demonstration.

While Newman's first emphasis was multi-agency co-operation, many observers felt police were forcing the pace by laying down a clear social policy while also insisting on maintenance of their own operational independence. However, his successor, Sir Peter Imbert, argued that the community, not police, should be the prime focus of police/community relations; emphasising heterogeneity, he accepted that 'relations within the community, between different groups, are significantly outside the control of the police' (reported in the *Guardian*, 8 November 1989). Further, '[i]t is the community who should, in the main, determine whether police are to be involved in resolving community conflicts'. Police should also not veto multi-agency decisions that do not suit them.

Although the emphasis may vary, senior police have subsequently sought a growing, proactive involvement in the community. The fruits of a growing involvement with community organisations include the prioritisation of a more effective response to racial attacks and domestic violence, experiments with multi-agency co-operation in problem estates, and increased co-operation with victims' organisations generally. Ultimately, these innovations hinge on the preparedness of the ordinary ranks to work in new ways, and on development of an effective supervision system with suitable encouragements to do so. Here the organisation, in its sincere efforts to effect change, is trapped by techniques and competencies imposed by the policies of the past.

The contingencies the police must deal with have led to the acquisition of sophisticated armaments and defensive systems. A 1970s Home Office working party, on which army nominees outnumbered police, led to new weapons, including a rifle rejected in New York as too dangerous for city use, and a pistol that could shoot someone through a door or car (Bunyan, 1976: 93). Equipment, such as metal detectors and infra-red surveillance devices, was made available centrally. Much equipment for use in civil disorder had been tested by the army in Northern Ireland. Yet some characteristics of 'minimal force' policing revealed continuing official ambivalence about paramilitary policing. For example, the long shields, unique in the world, made for slow advances: they were heavy and left police vulnerable to attack from the side or behind. Consequently, when using them police must re-group to turn corners, giving rioters every chance to flee (Waddington *et al*, 1989). In 1994, trainers stopped teaching recruits high-stepping Guards-style drill because in public order situations they kept hitting their knees on the bottom of their riot shields ('Police drop Guards-style drill', *Guardian*, 25 March 1994). Nor is all police equipment serviceable; in 1995 an Inspectorate review of 15 forces found that some revolvers had fractures, firing pins were worn, firearms were over-oiled and some forces relied on old weapons ('April start for DNA criminal database', *Guardian*, 17 March 1995). On average, police found it necessary to discharge weapons but six times a year in London in the early 90s (*Guardian*, 30 July 1993), although occasions steadily increased.

Surveys regularly reveal that a majority of the public favour more police power. After codes of practice were introduced, two-thirds said the police should stop and search anyone they think suspicious, 61% agreed they should fingerprint everyone in an area where a serious crime occurred, and 62% thought police should use plastic bullets, gas and water cannons against '*potentially* violent demonstrators' (Brewer *et al*, 1988: 37). All police forces have to face the conflict between the public order role and the demands and perspectives of locale-based routine enforcement. Police in some countries operate separate public order units. Where this was tried in the US the rationale was specialisation and the idea that it would free the rest of the force for community policing. These experiments generally failed because the officers assigned to the riot function complained that the work brutalised them and did not satisfy the reasons they joined the police. Britain has tried to compromise in staffing its riot squads. Postings are not permanent, training is available to all constables and they can opt (or, when demand is high, be assigned) to serve in a Police Support Unit-type body for quite brief periods. Nevertheless it was early recognised that holding groups of 12 constables in the back of a van for whole shifts was not only stultifying, but heightened the chances of 'incivility' in contacts with the public. Training and service in specialist public order and armed response units has a de-individualising effect.

The Metropolitan Police formed its Special Patrol Group (SPG) in 1965 and most forces followed suit, using various names (Lancashire's 'Commando Squad' being particularly epic). The 1973 killing of two Pakistanis waving toy pistols at India House illustrates how responding to people behaving suspiciously, with officers authorised to use lethal force, escalates minor incidents. If the SPG had been unarmed they would have had to deal with the men by clearing the streets and persuading them to surrender. They would have quickly realised the men were young and scared. Instead both were dead in four minutes. No one had even spoken to them. The case had uneasy echoes in many subsequent instances, as when Met police shot dead a 'marksman' in 1999 whose weapon turned out to be a table leg.

However, the involvement of the SPG and their successors in local policing shows the problems that come from training for the worst and then using those so trained for the mundane. A Police Support Unit (PSU) comprises two or three 'serials', each of 10 constables and a sergeant, headed by an inspector, and has transport, shields and helmets, trains for two or three days a month, is summoned for duty and goes into action together. When not PSU-tasked, the unit splits for normal duty, but the promotion of *esprit de corps* works against individual discretion, which plays no part in PSUs. Routine assignments are to high-crime areas, where saturation policing is applied against street crime. The concern is that the disposition of PSU-trained officers is more aggressive. This makes for more use of force, which can provoke citizens and thus inflate arrest rates for assault, obstruction and threatening behaviour.

The emergence of specialist 'armed response vehicle' (ARV) teams as the frontline response to all crime involving guns followed the 1987 Hungerford massacre. Forces actually cut numbers of firearms-authorised officers following the 1983 shooting of Stephen Waldorf, with a decline from 10,000 officers in 1985 to 6,000 in 1995, but with an accompanying attempt to professionalise the function, it being concentrated in tactical firearms units comprising a core of highly-trained officers. These units are complemented by the ARVs to provide rapid response; ARVs carry Hechler and Koch MP5 submachine gun carbines and standard issue Smith and Wesson .38 revolvers. ARVs are deployed in violent crime areas, such as Lambeth and inner city Manchester; guns are worn openly during patrol and the sight of openly carried submachine guns has grown familiar in anti-terrorist patrols at airports and in diplomatic protection work ('Fewer offices but more cars in frontline against armed criminals', *Guardian*, 21 March 1995). Budget constraints mean that ARV officers can be taken off their duty to assist routine traffic duties, particularly in smaller forces ('Armed response units "could do traffic duties"', *Surrey Advertiser*, 4 February 2000).

When Kenneth Clarke gave way to Michael Howard as Home Secretary in 1993, policy changed on police weaponry. Howard reversed Clarke's opposition to US-style expandable side-handled batons and trials took place of a range of truncheon options, despite evidence that 17% of officers would not accept the US batons and 32% thought the truncheons should be kept in vehicles rather than routinely carried ('Larger batons "will not help to protect police"', *Guardian*, 15 October

1993). Force 'self-defence trainers' received the manufacturer's recommended five days' training, others spent a day practising 'parrying, striking and restraining' (Home Office News Release 272/93, 23 November 1993). Side-handled batons were approved for issue to any force in June 1994 (*Guardian*, 21 June 1994). Equipment supplementary to guns includes CS gas, pepper spray, expandable side-handled batons, armoured vests and visored helmets. Within two years of the introduction of expandable 'Asp' batons, all but three forces had received complaints about their use ('No baton charges against Surrey Police', *Surrey Advertiser*, 8 January 1999). Few forces had amended the US training manuals to accommodate less confrontational methods and a report into their use noted 'an unnecessarily aggressive style of baton training' in 14 forces. The Police Complaints Authority (PCA) called for general amendment of the manuals, refresher training for all officers, and reconsideration of where people should be struck, avoiding the lower leg as it fractures easily. A police spokeswoman noted the batons were part of a package of non-lethal options including CS spray and negotiating skills. When Cleveland Police adopted 'zero tolerance policing' in the harsh terms it was understood by then-Chief Superintendent Ray Mallon, CS spray was used more than in any other police area, over 600 times in 1997. The force was the subject of legal challenges arising from high profile raids and campaigns against 'anti-social behaviour' (*Guardian*, 8 November 1997). In 2002, officers of a Surrey ARV were the first in mainland Britain to use a 'baton gun', against a man brandishing a sword and pistol and chanting 'one of you must die' (*Guildford Times*, 9 August 2003). When he reached for his pistol, a baton round was discharged into his abdomen; he was treated for bruising. His gun turned out to be imitation. Taser weaponry was taken up in 2005 despite US evidence that the 'stun gun' can be lethal and its availability lowers the threshold at which police use force. Trials of *defensive* devices are much less frequent. Each year one in eight officers suffers a head injury. A new toughened and squat police helmet was tried in 2004, but police complained the public laughed at them (*Independent*, 22 March 2004).

The extension of the scope for armed intervention is also complicated by the problem of replica weapons, as where armed police arrested a man for 'brandishing' a novelty gun-shaped cigarette lighter on a train (*Surrey Advertiser*, 14 January 2005). While 'brandishing' was the perception of the passenger who called police, the man was actually responding to another passenger requesting a light. The assistant chief constable's statement noted that a number of cases involving youngsters with replica BB guns had triggered armed police responses, but that procedures now in place gave police no option but to respond. '"Any report of a firearm in a public place is subject to a strict intelligence-led process and if there is any evidence to suggest it might be a genuine firearm than we have to send out specially-trained units to deal with it''', the officer stated. Quite how 'intelligence-led' a response to a 999 call could be was not explained. Although specialist vehicles and more weaponry have been added, contemporary practice has solved neither the issue of how to use specialist armed officers when not required for armed duties nor that of appropriate response to replica weapons.

The Special Constable Act 1831 gave Justices of the Peace (JPs) power to swear Specials prior to disorder and fine those refusing. In 1914 the law changed to include war duties. Specials were extensively used in the 1918 and 1919 police strikes. After the First World War the Bolshevik panic led the Home Secretary to urge forces to establish the wartime Specials as a permanent reserve. Each force had them by the 1926 General Strike (with other auxiliaries, 226,000 volunteers were available). Some 100,000 Specials were available in the 1930s (118,000 in 1938) and that figure became the authorised establishment, but by 1964 there were only 51,000, and 23,000 by 1975; 1989 enrolment was 16,000. Although numbers rose to 19,243 in 1993, when the Home Secretary announced a drive to make it 30,000 by 1996, they dwindled to 12,738 on 31 March 2001, down 1,609 (11%) in a year, falling to 11,598 by March 2002; about a third were female. About half of all Specials, and nearly all those under 25, join for the minimum time of service of two years before joining a regular force. The case of the Specials reveals declining public inclination to assist public order policing, although an entire police division was patrolled wholly by Specials for the first time ever in 1994, with regular officers using the day for paperwork (*Guardian*, 24 April 1994).

How the resources of the police in a public order role are deployed is a matter of 'legal-occupational' judgment (Jefferson and Grimshaw, 1984). It is for senior officers to interpret the law here, being guided by the notion of 'public interest'. This may be illustrated by the case of a National Front march in Leicester in 1979, policed by 5,000 officers from 23 forces. Chief Constable Goodson permitted the march despite opposition from MPs, councillors, and community leaders. He gave three reasons. First, banning a march might only mean it occurring in another force's area or going ahead in defiance. Permitting it meant one could plan for it. This line was directed to the police audience. Secondly was the defence of freedom of speech and demonstration. This is the 'sectional' doctrine discussed above: the democratic opposition to the march is inverted, so that the greater threat to democracy is banning a racist march. This argument was directed to the public. The third reason was that the march could be policed without serious disorder, of which Goodson had to be satisfied to meet s 3 of the Public Order Act. This argument was addressed to legal audiences. It implies that because of mutual aid and the pride of chief constables it is unlikely that a s 3 ban *need* ever be invoked. Justifying his decision, Goodson noted the low complaint rate, that many demonstrators were outsiders and thus it was not 'his' community that especially opposed the march, and the severe attitude of the courts, implying that the actions of his officers were lawful. Goodson listed time, place, likely numbers and community feeling as factors in applying occupational, democratic and legal criteria (Jefferson and Grimshaw, 1984: 77).

Heavy-handed routine policing is less visible, but no less provocative; it was widely cited as a cause of the 1981 riots. The Brixton riots' trigger was a police attempt to help an injured black youth during 'Operation Swamp', which was misinterpreted in a 'spontaneous act of defiant aggression by young men who felt themselves hunted by a hostile police force' (Scarman, 1981: para 3.25). The second day of rioting at Brixton saw six hours of violence, arson, and looting, 82 people arrested, 279 police and at least 45 citizens injured, 61 private vehicles and 56 police vehicles damaged or destroyed, and 145 premises damaged. Most rioters were young black males, but a significant number were white (Benyon, 1984: 38). Many looters were older whites, seen arriving by car after the evening news. The disturbances ended after three days; over 7,000 police had been involved. Four months later there was disorder at Southall between white skinheads and young Asians. Petrol bombs were used, there were 20 arrests and 130 police and citizens were injured. That night, in Liverpool, police chased a young black on a motorbike and provoked rioting in Toxteth, which lasted for three days. On the Sunday night 282 police were injured and there was extensive looting involving many whites of all ages. Police were attacked with scaffolding poles, bricks, beer barrels, oil drums, gas cylinders with open valves and firebombs. Disorder also occurred in North London, Handsworth, Sheffield, Nottingham, Hull, Slough, Leeds, Bradford, Blackburn, Leicester, Derby, Aldershot, High Wycombe and Cirencester. Rioting resumed in Brixton and there was further violence in Liverpool, in which a disabled man was killed by a police vehicle. Latterly, such tensions have marked Asian communities. In 2005, police asked Muslims celebrating the Eid festival in Southall and North London not to fly national flags (those of Muslim countries of origin are flown as a normal part of Eid parades; 'Ten O'Clock News', BBC 1 television, 12 January 2005). Young Muslims were angered, older Muslims accepted the flags could provoke disorder. The police insisted their request was 'guidance', not a ban.

Following the early 1980s riots, ACPO prepared its 'Tactical Operations Manual' with a range of manoeuvres and tactics for repressing disorder. It was a key event in the redirection of police methods from the individual-oriented tradition to that of the team, from a minimalist to a paramilitary approach. There was to be readier use of armaments and a shift from the reactive to the proactive. The manoeuvres include military formations, involving shield serials and mounted police breaking up groups and affording cover for snatch squads to make arrests. One is aptly called 'Mounted officers advance on a crowd in a way indicating that they do not intend to stop' (Manoeuvre 10). Another involves short-shield officers running between officers holding long shields into the crowd to disperse it and *'incapacitate* missile throwers and ringleaders by striking in a controlled manner with batons about the arms and legs or torso', a criminal assault if done by a citizen. The manual, consciously inspired by colonial policing, gives little indication of any variation if the disorder is industrial. It emerged without parliamentary or public consultation.

Disorder at Stonehenge in 1988 tested new legislation to meet public disorder. Section 39 of the Public Order Act 1986 was enacted specifically to give police new power to deal with travellers. It effectively made trespass a criminal offence. Instead of having to wait two days for landowners to obtain a possession order, police could move people on if the landowner had taken reasonable steps to ask them to go and if they had caused damage (urination sufficed), threatened or insulted the owner or had 12 or more vehicles. The Home Office had to issue a circular in 1987 warning chiefs to use the Act sparingly for fear of breaching the European Convention on Human Rights (*Guardian*, 22 June 1989). By 11 pm on the eve of the disorder a large number of semi-convoys were ready to move out, but found their exits blocked by police. A journalist was directed, along with thousands of solstice followers, into a narrow enclosure hundreds of yards from the monument and fenced with barbed wire. The side facing Stonehenge was lined with police and a police helicopter circled overhead playing an intense spotlight on the crowd (*Guardian*, 22 June 1988). Those who broke through the fence were detained, 'sometimes quite violently'. When it was realised this was as close as they were getting, there were renewed surges over the now-collapsed fence and missiles were thrown. When a journalist asked a PC for his collar number, he was asked 'which would you rather have, my name and number or your skull?' (*Guardian*, 22 June 1988).

The ensuing shambles illustrated the difficulty of marshalling police unused to combat. As riot police approached, the helicopter gave an indistinguishable announcement later found to be the Chief Constable's 'opinion' that there was danger of damage to property and people and the crowd should disperse or be arrested. Police could not tell the journalist what the message was either, but immediately pushed people back 'quite violently, causing them to climb the wire fence topped with barbed wire', which was difficult for women and children. Repeatedly the flanks of police got ahead of the leaders; apparently they could hear 'advance', but not 'halt', though on occasion crowd members who shouted 'halt' were pleased to see the officers obey. Such performances prompted calls to abandon the fiction of 'minimum force' on the basis that CS gas and water cannon could hardly be worse (P Waddington, 1989).

Britain's colonial past has produced numerous social conflicts, but Northern Ireland has proved the most grievous, and has exposed the failings of tactics evolved in the policing of Malaya, Kenya and Aden. The effect of the 'troubles' is not confined to the province. The Prevention of Terrorism (Temporary Provisions) Act 1974 allowed arrest without warrant of people wearing any item or displaying any article that associated them with a proscribed organisation and sanctioned exclusion orders and searches authorised by the police themselves rather than the judiciary. Unresolved social conflict disrupts ever-wider circles of society; it became illegal to report the words of IRA supporters. In 1988 this led the Independent Broadcasting Authority to silence the sound of a ballad, but to run the lyrics as a caption. Several million apparently sang along. The offending lyrics of The Pogues' 'Streets of Sorrow/Birmingham Six' were:

> There were six men in Birmingham
> In Guildford there's four
> That were picked up and tortured
> And framed by the law
> And the filth got promotion
> But they're still doing time
> For being Irish in the wrong place
> And at the wrong time.
> (*Guardian*, 14 February 1989)

Successful appeals by the supposed terrorists, following evidence of gross police and forensic malpractice, led to the release of men destroyed by wrongful imprisonment and unable to cope with life outside (Parker, 2004). In 2005 the Prime Minister offered a formal apology to these victims of British state terrorism ('Ten O'Clock News', BBC 1 television, 9 February 2005).

Brewer *et al* (1988), King and Brearley (1996), Waddington *et al* (1989), Waddington (1996), Morgan and Newburn (1997) and Reiner (1998) are amongst authorities who have traced changes in public order policing in recent years. All argue that traditional 'pushing and shoving' techniques for maintaining order in crowd situations have declined since the 1984–85 coal dispute in favour of more paramilitary tactics. Some analyses emphasise the protection of the majority against those who cannot claim full citizenship rights due to their marginal social status; travellers are an example (P Waddington, 1999). Peter Waddington (1994: 206) judges police practice generally to be 'remarkably benign', arguing that police are most powerful when they do nothing, provided they have adequate tools to act if required. Their focus in major public order policing is therefore on achieving consensual relations and clear planning in tandem with organisers. Other than planning, the key technique for maintaining control is incorporation of organisers. King and Brearley (1996) maintain that the police have increasingly acted proactively in responding to major public order problems, emphasising increased surveillance and intelligence-based techniques as well as paramilitarism, as seen in the 1991 summer riots across Britain, although these techniques signally failed in the 2001 Bradford riot. They also note the diversification of dissent as class-based politics has increasingly given way to interest group politics, and the potential this has for the new approach to be applied to the less socially and politically marginal, an analysis well-suited to circumstances where, for instance, judges, senior police, and other members of the high Establishment find themselves on the wrong side of the ban on hunting with hounds. Police legitimacy stands at issue the more there is recourse to surveillance and paramilitarism, and the wider the range of the public finding itself at odds with one or another government policy.

Mutual aid

The co-ordination of action by different police forces has long provoked fears of excessive government direction. The Police Act 1890 created the formal structure of mutual aid. A 'police authority' – watch or standing joint committee – was empowered to agree to exchange police with other authorities and delegate the power to chief officers. By 1900 there were over two million trade unionists and rising concern about Bolshevik influences. Co-operation between forces was on a large scale. The tendency towards central control was soon manifest. When coalminers struck at Tonypandy in 1910, the entire Glamorgan Constabulary of 500 officers joined the local force, with help from Swansea, Cardiff and Bristol; 100 mounted police and 700 on foot were brought from London. As London's police authority, the Home Secretary sent a battalion of police, but not troops as requested. After the strike the Glamorgan Standing Joint Committee (SJC) refused to pay the bills the coal companies, beneficiaries of the extra policing, presented for feeding and housing police. The SJC had not requested the aid and repudiated responsibility for the Met officers. A judge held that the chief constable acted as agent for the SJC and the latter had 'ratified by action' the agreement. The fact that the Met had remained constituted ratification. This was reversed on appeal, but the rest of the judgment was affirmed, an important legal recognition of the central government role in organising policing (Lustgarten, 1986: 54).

The Home Office Police Department set up after the Desborough Report co-ordinated the assignment of extra police in the General Strike. Section 14 of the Police Act 1964 provided for bilateral arrangements, leaving the Home Secretary a reserve power to direct chiefs to furnish aid if not volunteered and to settle disputes about payment. This enabled erosions of police authority power when the National Reporting Centre (NRC) at Scotland Yard emerged. Authorities were not involved in discussing the need for the NRC nor notified of decisions.

> The retention by the Home Secretary of ultimate financial adjudication was crucial in removing local financial influence and undermining budgetary sanctions; and the wording of the 1964 Act enabled the NRC to operate without reference to or input from the police authorities. (McCabe and Wallington, 1988: 45)

The 1984–85 coal dispute saw the NRC feature prominently, combining all 43 forces under central direction. The NRC, which had no statutory basis, has been fully activated on major occasions, including the riots of 1981, the 1983 Warrington printworkers' dispute, the coal dispute and the 2003 fuel blockades. It is activated by the President of ACPO in consultation with colleagues and the Home Office. The President is assisted by the Inspectorate and other ACPO members, and reports daily to the Home Secretary. 'The official view is that the NRC coordinates the deployment of officers, whereas critics regard its role as a controlling one ... providing Britain with a *de facto* national riot police' (Brewer *et al*, 1988: 19).

Local authorities have been concerned at this loss of contact with their policing arrangements. South Yorkshire refused to pay for the domiciling of officers drafted in during the Orgreave Steel Plant dispute. The same authority faced added policing costs of tens of millions after the 1984–85 coal dispute; nearly every English force sent men to Nottinghamshire and South Yorkshire. Even distant authorities had to find huge sums, mainly for overtime. After months of argument, the Home Secretary agreed to pay everything over a 75-pence addition to the police element of their community charge, leaving authorities like West Midlands to raise £3 million extra. Worse, the extra spending threatened to incur rate-capping penalties used by the Conservative government to stifle spending in Labour authorities. Cuts had then to be made either in the police budget or other services, such as education.

The coal dispute exposed dubious emphases in policing disorder in relation to training, priorities and strategies. The police played the central role in the complex course of the strike. Success in police terms came at the expense of distortion of police priorities, undermining of the local authority limb of tripartite accountability, serious nationwide depletion of normal policing, major damage to police/community relationships, and challenges to civil liberties. Because it was thought impolitic to use the 1980 legislation on secondary picketing in the coal dispute, police powers of control of the roads were used. This was challengeable outside serious crime, but ministers 'spelled out their view and, in doing so, publicly instructed police officers to use their powers to obstruct traffic on motorways and other arteries in such a way as to prevent the congregation of pickets at working pits' (McCabe and Wallington, 1988: 59). The Home Secretary, following the National Coal Board (NCB) injunction against secondary picketing in Nottinghamshire, went beyond the statutory Code of Practice on Picketing by directing chiefs' attention to control of the roads (McCabe and Wallington, 1988, 59–60).

The NCB strategy was that if enough of those who did not support striking, or could not afford to, could be enticed back to work, the strike would collapse. 'The strategy depended ... above all ... on a guarantee of safe carriage to and from work' (McCabe and Wallington, 1988: 60). This made police the key to the management strategy to defeat the strike. Added to this were frequent ministerial pronouncements that widespread disorder was the inevitable outcome of mass picketing, which made police involvement constitutionally justifiable. This diverged sharply from the model of legitimate policing long-espoused by police. It was de Frend and Uglow's analysis that:

> [t]he independence and autonomy of chief constables came under attack as there was direct pressure from the Prime Minister and the Home Secretary to adopt particular strategies and tactics; the traditional neutrality of the police disappeared as they overtly supported one side in an industrial dispute; finally, ... the structure of the conflict was shaped by a pre-determined, coordinated strategy with the consistent aim of neutralising the union's main weapon. (de Frend and Uglow, 1985: 65)

This latter refers to police establishing themselves at pickets as the sole authority. In these authors' observation of two dispute areas the police did establish themselves as sole authority, with senior officers deciding whether any National Union of Mineworkers (NUM) member was allowed to stand at the colliery gate, whether they could speak to working miners, and the words they could utter. Strikers complained of the ranks' lack of supervision, with actions normally subject to sanction going unnoticed. Many officers did not display collar numbers. Met and Merseyside Police displayed 'unusual arrogance and insensitivity', hurling coins at pickets, being drunk, following pickets on dispersal and assaulting them, forcing entry to houses and damaging property (McCabe and Wallington, 1988: 83). Mutual aid officers are under formal control of the host chief, and the relevant police authority later called him to account, but had no standing to question him as he retained disciplinary authority over his officers.

Most picketing was peaceful, yet there were 9,808 arrests (England and Wales), both absolutely and proportionately more than during any industrial dispute for 50 years, and not exceeded since. By October 1984 nearly 200,000 striking miners had been kept away from the Nottinghamshire pits. The turn-back tactic was adopted by officers against people whose destination was not a colliery, for example three Derbyshire ladies heading for the chip shop at noon (McCabe and Wallington, 1988: 70). Police denied passage to normal traffic by occupying all three lanes of motorways with convoys of lorries and escorts. Related actions included searching people and cars for specious reasons, aimless, confusing and obscure diversions and deliberate smashing of car windows. Later court decisions ruled some roadblocks to have been illegal.

Orgreave was something else. It had the making of a rout. South Wales miners were unfamiliar with the new shields and helmets and came expecting the usual pushing and shoving. Nearly 5,000 police with 50 cavalry and 58 dogs dispersed them through adjoining residential areas. McCabe and Wallington (1988: 77) contrast the guarded words of the official report and official film of the event: 'There had already been some scenes of violence and police officers in protective headgear and with shields had to be deployed to protect the police cordon from missiles being thrown by the pickets.' However, the official police film clearly shows, contrary to media coverage, that there were no 'scenes of violence' before mounted officers rode into the pickets. The pickets retaliated only after the charges. It was television that made the police victory dangerous: footage of violence inflicted on civilians in full retreat 'remains as a testimony to the retribution exacted by police officers' (McCabe and Wallington, 1988: 77). Orgreave did not end the strike, but it opened the door for heavier policing.

Riot and unlawful assembly cases were intended to have a deterrent effect even before charges were proved. Not one riot charge came up to proof in court. A number of defendants did plead guilty, advised they would thus gain non-custodial suspended sentences. Summary prosecution cases were marked by weak evidence. Witnesses were police centrally involved in the actions that gave rise to the charges. In one case a defendant was convicted of throwing a brick through a lorry window. No one saw the brick thrown, but the driver said the miner 'looked as if he had just thrown a brick'.

Government motives were plain enough. The Home Secretary indicated what he wanted from police by releasing all financial constraint, belittling police authorities, and giving speeches about offences carrying life sentences. The Attorney General encouraged the illegal roadblocks. The Prime Minister condemned the 'enemy within' (to a plainly incredulous interviewer who asked her whether such language was permissible even from the most 'rabid backbencher'; standing her ground, she cited the 'intimidation' the nation had seen – the dubious television footage); but chief constables acquiesced to a partisan role and were, generously, insensitive to the repercussions. The constitutional weakness of accountability facilitated the use of police to defeat one side in an industrial dispute. A decade later the official history of the Police Federation referred to betrayal by the Thatcher government and having been badly led by senior officers. Rank-and-file officers would have been incensed had they known that the NCB's chairman's tactic was to involve police in violent picketing incidents; many confrontations were avoidable. The history referred to 'secret political collusion' between the NCB chairman and the Prime Minister, Home Secretary and Energy Secretary, following the chairman's outrage at the neutral stance police initially adopted (Judge, 1995).

Although it liaised closely with the Home Office Public Order desk and the Inspectorate, the NRC was directed by successive ACPO presidents throughout the dispute. This was not the result of a police conspiracy, but because the Home Office established a structure using ACPO in this way. With no national force there had to be some co-ordinating body. Constitutionally, politically responsible government would require that this be by the Home Secretary, but that would contradict the concept of locally based policing and undermine the apolitical nature of policing. Putting the NRC in the hands of the ACPO presidents got the Home Office off the hook. Law enforcement's apolitical nature was preserved.

The NRC was later re-named the Mutual Aid Centre. Two chief constables revealed some years later that the NRC itself was set up on the instructions of central government and not in fact at senior officers' request ('Police report rewriting strike history', *Guardian*, 3 January 1995). The handling of the strike by the chief who led the NRC was 'insensitive and bordered on the belligerent'. An *ad hoc*, unconstitutional body is open to such abuse. The Police Act 1996 formalised what had been implicit, but changed little else. Police authorities remained paymaster, but with limited control over the circumstances of co-operation. Chiefs can ask one another for manpower or other assistance to meet any 'special demand' on their resources. The receiving authority normally pays, but where it and donor authority cannot agree, payment is determined by the Home Secretary. The Home Secretary may direct that mutual aid be arranged where it is believed to be in the interests of public safety or order and voluntary aid arrangements cannot be made. The extraordinary convenience of these arrangements for Home Secretary and chiefs may account for the endurance of local forces despite regular claims that a national force is inevitable. Mutual aid and collaborative agreements have been the basis of steps in that direction, such as the regional crime squads and National Criminal Intelligence Service (NCIS). It has been a vehicle for the centralising influence, but one more palatable than altogether sweeping away localism, with its advantage of plausible deniability of central direction.

A national force

Increased central funding of local forces and the establishment of a Police Department in the Home Office extended central control of police. Home Office influence came partly from the daily circulars sent to forces and partly from providing services single forces could not afford, including recruiting publicity, laboratories, equipment and training centres. Home Office inspectors chair regional committees of chief constables. Technological developments add to fiscal and statutory centralisation, an example being the Police National Computer (PNC), which requires standardisation of reported information. The danger of a national force acting effectively as the government's force stands in tension with the efficient preservation of the *status quo*.

The Report of the 1960 Royal Commission remains the authoritative, if now much-modified, word on the role of chief constables, police authorities and Home Secretary. It endorsed existing judicial dicta on constabulary independence, but understood the doctrine to have an application restricted to the 'enforcement of law in particular cases' (Royal Commission on the Police 1962: paras 86, 88). It endorsed constabulary independence in respect of constables' activities, suggesting that consequently 'this left the police largely free from legal control', a conclusion one may feel is more logically connected with its acceptance of the view that constables were formally no different from ordinary citizens. In light of discretion, the great range of non-law-enforcement activities, and maintaining public order, this view of constables as citizens in uniform was barely plausible even in 1962, before many powers were codified.

However, the real problem was higher up: in the Report's famous phrase, 'the problem of controlling the police can, therefore, be restated as the problem of controlling chief constables' (Royal Commission on the Police 1962: para. 102). They were accountable to no one at all in regard to 'general policies', the disposition of personnel, resource management, and methods of handling demonstrations. The commission did not think 'complete immunity from external influence' was necessary, nor regulation by local authorities. External influence should come from the centre. Legal responsibility for local forces should reside with the Home Secretary, and local authorities would have an advisory function to the chief constable with whom final responsibility rested. One member, Goodhart, famously objected that 'if local connections were unimportant in preserving liberty ... and not to be trusted as the locus of control where control was required, the logical solution was the creation of a national force' (Lustgarten, 1986: 51). The Commission accepted that high-level policing decisions were policy matters, requiring a political authority to be responsible, but neglected mechanisms to make that responsibility meaningful.

Since then, the recommendations that stripped boroughs of their established powers have been followed and subsequent Home Secretaries have encouraged amalgamation into ever larger forces. With police authorities left enfeebled and the Home Secretary standing aside, chief constables quickly filled the power vacuum. Amalgamation has increased chief officer fiefdoms. Their reduced number has raised each individual's status and made ACPO better able to act as a united influence on national policy. The only significant disagreement between ACPO and the Home Office was over the 'financial management initiative' (FMI), which threatened police interests that had remained unchecked since escape from local fiscal control after the Commission. It is interesting that the FMI came after the unions had been tamed and the Opposition had moved from socialism to a social democrat platform. In these comfortable circumstances, government found the will to ask chiefs what it all was costing.

In the early 1990s, Home Office denials of plans for further amalgamation became weaker; six 'super-forces' seemed the most likely number. The Commons Home Affairs Select Committee found the existing method of choosing senior officers 'haphazard and amateurish' and were 'deeply disturbed' by the number of senior officers who had not attended the Senior Command Course at Bramshill, recommending it be compulsory and that senior officers form 'a cadre of professional officers' attached to the Home Office rather than local authorities (*Guardian,* 20 May 1989). This was tactically presented as a way to increase numbers of women and ethnic minorities in higher ranks. Government rejected the proposal while accepting the call for more central supervision of chief officer selection and training. By 1990, the Home Secretary lent his support to a national detection agency on FBI lines, and police chiefs concluded that a national police force was inevitable in all but name. In 1995, the Met Commissioner called for a national police force modelled on the FBI (*Guardian,* 6 September 1995) as the only way to counter organised, international crime. It would work alongside the security services, Customs and Excise, and Inland Revenue, and build on NCIS and the regional crime squads; but Condon opposed amalgamation of smaller forces, instead advocating formal partnerships with local authorities and businesses. In 2003 the Met, Thames Valley, and Surrey chief officers called for the number of forces to be cut to 20 and for a national FBI-type agency against serious crime. There would be a three tier policing structure with partly-elected local policing boards to oversee the work of 'neighbourhood police chiefs' dealing with low-level crime and anti-social behaviour, then a border police tier, and above it the FBI-type agency. The three chiefs saw regional forces based on regions as large as the Northeast or East Anglia (*Guardian*, 11 October 2003). All chiefs backed the planned national serious crime agency, but it was not until 2005 that it emerged as the Serious Organised Crime Agency, and a national force still lurks in the wings.

Police and state

The consequences of tight state control of the police are clear enough in the case of public order policing. Instead of inaugurating a paramilitary force, Britain has preferred to extend central co-ordination gradually, not only for tactical reasons, but because it maintains 'an image of civility for both ... internal and external audiences' (Brewer *et al*, 1988: 3). We have seen that this is the strength of the constabulary independence concept. Legal debate turns on whether constables act in a master and servant relationship with higher authorities. The relevant case is *Fisher v Oldham Corporation*. Fisher was a victim of mistaken identity, arrested under warrant in London and taken to Oldham on charges that were dropped once the error was realised. He brought an action in tort for compensation for false imprisonment. He proceeded against Oldham Corporation rather than the arresting officers, probably doubting they could pay the damages. He had to establish that a 'master and servant' relationship existed between the watch committee and the officers. The decision was that this was not so. Cases in which public authorities avoided claims for the negligence of their employees were precedent, on grounds that they were carrying out functions mandated nationally or of general public concern. Lustgarten points out that the many areas where such claims have been rejected render dubious the heavy use made of *Fisher* to defend constabulary independence. These cases have not, for instance, been used to assert the unique constitutional status of sheep disease inspectors (or, in Australia, legal aid workers). Lustgarten (1986: 58) argues that '[w]hether or not a person is held for purposes of tort law to be in a relationship of master and servant with whoever pays him is simply irrelevant to whether he is a "servant" in the sense of someone who is bound to obey the command of the paymaster'. It seems a poor basis for so grand a doctrine, but the matter rests there, constables being held to act on their own authority subject to law, and that ambit being projected right up to the chief. The advance of central co-ordination has not altered the line on the responsibility of the police.

The position on police action in public order events is the same as in any ordinary act of policing. The overriding commitment is preservation of order, the prerequisite for the exercise of rights by all. Conflict elicits police insistence on the need to accommodate everybody's rights and avoid partiality. It is ironic that adherence to this abstract and legalistic conception of democracy, the defence of the rights of 'all', invariably leads to the suppression of the very forms by which democracy is manifest, that is, the expression of conflicting views. 'Upholding the law' by suppressing protest becomes the sole legitimate meaning of democracy. When entire protests are suppressed this may perversely create the very alliance of legitimate protest and provocateurs that police fear most, and enlist support for the cause among the uncommitted in reaction to heavy-handed policing. Public order policing may provoke the conflict it seeks to avoid.

Apparently, central co-ordination does not go far enough to impose political review on chief officer decisions about major public order policing, but does provide every kind of reinforcement when chiefs act against disorder in any way they can square with narrow legal and occupational criteria. It may be due to laudable timidity on the part of the Home Office, where the belief continues that there is balance in the present compromises. Officials join civil libertarians and police chiefs in abhorring central control. Chief officers and senior politicians are well-placed to recognise that Home Office civil servants are unlikely to act as mere ciphers for their political 'masters'. Reservations about a national force at top level may be more than attentiveness to fears of lost localism. As we have seen, the present arrangements offer advantages of deniability and autonomy to the principal actors when subject to their sharpest challenge in major public disorder. However, European convergence, globalisation and the threats of organised crime and terrorism have made the present structure increasingly precarious. The decline of class politics in favour of 'single issue' alliances, such as hunting with hounds or fathers' rights, make the public order landscape less predictable and the lines of social conflict less clear-cut.

4. Civil policing and order maintenance

Local civil order

Control over policing has been the cause of recurrent conflict. As the polity undergoes change, so has the relation between the police and judicial and executive institutions. Legislation from the 19th century maintained the subordination of the police to the magistracy, but became less relevant than the contest between police authorities and chief constables, with central government a shadowy, but increasingly influential, actor. More recently, central government has emerged more starkly from the shadows and we have seen the influence of chief constables rise, but as 'Chief Executive Officers' working largely in accord with central government. Local government influence has waned, accentuated by its general diminution under governments guided more by corporate state principles than their manifestos admitted.

The existence of local forces 'accountable' to local authorities has not proved a safeguard against a policing system with substantial and increasing national elements. On occasions of major disorder, the government can in effect direct the police, but this is seldom necessary because the fundamental perspective of chief constables has been consistent with the governing interest of the Home Office. The concern in this chapter is with the impact of these circumstances on the ordinary relations of police and public, particularly relative to other less-elevated considerations that influence routine order maintenance.

Public disorder need not be riotous to provoke official handwringing, media sensationalism and public disquiet. An example is alcohol-related disorder. The course of the recent alarm about the night-time economy and 'super-pubs' is reminiscent of Durkheim's argument that the eradication of crime is impossible because society continually redefines its criteria of deviance to the progressively more particular (a 'society of saints' would still have – and need – 'sin'). Since the discovery of 'lager louts' in the late 1980s, politicians and the public have perceived an increasing problem of drink-related violence, and not only in cities. In 1987 some 200 youths 'ran amok' at Crowborough after being asked to leave a wine bar, 170 youths rioted in Lincoln, and two gangs battled at

High Wycombe over New Year. The Association of Chief Police Officers (ACPO) reported that there were 251 incidents of public disorder involving 36,300 people in 1987 and that alcohol featured in 90 percent (*Guardian*, 5 August 1988). The trend has continued; the British Crime Survey reported 1.2 million incidents of alcohol-related violence in 1999, 15% of 12–17-year-olds reporting involvement in anti-social behaviour after drinking, primarily heated arguments and fighting, and that 36% of offenders are frequent drinkers compared to 20% of non-offenders (Harrington, 2000).

Home Office research revealed at an early point in the debate about drinking behaviour that rather than affluent 'yuppie yobbos' the mayhem was caused by the usual suspects: young, poorly educated workers in low-status jobs (Tuck, 1989). The problems of weekend drinking and disorder outside entertainment places had simply 'achieved new prominence through changes in population patterns and prosperity'. 'Old-fashioned hard-line policing' halved Woking's public order offences within two years (*Guardian*, 6 April 1989). Police in Brighton reported success by briefing doorstaff, brewery representatives and publicans on licensing law (*Guardian*, 26 June 1988). In 2004 Guildford police warned drunks using football-type penalty cards and issued mops to clear up vomit and urine, and in 2005 emulated pioneering-Leicester by projecting on town centre walls giant images of drunks who had broken the conditions of their anti-social behaviour order ('Persistent offenders face going to the wall', *Surrey Advertiser*, 11 February 2005). These strategies require investment of substantial police resources and the 1990s and early 21st century both saw ongoing demonisation of young drinkers and police claims that they could not cope.

When a Home Secretary dismissed Dorking, Lincoln and Aylesbury youth as dangerous brutes with 'an aimless lust for violence' who are 'one of the main factors undermining the peace of British society', journalists discovered that Aylesbury youth could not remember their last riot, 40 members of the main local gang had fled rather than confront a solo constable, and its members were preoccupied with school rivalries (*Guardian*, 11 August 1988). According to one perceptive youth:

> [t]hey said the same about mods and rockers, hippies and punks. They were all immoral. So I suppose if the Government runs out of people to blame they start picking on ordinary people who get a bit drunk on Saturday nights in small towns. (*Guardian*, 11 August 1988)

However, by fomenting alarm over drink and brawling, successive governments put the most pervasive and intractable problems of civil order on the agenda. That is precisely why these are called problems of *routine* local order. What this also did was to replace the stereotype of the typical offender as poor, working-class and unemployed with the credit card carrying 'lager lout' and the affluent 'binge drinker'. Any apparent causal connection between crime and social conditions was to be denied. If the general tenor of late 20th and early 21st century control was to be 'responsibilisation', the idea that we all must take our part in social control, we had to begin by shedding old preconceptions about crime and disadvantage.

Public, political and professional opinion divided over the likely consequences of the Licensing Act 2003, which legislated for an end to national licensing hours and the transfer of drinking hours responsibility to local authorities from 2005. Initially approved by ACPO on the basis that staggering licensed premises closing times would assist town centre policing at night, and by government as a means of implanting a 'continental café culture' in a regenerated urban Britain, second thoughts were aired as implementation loomed. It was suggested that local authorities could deal with alcohol-related disorder by withdrawing licenses from establishments where customers were sold drink while already drunk. With cities such as Nottingham having 3,500 licensed premises, the local chief constable pointed out that most of those involved would be unable to remember where they had been when sold one drink too many, and that controlling and investigating disorder would tie up his entire force forever ('The Today Programme', BBC Radio 4, 12 January 2005). Legislators hurriedly discussed a mandatory levy on licensed premises to pay for town centre policing but the drinks industry held that, with a £10 billion 2005/2006 budget for policing, and £22 billion in tax revenue contributed by the industry annually, they had a long way to go before needing to pay more ('World at One', BBC Radio 4, 13 January 2005).

Such political diversions and managerial considerations may have a short-term effect on the attention paid to a given aspect of policing, but have little lasting impact on routine police/public relations. Similarly the potential for abuse inherent in routine police business is resistant to external interventions. These include a perceived lack of sensitivity by police at incidents, particularly on-street stops; breaches of the codes of practice regulating the arrest, charging and interrogation process; the abuse of prisoners' rights, sometimes leading to deaths in custody; and accidents caused by police in hot pursuit. This is what is meant by the contrast in the potential for conflict between the sharp, but temporary, mass public order event and the pervasiveness of routine policing.

Organisational demands for high productivity measured by arrest contradict the requirements of strict adherence to legal rules. Such conflict encourages corner-cutting forms of occupational deviance, reinforced by the self-generated nature of the work and the virtual invisibility of frontline policing to supervisors. Most patrol is solo, and when pairs patrol they are generally both constables. In most incidents the only account available to supervisors is that of the officer directly involved; but the picture varies depending on the extent to which particular practices and duties are subject to the structure of law. Tasks marked by a permissive legal structure concern operational matters, and it is these which are most subject to occupational values, with such values gaining more purchase the more discretionary and ambiguous the legal matter. Administrative matters are much less subject to such informal norms and values.

It is, therefore, particular forms of police work that account for the largest volume of criticism – those associated with routine, unsupervised patrol and with permissive law. The 1983 PSI report gave a detailed account of the problems that legislation, such as the Police and Criminal Evidence Act, has latterly sought to address, quoting numerous people who, having been arrested, criticised police behaviour: 59% of arrestees had such criticism. Some 13% complained of assault/excessive force, 7% of threatening/abusive behaviour, and 14% of bullying or aggressive manner (Smith and Gray, 1983: 128). In 26% of arrests the suspect claimed police used rude or insulting language; 7% cited racist insults; 14% 'other insults' ('you useless junked-out bag of shit' was reported by a female heroin user). The report concluded that '[t]he survey findings strongly suggest that in a considerable minority of cases suspects are assaulted, threatened and verbally abused' and, while allowing for the inevitable resentfulness of arrestees, that 'this appears to be ... a pattern of conduct among ... a substantial minority of police officers' (Smith and Gray, 1983: 140). In 1995 the Met issued officers with 80 pages of advice on handling the public – the 'Good Practice Guide to Officer Safety'. Advice is given on deportment ('standing with arms apart and palms upward' is apparently friendliest). Officers feeling threatened should stand with feet a shoulder width and diagonally apart, knees slightly bent and hands above the waist and open. Behavioural differences between ethnic groups feature. '[F]or some Afro-Caribbeans it can be disrespectful to look someone in the eye. Instead they may look at you and then look down or to one side. If you mirror this there will not be a problem so long as you can see their hands' ('Hello, hello, the way to tackle villains may lie in body language', *Guardian*, 9 September 1995). The endurance of demeanour problems in contemporary surveys suggests they are intrinsic to the circumstances rather than a problem of the individual officer; for example, officers' manner rather than the fact of having intervened remains the top public complaint (Home Office, 2003b).

Conflict is exacerbated when malpractice is disproportionately suffered by one group. This is more subtle than overt 'bias'. Reiner cites three forms of institutionalised discrimination. A key case is directing extra police resources or hard tactics to areas of high crime and social deprivation. 'The result will be a greater probability of stop and search, arrest, etc. for those people living there who are vulnerable to police attention' (Reiner, 1985: 134). A second case is 'the use of indices of the probability of reoffending ... in a routine way to determine decisions such as cautioning or charging' (Reiner, 1985: 134). Indices of 'problem family' backgrounds, for example, may result in discriminatory decisions. A more clear-cut instance is the contemporary fixation on the idea that small numbers of persistent offenders cause most crime. A third form of institutional discrimination concerns the complaint about police inattention to racial attacks, which 'may indicate not so much a lack of concern as unthinking application of standard preconceptions and procedures which assume individual motivations for offences' (Reiner, 1985: 135). Routine procedures and assumptions indirectly disadvantage minorities.

An instance of Reiner's second case is indeed police and official response to research on repeat offending and the view that prolific offenders account for the great majority of crime. This led 21st century policing into highly targeted strategies. Targeting persistent offenders was said to have cut burglaries by 46% in Guildford. 'During 2000/1, 609 burglaries were committed compared to just 166 in the first six months of 2001/2. This reduction has been achieved by the arrest and conviction of six prolific offenders' (*Surrey Advertiser*, 12 October 2001). Targeting involved surveillance at a cost of £4,000 a day, with more being spent on technical equipment operators and on informers. In 2002, government research suggested that ex-prisoners were responsible for a fifth of all crime (*Guardian*, 18 June 2002). The 64% recidivism rate for ex-prisoners suggested another avenue for improving the situation than targeting the 'usual suspects'. Some forces later sent postcards to the home address of convicted burglars with an image of a prison cell and the words 'Wish You Were Here' (*Guildford Times*, 5 March 2005). Each card addressed the person by name and included the sentiment that 'as a known burglar your DNA and fingerprints are on file, giving us information to link you to any future crimes you might commit'. Recipients were also advised of the legal change permitting criminal records to be disclosed in court prior to conviction, and sent a leaflet on the degree of force householders can use against burglars. It is difficult to see how such harassment could not engender resentment and there is clear potential for a counterproductive effect on individuals seeking to reform.

Strict adherence to the letter of the law may be thought the best guarantee of fair treatment. In fact, such inflexibility would soon exhaust the resources of the constabulary and paralyse the courts. The police rely on public co-operation in many instances. This is the practical meaning of the notion that policing relies on the consent of the community, and may be one reason that police often refer to the fact of co-operation as indicating acceptance of their actions. We can see the importance of consent to the practical functioning of the police by considering the idea of 'helping the police with their inquiries'. This is frequently the result of action legally constituting false imprisonment.

However, genuinely voluntary consent in accompanying police would be a defence and 'consent is a very slippery concept'. The fact that the practice is general indicates how normal is the citizen's co-operation. This is not because of the benign regard in which police are held, but a result of ignorance about the limits of police powers. Research on warrantless searches shows that the consent of people ignorant of the law can easily be manipulated (for example, Lidstone, 1984). It should be recalled that police speak with fierce insistence of their accountability to the law, and not the state, as a proof of the case against greater political accountability and a defence of constabulary independence. Yet here we see that this ostensible subordinance to the law is no guarantee against malpractice, but instead evidence of 'consent'. The point would, perhaps, attract more critical scholarly comment were it not for its semi-whimsical treatment as one of several artful devices by which citizens are manipulated, such as reference to a mythical 'Ways and Means Act' (first noted in Manning, 1977).

The community plays the major part in the achievement of local public order. This relates to the fundamental distinction between informal and formal social control, where the former is imparted by socialisation processes involving bonds to primary groups (initially the family, then peers), and the latter by the police and other social agencies. There is little doubt which is more effective; the police are a stopgap whose work can be read as necessary when internalised controls are weak or degraded. Most of us are kept in line most of the time by our sense of right and wrong. It is no coincidence that societies marked by strong informal social control also have low crime rates. A number of Asian societies provide empirical evidence of the relationship. This is not to say that their citizens do not suffer other problems; harsh informal controls can be oppressive. However, as Komiya observed, '[t]he Japanese tolerate strong informal social control because in return they are supported and cared for by the (inner-circle) *uichi*-type group ... What is important for crime prevention is not to care about others, but to be cared about by others' (Komiya, 1999: 381–84).

Also an aspect of the community part in local public order is that the bulk of police patrol is spent in 'reactive' work, responding to public calls. Less trivially, proactive work also relies on public co-operation, although information-givers are seldom 'disinterested'; informers are an important resource to police. Of course, the reliance on consent can be seen dramatically in major disorder and *cause célèbre* that lead to alienation of important fractions of society. Chief constables reacted to the Scarman Report and the Macpherson Inquiry with a predictable clamour for more of what Lambert (1986) called the 'holy trinity' of policing: more personnel, more powers, and more equipment. This conception of police 'professionalism' is a sorry distortion of Vollmer's principles of scientific police management (Manning, 1982). It hinges on exaggerating the importance of law enforcement in the law and order dichotomy. Yet without order maintenance at the routine level, law would be impossible to enforce. Some senior officers are guided by what is known to them all – that no more than half of police time is spent in law enforcement (Singer, 2001) and that crime cannot be controlled by police on their own. These officers recognise why community involvement is central to effective policing. Despite a long history of lip service and intermittent support, in community policing we have the clearest descendant of the idea of a local force, responsive to local need, defined in local terms and directly accountable.

Policing and community

This is not to suggest that community policing would bring us back to some bucolic idyll. Indeed, adequate community policing would bring police into a relation with the public in which they would have to acknowledge the divisions in the community and in attitudes towards police. The 'decent citizen', 'proper villain' and 'scumbag' stereotypes presently remain unchallenged because patrol contacts are fleeting, with repeat calls conducted by the same officer being exceptional. It is true that police have more recently revived emphasis on community policing, supported by politicians of all hues, but the simple fact is that staffing is not sufficient to routinely deliver regular foot patrol to all our communities; even the new Police Community Support Officers are a specialist resource reserved for troubled areas.

Police generally see the 'community' unilaterally ('the public') or differentiated by population composition (for example, black versus white), crime-proneness (respectable versus criminal) or attitude to police (hostile versus supportive). These are ineffective distinctions if we are to grasp how 'the community' affects police behaviour. We should consider 'under what conditions are various "publics" ... able to have an effect on policework practice? ... [W]hich decisions in relation to which constituencies and which conditions are subject to extra-legal, "non-police" determinations?' (Grimshaw and Jefferson, 1987: 21). The constituencies need to be specified in their long-term relation to police and the nature of their situational involvement with police.

To do this it is necessary to differentiate between the roles in which sub-groups of the community can come in contact with police. This could be as situated role-bearers (witness, complainant, victim, etc), as representatives of the community (elected or self-appointed, etc) or as organisation members (social workers, school staff, journalists etc). Where law is permissive, officer and citizen demeanour are crucial elements determining the outcome of disputes. Thus, '[w]e would expect some difference in the ability of citizens, according to the nature of their "contacting" role, to influence police behaviour, with, for example, contacting roles spelling "trouble" or "inconvenience" less likely to influence behaviour' (Grimshaw and Jefferson, 1987: 21–22). Community policing can provide a mechanism to act on poor relations with troublesome categories. In a somewhat desperate attempt to establish bonds, some police forces inaugurated a scheme in 1996 whereby Specials and police cadets were tasked to mix with young people attending sports and leisure events (*Surrey Advertiser*, 22 November 1996). 'Street credible outfits' were provided. It is noteworthy not only that there was a decline in petty misbehaviour at the venues where this was done, but that police chose those other than regular officers to carry it out. There are further differentiations to make in attuning to community variation.

> Citizens in each 'contacting role' can be seen as respectable or otherwise ... The nature of the contact can be reciprocal, with each party having items of value to exchange, or one-way, and can be either sporadic or recurrent. Furthermore the nature of the issue bringing citizens and police into contact can be one about which there is a high degree of consensus, or it can be highly contentious. (Grimshaw and Jefferson, 1987: 22)

We can thus assume that least influence is exerted by 'non-respectable individual strangers who have nothing to exchange and with whom contact is sporadic and contentious'. The closer the police are to the community the better able they are to estimate not just the broad reaction to their interventions, but individuals' likely reactions to a specific intervention.

The important point here is that even in the high crime estates that account for much patrol time and many interventions, the public is neither all-criminal nor is the criminal public 'criminal' all the time. Most residents share a common goal to live free of predatory crime and disorder. We know from ethnographic research on high-crime neighbourhoods that this consensus value exists even in such environments. For example, gang leaders and drug dealers have been shown to engage in efforts to thwart crime in their *own* neighbourhood (Pattillo 1998). Pattillo reports how the leader of a major ethnic gang was a long-term resident who engaged in social control actions (monitoring, threats) to keep his neighbourhood free of street crime and signs of disorder such as graffiti, vandalism and prostitution. There is, of course, an anxiety on the part of such people both to control their own 'turf' and not to draw unwanted attention to their criminal activities. Similar data is available from research on drug dealers in the UK (Fountain, 1992) and much longer-established evidence concerning members of organised criminal and syndicated crime groups (Whyte, 1943). Studies of high-crime estates challenge the assumption that informal social control is always absent in such areas (Foster, 2002); rather, 'high crime communities are often simply dismissed as apathetic, chaotic, disorganised and demoralised (thus letting agencies conveniently "off the hook")' (Foster, 2002: 184). That is, those charged with crime prevention on such estates are apt to resort to technology on such assumptions. Technology, such as CCTV, appeals because it is cheap, despite evidence that schemes that use people as preventive tools, such as concierge schemes, are more effective. Writing of the impact of a major estate-improvement programme, Foster makes the important further observation that the programme 'had not "rekindled" *all* the people (and indeed the future of the estate was premised on a belief that *some* people should be forcibly removed and excluded)' (Foster, 2002: 184). The trick for police is to know the community well enough not only to know who is prepared to watch, record and act, but who will help on each particular occasion in relation to each particular kind of offence. Fountain's (1992) telling instance is that of a drug user on such an estate who was willing to let police use her home as a surveillance site during a spate of indecent assaults nearby; they simply had to ignore her smoking cannabis. They did, and she later became a Neighbourhood Watch organiser.

These considerations move us substantially beyond the idea of 'the community' and its relation with police. The important point is that the 'community' be seen not just as a convenient heuristic unit, but one comprised of the collective sum of variable situated experience over time and space. It is worthwhile considering what form social control can take in a police/public relationship where understandings have been built up over the years, through the process of 'give and take'. We have already seen that the police rely on 'give and take'. When the public can also rely on that from the police, an accountability more real than any statutory mechanism is in sight.

Rural policing

It is commonly thought that such ongoing, negotiational relations are more likely in rural areas, a view that suggests the origin both of stereotypical understandings of 'community' and of the mythology of a lost golden age of policing. 'The police and public are conscious of what each expects of the other, and this is more apparent in rural areas, where contact is closer and more personal' (Evans, 1975). The archetype of old-time bobbying is periodically rediscovered by the media. One epitome had patrolled his village for 13 years (*Sunday Express*, 13 July 1988). He cycled everywhere, arguing

> [i]t's difficult to lean a car against a lamp post to pass the time of day.' Mums worried about their boys getting into trouble treat him as a caring uncle. Youngsters complain to him about lack of play areas. Pensioners seek reassurance about vandalism and break-ins.

The PC drove an ambulance for the disabled, helped with youth work, attended church and council meetings – 'sometimes it seems I do very little policing. I'm more of a community worker.' He read stories at a nursery school and took the children on 'safety walks'; but he had also recently arrested three youths for burglary – 'their parents were angry at first and said they would never talk to me again. But they soon came round.' A nearly identical account, this time of a Surrey officer (now tagged a 'Designated Neighbourhood Specialist Officer'), appeared in 2002 (*Guildford Times*, 24 August 2002).

Rural/urban differences are real, albeit in a more complex way than this, and, importantly, as much to do with organisational and occupational differences as with the kind of contact (Cain, 1973, is the seminal authority). We should not exaggerate the warmth of rural police/public relations. Evidence from the 19th century suggests that constables – borough and county – were largely cut off from the community by public reserve and police regulations. In 1857, Buckinghamshire's Chief Constable ordered that plates inscribed 'County Constabulary' be displayed over the doors of all police cottages. Until the mid-1860s police had to wear their uniform off duty. 'The concept of being off duty ... was not recognised until the 1890s, when the larger forces instituted regular days of rest' (Steedman, 1984: 119). Police could not drink, gamble, or smoke in public. They could neither attend fairs nor race meetings. Senior officers could no doubt count on most of their men knowing what that sort of community life was like from prior experience. Their concern was that there be less opportunity for backsliding.

It is an enduring perspective. A constable whose contacts were too close might be vulnerable to undue influence. This was starkly profiled in the 1993 sacking of a mixed race WPC for making too few arrests and street stops. Posted to Brixton, near her home, she emphasised that her arrest record reflected the sensitivities of the public in Lambeth, informed by her background and understanding of local residents. However, an internal report referred to her '"gullibility in accepting any story told to her (and) reluctance to look for further offences or question the veracity of what she has been told"' ('Mixed race PC sacked for lack of arrests', *Guardian*, 10 June 1993). To see how this perspective obstructs the potential of community policing we might consider a remark made by Evans:

> The beat policeman has to be able to chat to people, so as to know what is going on. Because they know him as an individual, people in a village do not resent the fact that, living amongst them, he knows so much about them. They trust him. (1975: 44)

In a trusting relationship there is negotiation and a presumption that the other party will try to grasp the constraints applying to one's own action. The idea that a close relationship should be shunned in case leverage is exerted assumes that in a 'trusting' relationship compliance with the demands of the other is automatic. Close relationships, whether in town or country, are indeed marked by 'give and take'. Sometimes you win, sometimes not; over time you both win. The preference for detachment is an invitation to engage in guarded relationships in which interaction is so stilted as to make all tendered information dubious and to make it impossible to know enough about an informant's normal manner to determine when the information is honestly given. In short, trust will not be given if the constable does not reciprocate, and, without trust, consent can only be obtained by pressure and force.

Urban community role

Such circumstances are thought to characterise urban life, although their achievement in rural areas declined heavily during the 1990s as budget constraints and performance indicators dominated by arrest rates and response times distorted service delivery. In urban areas the police/public relationship has long been seen as problematic because of urban reserve and anonymity, diversity, and impermanency. Yet Herbert Gans famously profiled the 'urban village', and the bread of every estate agent is that each cherished bijou nestles in a 'little Soho'. Cities are aggregates of bounded locales. There are 'anonymous' estates, but, when one delves closer, one finds that even in the worst there is a measure of sociality (Foster, 2002). It is not 'the city' *per se* that chills the police/public relationship. It is the manner of policing it. Reactive ('fire brigade') policing makes for fiscal savings, but with an equivalent social deficit. It makes it harder for residents to get to know the police, and this makes police seem anonymous. Moreover, it insulates police from responsiveness to public requests other than emergency calls for service. Because officers have only intermittent contacts with the public, mostly at times of crisis, it is harder for police to take into account their character and perspectives. Snap judgments are made on gross characteristics, such as appearance, and officers have fewer resources with which to decide whether information given is reliable. Community policing (CP) involves regular face-to-face contact with the same residents. Insofar as they do achieve high contact with local people, community constables have an extra line of accountability: 'community residents have demonstrated that they will complain loudly about a CP officer they think is lazy, corrupt or ineffective' (Trojanowicz, 1988: 3).

While the community may be a source of new ideas, it is no guarantee of wisdom, and some widely touted community policing successes have a distinct downside. An indicative case is the periodic efforts to clean up entrenched red light districts. A multi-agency, community-based strategy was used in Finsbury Park, with the residents' association playing an important role. The principal method was road closure by councils, and police surveillance/harassment of kerb-crawlers. There was public concern that this would displace the problem, and residents of neighbouring areas opposed road closure for that reason, as did traffic police. The vice squad worked with the residents' association to identify brothels; a senior officer found jobs and accommodation for the prostitutes. The idea spread in London and a similar scheme was tried in Luton, where council workers locked and unlocked gates across residential roads at dusk and dawn. There the prostitutes simply moved on and the council had to consider closing a second set of roads to stop the new red light district. In London, displacement had not occurred: known names were not found on the charge sheet.

However, specialists working with prostitutes suggest such schemes have several dysfunctional effects. Workers with AIDS charities have pointed out that streetwalkers are easier to contact than sex workers operating from call girl agencies or in saunas, and if higher fines are imposed for prostitution, women may engage in unprotected sex, for which clients will pay more. Also, if sex workers are regularly moved on they may fail to re-register with AIDS clinics in their new area, because of the stigma of having to admit again that they are prostitutes. Evidence from a mobile AIDS clinic in Plymouth indicated the health benefit of an approach that relies on prostitutes being identifiable rather than driven underground: only two cases of gonorrhoea were reported in its first 19 months, compared to four a week previously (*Guardian*, 13 December 1989). In recent years the Home Office has considered licensing small brothels in prostitution 'tolerance zones', and establishing a state register of sex workers. However, in 2004 chief constables warned against the plans and instead advocated safe houses for prostitutes who wanted to testify against clients and 'exit schemes' for prostitutes after closing brothels masquerading as massage parlours and saunas (*Guardian*, 11 December 2004). In fact, prostitution had become a low priority for most forces, with the number of women cautioned for soliciting falling from 3,323 in 1993 to 732 in 2000. Child prostitutes are no longer prosecuted, but treated as child abuse victims, with the emphasis instead on prosecuting men who were kerb-crawling.

Anti-crime drives under the aegis of community policing must see social problems in the round. Community policing only makes sense if constables believe there is more to policing than enforcement of law by the imposition of legal force. This belief is related to their experience of public interaction, which varies according to ecological matters such as the ethnic composition and prosperity of an area. These facets of community policing schemes may also be limited by organisational considerations. Senior officers use accommodation allowances as a means of control, ruling out certain areas in which the ranks can buy houses by denying eligibility for allowances, and ruling out sharing with groups such as students. While the community policing rhetoric emphasises local ties, force housing policy can encourage isolation of police from the urban community. Longer assignments for local officers could build trust in the community; so would recruitment from within the area. Some forces assign local recruits to beats where they live, not only building links, but helping young officers resist the canteen culture.

Community constables do not work the whole range of shift duties, and under normal circumstances only attend their beats eight hours in any 24-hour period. Their involvement in duties such as school visits also suggests that they cannot be expected to provide significant response cover to their beats. Because of their specialist function and because their activities may not be co-ordinated by relief supervisors, they are not regarded as part of a station's response capability, even though they spend much time investigating beat crimes. These factors affect how other police see CP officers and their work. Research evaluating CP has to be carefully weighed, not least because of the scepticism of police about its effectiveness. The core of CP is regular patrol. Sherman (1992) examined the effects of increased, 'directed' patrol on levels of reported 'hard' (predatory) crime and 'soft' crime and disorder at 110 crime hotspots. A 250% increase in directed patrol had only a modest deterrent effect on robbery calls and no significant impact on 'hard' crime calls generally. However, when the much larger number of 'soft' crime calls were added, a 13% reduction in total calls for service was observed. Enhanced, visible police presence had little impact on crime, but tangible impact on disorder. Moreover, Bennett found that a UK scheme involving the police seeking more direct contact with citizens had little effect on crime or reporting rates, but did substantially improve public satisfaction (Bennett, 1991a and b).

The divided community

The community is highly diverse. Factions and groups make competing demands. Some are incompatible. Officers functioning as part of a community can arbitrate such demands, developing respect for police by the sensitive use of discretion. It should not be assumed that the police are unaware of their ability to legitimise some groups against others, or will be timid in doing so. Sensitivities may be such that well-meaning efforts to differentiate the community become counterproductive. A chief superintendent in charge at Notting Hill wrote to the leader of Kensington and Chelsea Council about its grants to community organisations: '"With only limited public funding available, care has to be exercised ... I am concerned that organisations which create divisiveness in the community are not encouraged by receiving public funding. [The] ongoing nurturing of the community [could be threatened] if highly emotive and, arguably, politically extremist organisations are given a public funding platform"' (*Guardian,* 22 March 1989). His representations occurred in an area where research had revealed failure of an expensive community policing scheme due in part to community resistance (Irving *et al*, 1989). Such a lack of circumspection is particularly dangerous where divisions between police and public can be expressed on gross demographic criteria, placing police in an oppositional relationship with whole categories of people, such as 'ethnic minority youth'. Petty involvement in crime is a much more general experience than police may assume in attributing it to an identifiable and discrete group. A 1988 classroom survey on shoplifting revealed that some 46% of 11–15-year-olds had stolen something at some time, 52% from shops (*Guardian,* 30 November 1988), and in 2005 the Home Office self-report survey, discussed in Chapter 1 of this book, found that a third of teenage boys were active offenders (Home Office, 2005), albeit with caveats about seriousness.

The potential of community policing to make officers more sophisticated about criminal stereotypes and labelling is affected by who they take as representative of the community. In inner-city estates with high ethnic minority concentrations the community constables make a point of maintaining liaison with tenants' associations, pensioners' groups and the like. These are chiefly white organisations. Links with the black population are largely through ethnically-based youth clubs. White tenants are cast as potential victims, black youths are cast as potential offenders. Within these communities there are serious differences of perspective. Blacks see inner-city problems as unemployment, poor housing and facilities, whites as drug-dealing and street crime. Local order is thus seen as a 'black' problem, even though many of the drug users are white; the police take the drug problem as a legitimation of extensive stop and search. Police often complain that efforts to secure better community relations are obstructed by the apathy and disorganisation of people on 'problem estates'. Yet they also say that the integrated, cohesive Asian community is an obstacle to community-building because it is impenetrable.

Real CP means addressing the problems raised by communities. There was official knowledge about hate crime over 20 years before it became a police priority. In 1981, a Home Office survey found that 70 Asians in every 100,000, and 51 Afro-Caribbeans, could expect to be victims of a racially motivated attack in any two months. In 1987, Leeds Community Relations Council found 305 cases of harassment over an 18-month period in a sample population of 4,000, suggesting a harassment level 10 times the 1981 estimate. Ethnic minority people remain considerably more likely to be victims of racially-motivated offences; people of mixed race have a 4% risk of racially-motivated victimisation, Asians a 3% rate, blacks and Chinese a 2% risk and whites under 1% (Home Office, 2004a); see Table 1. Some ethnic minority people are also over-represented amongst victims of crime generally; for example, while blacks and whites have a 25% rate for 'household crimes' (including burglary), Indians and Pakistanis have a 28% rate (Home Office, 2003b).

Where police and other agencies work together on problems of real concern to local people the impetus can overcome previously bitter relations. When local police instituted a tough policy on racial harassment in the late 1980s, Islington Council backed them vigorously (Council press

Table 1: Victimisation and ethnicity

	All household crime	All personal crime	All BCS crime	Unweighted base (respondents)
White	23,000	76,000	99,000	34,525
Mixed	8,000	5,000	13,000	363
Asian or Asian British	27,000	31,000	59,000	2,190
Black or black British	10,000	12,000	22,000	1,536
Chinese or other	3,000	10,000	13,000	649
Total	71,000	135,000	206,000	39,263

Source: Salisbury and Upson (2004)
Note: Estimated numbers (to the nearest thousand) include multiple victimisation.

release, 5 October 1989). The effort saw the first successful prosecution for racially motivated crimes, and a consequent higher reporting rate, suggesting increased public confidence. A racial harassment steering group with senior officers, chaired by the Council's Chief Executive, tightened co-operation, so all race cases, handled by police or Council, were cross-reported. In 1988, 103 cases were reported with no prosecutions, but by October 1989 some 125 were reported and five had been prosecuted, with sentences including two years jail. In the face of minority people being stabbed, spat at and firebombed, both agencies accepted 'a victim-centred definition of race harassment'. Here was a problem where police accepted divisions in the community and were prepared to 'take sides'.

The answer to the undoubted difficulty of 'community-building' may be to focus effort on providing services requested by local people. Although there are analyses, such as FitzGerald et al (2002), that put a different cast on the matter, a major obstacle police have faced is the suspicion caused by the higher likelihood that minority people face of being questioned as they go about their business. Blacks remain far more likely to be stopped and searched: 100 per 100,000 population in 2001–02, compared to 38 for Asians and 15 for whites (Home Office, 2003b). If arrested, blacks are less likely to receive the relatively mild outcome of cautioning: some 16% of whites and 17% of Asians arrested are cautioned, but 13% of blacks (Home Office, 2003b). While ethnic minority people have broadly similar perceptions of the criminal justice system as do whites, they feel they are seen as an underclass by police and are unfairly targeted. They are actually *more* likely than others to see the criminal justice system as doing a good job, and have more confidence than whites in the courts and prosecution service, but less in the police (Home Office, 2003b).

Overt discrimination dominated early concerns. Staffordshire Police were convicted of encouraging racial discrimination by publishing a crime prevention leaflet in which householders were advised to note registration numbers of cars driven by 'coloured people' (*Guardian*, 23 June 1988). The judge remarked that it was beyond his comprehension that anyone could have published such a statement. The police said the officer responsible had not yet undergone community relations training, an excuse no longer available. Institutionalised discrimination dominates contemporary concerns. The significance of institutionalised discriminatory practices is that their routine nature masks iniquitous treatment. Cautioning procedures, charging policies and the need for photographing and fingerprinting offenders are points of routine tension. In one case, three black children, aged nine, 10 and 11, who were caught stealing sweets, spent five hours in a police station, and the two eldest were charged, photographed, fingerprinted and obliged to make signed statements, acquiring a criminal record that would last until age 17 (Thomas, 1989: 12). The legality of the nine-year-old being taken to the station (below the age of criminal responsibility), the acceptability of a social worker acting as 'appropriate adult' within the Codes of Practice, and a 'standing order' in the station that all juveniles have prints taken (when s 61 of the Police and Criminal Evidence Act (PCEA) refers to 'a person' rather than persons) were all dubious. Social workers requested that the children be 'reported' and allowed to leave, but the police preferred cautioning, which left no further police action, but put their record on computer. At 10.30 at night an inspector cautioned the children, including the nine-year-old who should not have been present, but was clinging to his slightly older brother and sister. Access to a solicitor was apparently not considered. Because such incidents relate to minor crime they seldom achieve the notice given *cause célèbre*, such as the botched investigation of the murder of Stephen Lawrence, but they are more pervasive and equally corrosive.

The Stephen Lawrence case was a watershed in identifying the divisions of contemporary urban Britain. The murder itself exposed the fissures present despite a superficially multi-cultural tolerance, with a widespread perception that the family's civil action, despite its ultimate failure, had identified the perpetrators, white youths whose repellent behaviour at court and in front of cameras revealed the casual brutality of attitudes in a section of the white working-class. The Macpherson Inquiry resisted labelling the failed police investigation as the result of bumbling incompetence. This was not merely a muddled investigation, or even a reflection of an offhand attitude, but the result of institutionalised racism (Bridges, 1999). The Met Commissioner accepted the verdict and chiefs across the country followed suit. Police culture needed to be overhauled, and clear objectives to be set by forces to deal with racist crime, a view reinforced in the Inspectorate's thematic review based on the position in 15 forces ('Police chief in pledge to tackle racism', *Surrey Advertiser*, 5 March 1999), and the government's new interest in ethnic minority recruitment quotas.

By emphasising constructive applications of discretion, community policing focuses on the grey areas between the binary legal logic of guilty/not guilty. We have seen that heavy-handed policing can provoke unity in groups that are otherwise seething with variety, by drawing them together against police. The police are plainly aware that internal divisions on grounds of competing interests mark the inner city. A proliferation of policies accepting and even valuing 'diversity' has marked recent times. The chief value of glossily presented policies is not that they bring about non-discriminatory policing, but that they give the public a tool with which to confront police when the policies are breached.

Providing a service

The social service function of the police is well-recognised, as is their avowed dislike of it. Punch's classic analysis (1975) argued that this stems from fear at becoming a repository for diffuse and distasteful tasks shed by other agencies and from the low esteem in which the social services are held. Despite enduring antipathies, the police and social workers share a clientele – 'the drunk, the delinquent, the homeless, the drug addict, the problem family, the battered wife, the immigrant' (Punch, 1975). In fact, the negative view of social services is often shared with the public. In crisis, people generally turn to the police first. Cummings (1965) long ago found that over half of calls to police were for help in personal or interpersonal problems. In Punch and Naylor's similar study in three English towns, the proportion of 'service' calls was over half in two and nearly three-quarters in the third, which contained a rural area (Punch and Naylor, 1973). Officer time spent in different activities for 2001 appears in Table 2, where it can be seen that only 9% of time is spent directly in crime-related work. If, crudely, this is summed with the 23% of time spent attending incidents, about a third of police time may be directly crime-related. Much of the remainder will be social service-type work. General provision of assistance – dealing with disputes, lost and found property, missing persons, information-giving and so on – may hinder their strict law enforcement role, but brings police in contact with people who provide information; these low-key interventions may de-escalate problems and reduce the police burden later.

However it is not only the share of police time spent in social service work that continues. The endurance of the pattern where such work is regarded as secondary is shown in recent police efforts to get citizens to report 'non-urgent' matters to special call centres or via the internet and email. Similarly, a number of police forces, including Greater Manchester, ceased automatically sending uniformed officers to all 999 calls in the early 1990s, citing a wish to 'target the criminal and not the crime' ('Minor offences lose 999 status', *Guardian*, 27 June 1994). Thefts from cars, criminal damage, burglaries from outbuildings and cycle thefts would be judged over the phone and officers might respond at a later time. Victim Support counsellors rather than police would visit victims of minor burglaries. In 1995, ACPO set new guidelines for forces that meant police no longer respond to every burglar alarm call, due to excessive false alarms; there were 1.9 million false alarm calls a year, but only 80,000 were genuine. Calls would henceforth get a police response if the

Table 2: Officer time use

% of respondent time by activity	
Working inside the police station	
Relief management	7.0%
Prisoner processing	5.7%
Prosecution, file and enquiries	6.2%
Cover duties	3.5%
Dealing with public	1.2%
Individual administration	0.5%
Station based training	0.7%
Break	5.1%
Other	13.1%
Working within the community	
Community support	1.7%
Patrol (including uncommitted patrol and travelling between pre-planned tasks)	17.0%
Attending incidents	23.3%
Crime related	9.0%
Other duties	3.3%
Policing events	0.5%
Break taken outside station	0.3%
Other work in the community	1.0%
Working with the criminal justice system	
Within the police force (other than own police station)	0.2%
At court	0.6%

Source: Singer (2001)

caller could see lights on in a supposedly empty property or figures moving in a garden, but there would be no response if callers were uncertain of the alarm's exact location ('Police to stop automatic response to burglar alarms', *Guardian*, 22 March 1995). The policy was seen as part of a greater emphasis on concentrating resources on CID, with greater use of new technology and less patrol. Whether the police want to keep at arms length from such demands or to engage in a partnership response, service-type demands are rising. In 2004 a quarter of the criminal justice budget for violent crime was spent on dealing with domestic violence (*Surrey Advertiser*, 28 January 2005).

Despite the police attitude to such work, there is long-established evidence that police can be effective in a social role. One of the earliest examples dates from 1955. In Greenock, with a population then of 80,000, some 900 children were appearing before the juvenile court each year. Community facilities and playgrounds were widely vandalised. 'The police introduced juvenile liaison which kept back from overworked courts a host of minor offenders, many of whom were helped by the police' (Punch and Naylor, 1973). Police initiated physical improvements in poor neighbourhoods and secured a reduction in vandalism, and improved sporting and social amenities, working with residents, school staff, local authorities and social agencies.

One of the most sustained CP initiatives, Chicago's CAPS (Chicago Alternative Policing Strategy) programme, offers massive evidence of the value of CP based on integrating city services – police, housing, social services – and involving residents (Skogan, 1990a). The benefits have not generally been in crime control, but in service-type improvements. Municipal workers and police led problem-solving training sessions for the public. CP expands the police mandate: citizens raised social disorder problems dominated by unlawful activities police had customarily not prioritised – graffiti, public drinking, vandalism, truancy – and activities on the fringe of legality – loitering, begging, non-violent domestic disputes. Police found themselves involved in neighbourhood clean-ups, inventorying dilapidated structures and tracing the owners. Police accompanied residents at prayer vigils where drug-related shootings had occurred, guarded barbeque 'smoke outs' at drug-dealing locations, and noted broken street lights and trees that needed trimming.

After two years of CAPS, about a third of residents had attended a beat community meeting and three-quarters of these reported that actions were taken or they noticed a change in their neighbourhood as a result of the meetings. Those reporting police doing a good job increased with participation in CAPS programmes. The beat meetings chiefly provided information to police on the basis that it was for them to act. Residents proved most active and successful in tackling troublesome or abandoned buildings. They contacted landlords, worked with city legal departments to evict problem tenants or secure demolition of abandoned buildings, and put addresses on the backs of buildings so officers in alleys could specify their location. A key instrument was a one page City Service Request Form covering all service requests and available online or from police and community organisations.

Problem measures declined about 7% over the period from inception to 1999, with a 10% fall (to 45%) in residents reporting gang violence problems. The property and street crime index fell (from 40% to 31%), the largest decline being in robbery and assault on the street. Burglary, car theft and car vandalism declined by 8%. The physical decay index fell 6%. These are not spectacular improvements, but disproportionately registered with those most in need, particularly African-Americans. From 1994 onward there were sustained if unspectacular decreases in fear of crime. Feeling safe outdoors, while alone after dark, increased nearly 10%. Reports that nearby areas were safe increased from 45% to 56%.

Before CAPS, less than 40% of Chicagoans had an optimistic view of police responsiveness to community concerns. Under CAPS, the index rose 20%. Those who thought police were doing a good job working with residents to solve problems rose 20% (to 59%). Chicagoans rating police as doing their job well rose from 36% to 50%. Reports that police were doing a good job assisting crime victims rose 20% (to 57%). Highest marks were given for keeping order: positive scores hit 66% by 1999, from 56% in 1993.

The gains seen under CAPS do not imply that CP's focus on social disorder will directly impact on serious crime (the 'broken windows hypothesis'; Kelling, 1998). Rather, disorder and crime have similar causes, and social cohesion reduces disorder and, to a lesser extent, crime, by disabling the forces that produce them (Sampson and Raudenbush, 1999). Sampson and Raudenbush found that disorder is a moderate correlate of predatory crime, but varies consistently with antecedent neighbourhood characteristics. Eradicating disorder may indirectly reduce crime by stabilising neighbourhoods, but a direct link to crime is unlikely. Community policing can bring benefits of social integration, responsiveness of city services to residents' needs, and improved handling of urban decay. While the best research tells us that working against social disorder does not impact on serious crime, it also tells us that working against social disorder impacts positively on public reassurance.

Such initiatives are important against the increasing use of public satisfaction measures to evaluate police performance. Crime survey data indicate a majority satisfaction with police performance by victims, but with a declining trend. Those very or fairly satisfied were 68% in 1984, 60% in 1988, 65% in 1992 and 67% in 1994. Whites were more satisfied (68%) than blacks (59%) or Asians (59%), manual workers (65%) were less satisfied than non-manual (71%). Victims of low seriousness offences were most satisfied (78%), and those of highly serious offences least (62%), with medium seriousness at a 69% satisfaction level (British Crime Survey, 1994). Some 24% rated local police very good, 58% fairly good, 13% fairly poor and 5% very poor. By 2003–04 overall victim satisfaction had fallen to 58% (British Crime Survey, 2004).

Disposition and demeanour variables are known to be highly influential on satisfaction. In 1994 when 92% of BCS respondents rated police as very/fairly polite, only 60% thought they had showed enough effort, and only 34% felt police had kept them well-informed. There have been force-specific initiatives aimed at particular victim groups. In 1993 the Met inaugurated two homophobic violence units in areas where there were attacks on gay men and gay pubs (*Guardian*, 26 February 1993). Homophobic violence had been monitored since 1991 and the units aimed to raise victims' confidence in police. In 2001 the chief of a force criticised in 1996 for repeated sexual discrimination, and whose predecessor was facing disciplinary action over discrimination when he retired, appeared at a press conference to celebrate the presence in his ranks of two '"good, effective – and transsexual"' officers. The officers declined to answer questions, but the force diversity officer said that one of them had the medical condition gender dysphoria ('Police chief celebrates transsexuals', *Guardian*, 21 July 2001).

Police involvement in an increasing range of multi-agency liaison groups offers them scope to more effectively prioritise and value social service-type work. While still patchy and contentious, increasing police participation in partnership work reflects a growing acceptance that an institution that often warrants the pursuit of its own interests by reference to the need for the professional exercise of discretion can hardly argue that its role in community development is strictly circumvented by its legal brief.

Discretion and order

This returns us to the police role in the achievement and maintenance of civil order. The policing of major public order events suggested that the police have considerable latitude for action and a privileged claim to interpret the law in practice, as well as the sole claim to determine what is occupationally warranted. This latitude emanates from the discretion they are granted. The importance and dilemmas of discretion have been the focus of recruiting campaigns, such as a well-known late 80s advertisement featuring an officer having to decide what to do at an off-duty party when he realises cannabis is being smoked by a friend – 'Do you turn your back or turn him in?' The copy well-approximated the wise-guy punchiness often heard among police.

> You don't want to lose a friend. You don't want to break up a party. You don't want your face smashed in. On the other hand you've sworn to uphold the Law ... Now observe the first law of diplomacy, 'engage brain before opening mouth'. In other words, consider the options ... Here are three that would most impress us if you were trying to join the Metropolitan Police. (1) Have a quiet word with the host, explain your predicament and his liability, then ask him to put a stop to it. (2) Pop out to the nearest police station and report the incident. (3) Stay at the party for a while, identify the offenders and tackle the situation later, having consulted your superiors. Do you begin to see how much responsibility you'll have?

As another advert declared, 'for many of the incidents you'll come across there are no rules, just guidelines'. Police were subsequently prominent, if reluctant, advocates of a change in the status of cannabis (Warburton *et al*,

2005), but recruiting campaigns continued to highlight discretion, as in a late 1990s campaign about how to deal with homeless people (who were also petty criminals and class A drug users).

Goldstein's classic article (1960; see also Wilson, 1968) established that the police are nearly alone among bureaucracies in that the degree of discretion is greatest at the lowest level and that decisions by officers in contact with the public are marked by 'low visibility', thus being invisible to superiors and effectively 'unreviewable'. This is especially true when they have decided *not* to arrest. Lustgarten asserts that the point reflects the more fundamental fact that 'in taking the sort of decision that is the quintessence of their work, the police are guided by virtually no legal standards at all' (1986: 10). Subject to the broad restraint of civil and criminal liability 'they act within an almost infinite range of lawful possibilities' (Lustgarten, 1986: 10). Lustgarten's example is a fight between two men with the constable summoned to the scene. The constable can choose to (1) stop the fight, dispersing the men with an informal warning, (2) stop the fight and attempt to mediate, (3) formally caution one or both men, (4) seek the cause and arrest the man he holds responsible, or (5) arrest both, choosing from charges relating to public order and/or several degrees of assault (1986: 10–11). Choice depended on the constable's role concept.

> If it is solely and simply law enforcement, the first two possibilities are excluded: the law has been broken and the offenders must be penalised. If considerations of maintaining the peace and public good will predominate, any of the responses is permissible and may depend upon the character of the people involved, where the fight took place, reactions of others in the neighbourhood, and numerous other highly idiosyncratic factors. Still other facts, notably the dangers of overloading the capacity of the criminal justice system and the cost of processing offenders will also be relevant ... (1986: 11)

Since all these options are within the constable's legal power, it is meaningless to say that the constable must 'uphold the law'. The 'law' is supplanted by considerations of the worthiness of those involved, public feeling, seriousness, or the costs and benefits of various sanctions. Lustgarten notes that there is nothing in the decision that a lay person could not do. It is the context of the decision that requires a constable to take it and, indeed, makes it less susceptible to guidance by supervisors.

> The sheer idiosyncrasy, the fact that every decision will require the weighing of different factors, means it may be difficult to subject it to preordained rules drawn up by hierarchical superiors. The speed with which the choice must be made is largely responsible for this, for where other highly personal judgments are governed by complex rules – for example, entitlement to supplementary benefit – decisions often take days. (1986: 11)

So the unique character of police discretion springs from the need to make decisions sensitive to the situation while it is in progress and not from its 'legal' character. This combination of a swift, highly personal decision in relative isolation based on criteria only partly related to law also heightens the possibility that it may be seen by outsiders as arbitrary. There is a last, vital point to balance the impression of great latitude. The police hierarchy is quasi-military: its standing orders are noted for detail and breadth. Arrest decisions are reviewed, charges may be rejected, an arrest may be required where a caution was put forward. Goldstein's point is strongest when a constable chooses *not* to invoke the law.

Young constables are often so mindful that discretion is reviewable, at least where charges result, that they prefer to use their discretion very tightly indeed; but discretion at the bottom and top shares the characteristic that room is permitted for 'highly personal', subjective judgments. At chief officer level we can see this in two instances. The first is the caution. Since the 1980 Royal Commission on Criminal Procedure, divergence in cautioning policies has been noted; the Commission heard that in 1977–78 Northumbria cautioned 18% of its suspected young offenders, but at the other extreme Dyfed-Powys cautioned 68%. More recently, cautioning varied from 23% in South Yorkshire to 48% in Gloucestershire (Home Office, 1999). While offence category, personal characteristics of suspect and the requirements of a successful prosecution standardise decisions, the chief constable's conception of crime is another influence, accounting for considerable variation when similar cases are compared across jurisdictions. Chiefs have taken a definitive line for or against wider cautioning and it is widely held that sentence variation reflects their different preconceptions. 'Most important is the general ambience prevailing throughout the force regarding attitudes to young offenders – the ideological atmosphere promoted and supported by the chief officer's views, in internal force orders, in resource commitment and in public statements' (Brogden, 1982: 141); exactly the same point can be made regarding drug offences (Warburton *et al*, 2005).

It is to be recalled that the justification for individual officer discretion was the need for swift decision, having regard to the circumstances. Such criteria seem strained in the case of cautioning. Here, senior officer discretion makes for inflexibility. It accounts for wide variations despite clear Home Office guidance. There may be some limited sense in which the particular characteristics of a jurisdiction's youth suggest a particular policy, but the evidence is that it is not a judgment on 'local knowledge' so much as the personal philosophy of chiefs and senior officers that is operating. In any case, that presumes geographical variation in the maturity and/or culpability of those cautioned, which strains credulity.

The issue is similar regarding public order offences, in this case the minor infringements that are the very stuff of civil order, rather than high profile disturbances. These offences are highly contingent on police initiatives for much of their recording and prosecution. Summary offences like prostitution, petty drug misuse and drunkenness are particularly likely to be influenced by the policies of the chief officer, the views of the prosecuting officer and conventions in local workgroups. These are 'crimes without victims' and so come to light only as a result of proactive policing. At one point betting and gambling prosecutions were six times more frequent on Merseyside than Thames Valley, and while Thames Valley prosecuted five times as many drug users as Northamptonshire it could not find a single case of prostitution worth prosecuting. In the 1990s a single pair of youths accounted for almost all of one force's arrests for underage sex; the enraptured couple admitted to over 300 acts (the Home Office deterred the force's attempt to count this as the successful detection of 300 offences, deeming it amounted to just one). Warburton *et al* (2005) found that the three principal influences on the action taken by police when encountering drug-taking were length of service, police force area, and officer attitude. The latter was the strongest predictor, and was mediated by the officer's personal experience of drugs. The reality of local civil order as it is experienced by ordinary people is much marked by variation in police practices whose legal warrant is dubious and whose grounding in personal standards is not effectively reviewable. The themes established in the harshly conflictual setting of the policing of major public disorder are visited again upon a wider population in the production of local civil order, but with greater obscurity.

5. Managing social conflict: armaments, alliances, divisions

How far should preventive policing go?

The two broad forms of public disorder – dramatic, temporary and discrete events, and mundane, enduring and cumulative processes – both express social conflict. This chapter examines the experience of different policing techniques by police and public, contrasting the apparatus of forceful social control with contemporary approaches to community policing, and considering their points of convergence. Placed deliberately between discussions of the paramilitary apparatus of policing and discussions of partnership work and community policing, a discussion of internal divisions within forces and the stressful effects of police work represents the police workforce as the locus of unresolved tensions between the competing approaches. Graphic testimony that a weak force enjoying public support is more effective than a powerful force without is conveyed by the England and Wales police ratio of 2.4 officers per 1,000 population compared to 5 officers per 1,000 in Northern Ireland (Department of Justice, 2003); in the late 1970s, though, the ratio was 2 officers to 1,000 on the mainland, 20 to 1,000 in Northern Ireland (Alderson, 1979).

Post-Scarman formulations of the police function have emphasised the pre-eminent need to maintain the Queen's Peace. Police have often distorted such principles by elevating crime control as the supreme police function, and have been readily encouraged to do so by politicians. While this approach has proved useful in public relations and securing larger budgets, it is contradicted by law and history. The Queen's Peace doctrine has a long lineage, reinforced prior to Scarman by the 1960 Royal Commission, which declared that:

> [t]he police in this country are the instruments for enforcing the rule of law; they are the means by which civilised society maintains order, that people may live safely in their homes and go freely about their lawful business. Basically their task is the maintenance of the Queen's Peace – that is, the preservation of law and order. Without this there would be anarchy. (Royal Commission, 1962: 21)

Much of the conventional ideology of policing is packed into those assertions. Policing and progress towards a civilised way of life are elided; before police there was not the relatively enduring community control of common law, but 'anarchy'. Popular respect is secured by the independence of law and police from 'sectarian' interests, guaranteeing individual liberty. The ideology particularly de-emphasises the police role in securing a social order conducive to established interests. Securing public order was essential in regulating the struggle of the working-class for equal rights. Law was hardly a neutral resource. While crime was seen as linked to deprivation and could be regulated through schemes administered by the Poor Law Guardians and latterly the Welfare State, public order required organised force. Outright military force was counterproductive. From the earliest times, policing was imbued with the doctrine of neutrality and identification with a strongly reified conception of law. When reference is made to the anarchy of pre-police times it is not law enforcement, but order maintenance that is being invoked. The 'Queen's Peace' refers pre-eminently to civil order and not crime control.

The emphasis on neutrality, independence and legal authority is important because of the obvious potential for public order policing to be taken as protecting those sectarian interests which already control most of the community's resources. The 'peace' is that of the *status quo* and the 'order' that of the established order. The old relation of constabulary and community under the common law, from which routine policing is supposed to derive its inspiration and essential qualities, was long ago undermined by social change, but police and government drew the lesson, from the police strikes and urban riots, that the community could not and would not police itself. When some took the opportunity to loot, burn and riot, it was seen not as a moral holiday, but as society's normal state when free of police.

This suggests why community policing, partnership and citizen involvement has proved such a quandary for contemporary police forces. Blanket policies for policing in partnership with the public obscure the need to negotiate variations in communities. For example, the demand for public order policing varies greatly according to characteristics of the area, and requires flexible policing techniques. This undermines blanket statements such as the canonical endorsement of preventive policing in the Metropolitan Police Instruction Book.

> The object to be obtained is the prevention of crime. To this great end every effort of the police is to be directed. The security of person and property and the preservation of a police establishment will thus be better effected than by the detection and punishment of the offender after he has succeeded in committing crime. (Quoted in Dear, 1975: 31)

Preventive policing depends critically on the characteristics of the area's population. In that sense, policing does have to be attuned to the community and its 'establishment' cannot simply be derived from broad statements of the police function. Nor can the tools and training of forceful social control be turned on and off according to circumstances.

Using 'all legal weapons'

It is tempting to see the proliferation of units like the Police Support Unit (PSU) as a militarisation of policing; but paramilitary policing is not only a question of capability, but of demand, or, more accurately, what the community will accept. It is not just what citizens will tolerate, but what the police will, too. Militarisation is resisted by the police partly because of belief in public consent and because police are concerned that carrying guns would heighten danger as criminals matched police firepower. Worry over the effect on the regular force's image of being identified with paramilitarism holds in check what police technology makes easily achievable, but is increasingly eroded by terrorism.

The strongest spur to paramilitarism is the knowledge and equipment put into police currency through the conflict in Northern Ireland. Street battles in the Bogside in 1969 gave early experience with water cannon and CS gas. The gas was applied as collective punishment to make the community politically ineffective, but instead crystallised resistance and provoked further disturbances. It should not be a hard lesson to grasp in a country whose wartime resolve was hardened by overwhelming enemy strength during the Battle of Britain; but the taint from exposure to such methods spreads. The army drew on experience of colonial insurgency, the Royal Ulster Constabulary (RUC) drew on the army, and inter-force co-operation made paramilitary armaments more widely available. The RUC applied the army's knowledge of 'advanced' interrogation techniques during internment, including total sensory deprivation.

The early nineties saw renewed sectarian violence in consequence of the republican movement's refusal to accept the Downing Street Declaration of December 1993 and government intransigence in the face of calls for its clarification. By 1994 there were no resident police officers in half the land area of Northern Ireland; in the first quarter of the year, three RUC officers were murdered, six injured, there were attempted murders of two senior officers, and RUC stations sustained 15 armed attacks ('Police find rewards in softly softly approach', *Guardian*, 30 April 1994). RUC officers noted that republican community accusations of police collusion with loyalists rose whenever Catholics were murdered, but this obscured an important fact. There was a general acceptance of police in their non-public order role, and *most* republicans and Catholics accepted even the public order role. Even so, a case study to illustrate acceptance for RUC community policing had to be published with the village's identity disguised and the officer appearing under a pseudonym ('Police find rewards in softly softly approach', *Guardian*, 30 April 1994). The 1995 IRA ceasefire allowed the Met to drop preventing terrorism from its top two priorities (the other was burglary), but the structure of anti-terrorist operations was kept in place and the only tangible change was cessation of armed roadblocks (*Guardian*, 8 March 1995). Following the '9/11' attacks in the US the full structure was restored and enhanced.

Following the murder of 16 people by gunman Michael Ryan, the Police Superintendents Association called for armed response teams on 24-hour patrol throughout Britain (*Guardian*, 22 September 1988). An Inspectorate report on the Hungerford massacre that said forces should consider special units with armoured cars manned 24 hours, more helicopters, body armour and a communications satellite (*Guardian*, 28 July 1988) proved an accurate augury, bar the satellite. The upgrading of armaments and weapons training proceeded without parliamentary consultation or taking account of the views of police constables. Surveys in the 1980s found some 77% of constables opposed the arming of the police when they joined the police, rising to 89% in their second year of service (Fielding, 1988), and advertising by the Met stated that the number authorised to carry guns had been reduced from 5,000 in 1985 to 3,000 in 1993, or one in ten; 'we're proud of the efficiency we've achieved, but we are even prouder of the fact that 90% of officers still aren't armed at any time'. By 1994, a national sample survey showed that the public was keener than the police to see police widely armed; 67% of the public, but 46% of police ('Public keener than police for guns on beat', *Guardian*, 18 May 1994). Routine arming was still opposed by the majority of both groups. Arming officers at all times was accepted by only 5% of police and 8% of the public, and 68% of the public said arming more police would make them less approachable. Serious assaults on police officers had not dramatically risen. In 1993, guns were used in 4,682 incidents, in 10 cases against police. Five officers were killed between 1990 and 1995. Of the 5,625 occasions when police were issued firearms in 1993 they fired shots on six occasions, killing four and injuring three (*Guardian*, 21 March 1995). The Association of Chief Police Officers (ACPO) confirmed its continued opposition to routine arming. The Home Office decided to test CS gas instead. Forces were seeking a new measure of protection, 'somewhere between a truncheon and a gun'. Pepper sprays could temporarily disable attackers, but could have effects on asthmatics and pregnant women (*Guardian*, 16 March 1995).

The Federation balloted its members in 1995 and found that they remained more reluctant to carry guns than was the public to see them armed. Nearly 74,000 officers responded, 60% of Federation membership; 79% did not want to be routinely armed, although 83%

wanted more officers firearms-trained. A parallel survey found that 26%
of the public favoured routine arming (*Guardian*, 16 May 1995). Officers
remained concerned over their safety. In the previous two years, 52,000
had their lives threatened on duty up to 10 times, 48,000 were personally
threatened with weapons up to 10 times, and 55,000 were injured by
assault between one and 10 times; but 6% would resign if required to
carry guns, and 46% would go armed only if directly ordered. On the
survey's last day a London constable was shot dead and Scotland Yard
announced all officers would be issued body armour, choosing between
bullet-proof or knife-proof vests. They also received alarm radios to send
distress signals to the nearest police station (*Guardian*, 10 May 1995). The
number of Armed Response Vehicles was doubled. The Home Secretary
announced he would back any chief who changed force policy to equip
all officers with body armour (Home Office News Release 108/95, 17
May 1995).

It is not only in order maintenance that chosen techniques may
provoke or aggravate the situation. Pressure to deliver on crime control
can also lead to provocative methods. Rioting in Wolverhampton in 1989
was attributed to police staging a drugs raid on a pub that prompted
trouble in which the Council's rent office was destroyed. Police vented
their frustration on bystanders (*Guardian*, 24 May 1989). The drug raid
was by 120 officers who arrived in vans; witnesses alleged they saw 10
police beating a black man, and that damage to the pub had been caused
by a heavy-handed search for drugs. Over subsequent weeks saturation
policing was applied to the area, with police kicking their way into flats
at dawn and searching sleeping children's beds for drugs (*Guardian*, 20
June 1989). The local vicar spoke of 'intimidation and straightforward
racist policing' and residents saw the raids as attempts to justify the
policing of the 'riot'. Misjudged incidents can undermine carefully
cultivated relations. In 1992 a black vicar pinning up police recruitment
posters in a community centre was caught in a brutal drugs raid in which
police threw him against a wall and then restrained him by standing on
his neck. The reverend survived, but the Moss Side ethnic minority
community was outraged (*Guardian*, 21 September 1992). Ironically one
of the officers involved sat on the same police community liaison group
as the victim.

The danger of 'saturation policing' as a strategy against crime, as
opposed to disorder, is apparent in police campaigns against street
crimes such as mugging. Police claim that the nature of the offences rule
out conventional strategies based on eliciting information from the
public. Police instead use their wide legal powers in a deterrent, 'pre-
emptive' way by deploying in large numbers. This withdraws police
from situations where they could get information co-operatively, and

can convert community ambivalence into solid hostility. Heavier use of stop and search powers for stolen property, drugs and weapons can also excite resistance during such campaigns. These were the ingredients of the 1980s riots.

The Brixton riots gave the Scarman Inquiry a clear run at the balance between crime control versus civil order. The police resort to 'all legal weapons' had contributed to serious disorder. The police strategy founded on (assumed) absence of community co-operation was ineffective against street crime while also provoking riots. Scarman advocated tough crime control in consultation with the community by 'knowing exactly, through judging the community temper, when you can get away with an SPG [PSU-type] visit' (Jefferson and Grimshaw, 1984: 102). Police thought this did not resolve the dilemma because Scarman did not speak to their absolute duty to enforce the law, which outweighed any requirement to operate only with community consent. This is unconvincing, both legally and practically. Discretion is embedded in the legal powers of constables, and the constabulary independence and original authority arguments imply this can be extrapolated from the ranks to senior officers. Discretion is equally well-founded practically. The 'unique' character of the office of constable is not due to special legal knowledge, but the extreme contingency of the situations about which they must reach decisions. In practice there is no 'unconditional requirement to enforce the law'; if there were, householders would still be charged for failing to wash their doorsteps. To argue that the police could not have deployed otherwise, 'given the current system of accountability that is based on an unconditional duty to enforce the law', is to depict police governance as rigid as well as unambiguous, whereas the accountability literature emphasises flexibility and recurrent adjustments in the powers of the parties to the tripartite system.

The 1980s riots persuaded chiefs that new strategies, weapons and laws were needed. The Public Order Act 1986 created new statutory offences of riot, affray and violent disorder. The old, much-used s 5 of the Public Order Act 1936, 'conduct likely to lead to a breach of the peace', gave way to a wider new offence, covering threatening, abusive or insulting words or behaviour which the perpetrator could reasonably foresee would lead to harassment, alarm or distress. This much enhanced police discretionary power. Powers to regulate processions and, for the first time in statute, to control the location, duration and size of stationary assemblies of over 20 people, were added. Control over size, location and duration of demonstrations was vested in police decisions and free from judicial review. There are no means by which the annulment of a police decision on the spot may be effected; one submits or is arrested.

Among the provisions of the Criminal Justice and Public Order Act 1994 were empowering councils on application by chiefs to ban gatherings of more than 20 people on a highway or any land without the owner's permission, disbanding of 'raves' where music is played at night and out of doors if a senior officer believes it may cause serious distress; a reduction to six in the number of vehicles above which police can require persons trespassing with vehicles or who damage property to leave, even where the owner consents to their presence; abolition of the local authority's duty to provide sites for travellers; introduction of an offence to attempt to disrupt or obstruct an activity taking place in the open air (aimed at hunt saboteurs); and the granting of additional powers to authorised representatives to force entry, with a requirement that squatters leave immediately. Hunt saboteurs claimed that hunt members saw the Act as implicitly approving assault on them; security firms hired by hunts had become increasingly violent. Police saw the anti-saboteur measures as an excessive call on resources, a theme repeated when hunting with hounds was banned from 2005. The Home Office confirmed that the 2,000 officers of Special Branch would henceforth spend more time monitoring demonstrations and marches to assess their public order implications: better assessment could save £750,000 a year by replacing full-scale operations against trespassers and ravers by smaller preventative operations.

However, chiefs indicated a wide use of discretion in implementing the new powers against travellers, ravers and squatters. ACPO's public order spokesman said '"[i]f justice is to be available to all the corners and crevices of our society it must be seen to be fair and not to discriminate against particular groups ... We must not ignore the ever-present generation gap between the freedom-loving young and their restriction-preferring elders'" ('Ravers left in firing line, amid concern at police powers', *Guardian*, 5 November 1994). Within a week of the Hyde Park protest at enactment of the law, police were analysing videotapes to match them to photos at previous protests so as to identify 'the most violent regular attenders' at London demonstrations. The photos were of the 1990 Poll Tax Riot and an anti-BNP protest (*Guardian*, 21 October 1994). Juxtaposition of the ACPO spokesman's benign perspective and the use of Special Branch to regulate rights of assembly and protest suggests the dangers in relying on police discretion.

Information, technology and trust

The police tendency to use 'all available means' in response to crime and disorder partly stems from an honourable preoccupation with controlling crime and protecting the public. Public opinion can reinforce or mitigate the tendency. Whether or not Garland and Sparks (2000) are right that it has come about due to the conditions of late modernity and the dismantling of social class distinctions, public opinion has largely reinforced the tendency in recent years, as the public has looked to police to assuage an apparently ever-increasing sense of risk and insecurity. Amongst the complex of attributes Giddens (1990) and Beck (1992) identified as characteristic of late modernity, those relevant here are risk awareness, political scepticism, economic globalisation, and the quickening of information exchange and communication by new technologies. It is not hard to see how these elements can combine to convince people not only that crime rates are rising out of control, but that they are personally more likely than before to be victims. Factual accuracy is not at the heart of such concerns. Although Britain has relatively high crime rates by international comparison, these have been falling since their historical peak in the 1990s and contemporary crime rates represent a lower absolute risk of victimisation than that experienced by the Victorians. However, worry over crime and insecurity is not fed by facts, but by perceptions. It is to the 'crime complex of late modernity' that Garland and Sparks (2000: 17) attribute 'the primary themes of the new penal policies – the expression of punitive sentiment, concern for victims, public protection, exclusion, enhanced control'. It is possible to see the origin of the crime complex in things more tangible than a less certain class structure. The world appears a more dangerous place than formerly because we are constantly reminded of the risk of victimisation by crime prevention technologies, public awareness campaigns displaying the production values previously only found in Hollywood features, and a mass media so ubiquitous that it broadcasts from our mobile telephones.

A public that increasingly demands precise assessment of the risks it faces in its search for security readily seeks comfort in technology. Technologies such as CCTV, computer databases of crime information, and voice and face recognition celebrate the estimation and control of risk. Surveillance becomes ubiquitous, automatic and undetectable. Policing is thus carried out by technology itself (Norris, 1995). Indeed, surveillance is now 'the cement which binds together the various risk-based strategies' in policing (Johnston, 2000: 61). However, the turn to technology is also a turn away from a reactive police effort, activated when the public wishes, toward a proactive posture, that silently observes whether the public wish it or not. 'Risk management is actuarial, proactive and anticipatory, the application of those principles requiring the collation and analysis of information obtained through systematic surveillance of those at risk or likely to cause risk' (Johnson, 2000: 56).

Proactive investigation employs systematic analysis of records of suspects' movements, financial dealings and associates. There are interceptions of communications, planting of listening devices, tracking and tracing devices and video surveillance (Bowling and Foster, 2002). While commentaries concentrate almost entirely on the use of surveillance technologies in monitoring the public, it is worth noting that they are also used against police and other law enforcement agents. General directives to forces include an 'essential requirement' that covert police units be able to disguise their communications not only from 'sophisticated criminal elements', but from 'unauthorised police units', indicating that advanced surveillance routines are used in internal as well as external investigations. In addition to surveillance technology, proactive policing involves informers and undercover officers (Heaton, 2000). Proactive policing methods and the technologies they use have developed more quickly than the regulatory framework (Maguire, 2000). The Regulation of Investigatory Powers Act 1999 confronted circumstances where there were few controls on intelligence-led policing; the framework was 'patchy, inconsistent and out-of-date, and did not provide adequate safeguards or remedies against abuse or misuse' (Bowling and Foster, 2002: 995). The official view was put by the Home Secretary in parliamentary debate over the bill: '[c]overt surveillance by police and other law enforcement officers is as old as policing itself; so too is the use of informants, agents and undercover officers' (Home Office Press Release 022/2000). The implication was 'so why complain, just trust us'.

The policing of the 1992 Castlemorton Common 'rave' featured surveillance and intelligence-gathering methods that were a catalyst to the Criminal Justice and Public Order Act. The actuarial style of control makes the police 'information brokers' amongst agencies having a policing function (Ericson and Haggerty, 1997). However, while it is important to recognise the increasing extent to which 'policing' occurs by surveillance technologies and multiple state, quasi-state, and private organisations, with the 'National Intelligence Model' forming a 'business model' for multi-party policing (Maguire, 2003), there is little doubt which is the key agency. That agency also happens to be the only one over which the public has any significant purchase.

The frail and obscure arrangements through which the police are accountable have long left much being taken on trust. There is no doubt that police databases are a vital resource; but there are doubts both about data quality and third party access. A group of police were imprisoned in 1989 for corruptly using the police computer on behalf of private detectives, some of whom were connected to the South African secret service, and in 2005 a case against two constables who raped a woman they were escorting home revealed evidence of illicit use of police computers (*Surrey Advertiser*, 5 March 2005). The Met 'SID (System for Intelligence and Detection) initiative' against serious crime, launched in 1994, relied on computer systems manipulating a database of video images of suspects and tape recordings of their voices, using these to trace suspects rapidly, with a new Directorate of Intelligence and dedicated units for drug-related violence and sexual attacks. The local intelligence officer role was upgraded so they could recommend action rather than acting only as collators. SID also involved more use of informers ('Met in shift to "21st century policing"', *Guardian*, 10 January 1994).

Concern over drugs and illegal immigration has prompted a change in police record-keeping from concentrating on selected suspects to surveillance on selected groups. The National Drugs Intelligence Unit and the National Immigration Intelligence Unit (later part of NCIS) have a 'pre-emptive' function, collating information on suspects as well as offenders, and taking information from informers and raids where address books are seized. Both units were set up without reference to Parliament. The NCIS database had 360 organised crime figures, with 3,000 more under investigation, and had played a part in arresting 1,134 'significant British criminals'. Two geographically based police intelligence units compiled computer databases containing information on 'New Travellers' (FFT, 1996). The routine operation of systems with the capacity to disperse unconfirmed information electronically and leak it to non-police personnel may quietly prejudice the well-being of more citizens than major public disorder.

Buzzwords may have changed since the Home Secretary announced plans to 'spin a "wire web" across the country to help police trap the criminal' (Home Office News Release, 6 October 1988), but reliance on unchecked information has not, according to research on 'intelligence-led policing' (Innes *et al*, 2004). The Police National Network (PNN) for data communication allows forces to exchange data directly. Patrol officers have direct access to all police computers, including other forces' crime reporting systems and that of the Home Office. In 1995 the records of four million offenders became available to police on their new national computer 'Phoenix'. There is a national automatic fingerprint system and national collection of photos of convicted people and stolen property, the latter now available on the Web. In 2002 the PNC held 50 million vehicle and 6.1 million criminal and missing persons records (HMIC, 2002). In 2001 police and other law enforcement agencies demanded access to all telecommunications – phone calls, email, faxes, internet usage and website content – ostensibly to combat child pornography, racist material and organised crime. Network and service providers were only required to keep communications data at the time for billing purposes – generally three months – but UK, EU and G8 law enforcement agencies wanted the data kept at least seven years (Bunyan, 2001).

However, it is as important to recognise the constraints on technology as it is to be mindful of its potential misuses. While impressive new technologies have certainly come on-stream, there is considerable evidence that when the time comes for action on the basis of the information held it is done in much the same way as before. Research by Maguire and John (1995) and Amey *et al* (1996) demonstrates the enduring predisposition to response-led rather than proactive policing. For example, the computer database information kept on New Travellers has thus far been proactively used only when a rave is notified as likely to occur on a traveller site (James, 2004). Even when police have advance intelligence of travellers arriving in their area they respond pragmatically and using conventional public order methods. Nor do they pass such information systematically to other forces or agencies. More significantly, they respond with a sense of the (low) threat posed by travellers and an awareness that transient people both have to be somewhere and that they will not stay anywhere forever. Another example is the problems over implementation of computerisation. Arresting someone keeps the arresting officers off the beat for 3.5 hours on average. One event can often necessitate entry of the same information on many separate records. Researchers found that '[w]here forms are available electronically, little officer time is actually saved because the IT system applications are mostly antiquated and do not talk to each other' (Singer, 2001: vi). Knitting new IT with the patchwork of existing systems is an ongoing challenge, posing a danger that 'much of the potential of the new IT will be squandered' (Singer, 2001: viii). The real considerations are not the simple existence of surveillance technologies, but the quality of information and the action taken on information received.

Problems of logistics and accuracy arise from too much information being held. The Audit Commission found gross inefficiency in the use of fingerprint services. Fingerprints are taken in millions of criminal cases a year, but offenders are identified by fingerprint evidence in only a fraction. There can be serious imbalance between resources for collecting and searching fingerprints: in some forces under 10% of fingermarks submitted were searched and one force had a four year backlog of prints waiting to be classified and filed. Its fingerprint collection was 'virtually useless' (Audit Commission, 1988).

The 1995 Home Affairs Select Committee inquiry into the private security industry set in train the transfer of responsibility for answering employer checks on criminal records to an organisation having agency status. The original idea was a commercial agency with the power to sell details of criminal records for vetting purposes. The inquiry backed state regulation of the security industry (*Guardian*, 16 January 1995), noting that in one company with 26 staff, 11 had convictions for a total of 74 crimes including rape, firearms offences and threats to kill. Home Office testimony strongly resisted any new state intervention in the industry and put the records check idea forward as a means for security companies to check their own employees' records. Recent times have seen government distance itself from responsibility for the accuracy of criminal record information by entrusting such work to quangos, private companies or foreign multinationals.

Response to terrorism, international crime and domestic activism has seen a proliferation of specialist units supplementing the Special Branch. Each force has a Special Branch; total strength was 870 in 1985, of which 379 were in London. In 1994 there were 520 in the Met, 1,400 in England and Wales outside London, 100+ in Scotland and 280+ in Northern Ireland. By 2003 there were 552 in London, 2,911 in England and Wales outside London, 100+ in Scotland and 684 in Northern Ireland. Under 1995 Special Branch guidelines the Branch co-ordinates with the security service MI5. Information about terrorism obtained by Special Branch goes to MI5. The guidelines also set more emphasis on public order, a key role being 'maintaining the Queen's Peace', with animal rights activists singled out for attention. The National Public Order Intelligence Unit of New Scotland Yard co-ordinates the 'collection, analysis, exploitation and dissemination of intelligence on the extremist threat to public order' (Statewatch, 2003). The Branch is focal point for immigration work, too, notably gathering intelligence for immigration raids. A Regional Special Branch Conference, chaired by a chief constable under mutual aid provisions, serves as a liaison mechanism with regional MI5 offices. Periodic indications of the kind of information collected suggests that much of it is unnecessary or unreliable. Of the several hundred files in one force's collection, only 20 were actually necessary for police purposes. This is not highly sensitive information carefully garnered by covert methods; the majority is publicly available or freely given. Political activists' names appearing in the media are indexed, and officers cultivate journalists looking for additional information such as the addresses of people expressing radical sentiments in letters to the editor, and the details of people attending local trades councils. Those signing petitions to Parliament are indexed. Information may be taken from informers motivated by grudges or payment.

It is important not to demonise technology or the police use of it. The breadth of the police role makes for some non-obvious technological applications. Police were early adopters of database solutions for schools project work, recognising that email could be used to satisfy non-urgent requests from schools. Cambridgeshire Constabulary linked local schools to a database of police-related materials fitting National Curriculum projects ('Police go online to boost school links', *Guardian*, 29 June 1993). Despite such benign applications, information technology can reduce respect and trust. In 1989 the Data Protection Registrar upheld a complaint against Sussex Police for failing to tell thousands of people interviewed before the Conservative conference in Brighton that the information would be held indefinitely and shared with other forces policing conference venues (*Guardian*, 1 June 1989). Information on 27,800 of the 50,000 interviewed was retained. Council employees, residents of neighbouring streets, and guests and staff of nearby hotels had to give it as a condition of entry to the 'secure zone'. A more recent instance is that of DNA testing. The UK set up the first national DNA database in 1995, initially logging only those charged with violent offences or burglary, but with police legally entitled to take samples from everyone arrested for a recordable offence ('April start for DNA criminal database', *Guardian*, 17 March 1995). Mouth swabs or hair samples can be taken forcibly if suspects fail to co-operate. Since then, over a million samples have been taken – arrestees are routinely sampled. Only those convicted were supposed to have their samples retained, the rest being destroyed after two years. However there have been a number of cases in which it emerged that samples were not destroyed and in one a murder trial was halted when it was revealed that an out of date sample was used to identify the suspect. Samples can now legally be retained indefinitely.

In 1999 the number of closed-circuit television (CCTV) cameras in Britain's public places passed a million ('Smile, you're on 300 candid cameras', *Sunday Times*, 14 February 1999). In urban areas this means that individuals are captured on tape 300 times a day. Evidence that privacy thresholds are lowering is the increase in private use of CCTV, as in the monitoring of children and nannies by parents, and use by employers in work environments. A Parcelforce employee was sacked in 1999 after being filmed playing frisbee during working hours. Indeed, police have expressed concern at how often tapes are used against them in disciplinary proceedings (Goold, 2005). Virgin Megastores used CCTV to monitor customer characteristics and purchasing behaviour. The police have pioneered applications such as the Automatic Number Plate Recognition (ANPR) system that records vehicle number plates and the Mandrake system used to match suspects to criminal photo databases. The use of security CCTV in public space, retail settings, domestic settings and as a source of entertainment footage suggests a steady erosion of public sensitivity that may help condone law enforcement uses of CCTV that would in the past have been unacceptable. Other techniques that are information-hungry may draw in data on large numbers of people unconnected with an investigation, but on whom information is available from images and tracker databases such as mobile phone logs.

The argument about trust and technology is circular. The resort to computer technology can itself be seen as compensating a reduction in freely-volunteered information from the public. The process can aggravate distrust if the public believes low-grade information is being disseminated across computer networks. Among the consequences is the need for plainclothes agents to create networks, the 'institutionalisation' of informing. Following an influential Audit Commission report, the 1990s saw much more emphasis on informers as an asset of intelligence-led policing. Street stops are increasingly used for information-gathering rather than direct attempts to catch suspects. These trends leave police increasingly working from circumstantial information instead of publicly-witnessed testimony, which impacts on the character of interrogation, contributing to pressure to use a cajoling, threatening approach to bring about confessions. Informers have been central to prominent miscarriages of justice, as in the case of the 'M25 Three', falsely convicted of murder, a stabbing, and robbery. The Appeal Court judge said that the police and a paid informer had been involved in a 'profoundly disturbing' conspiracy to give perjured evidence ('Guildford Four similarities seen in case of M25 Three', *Surrey Advertiser*, 28 July 2000).

These are not Luddite objections. Information technologies could be used to exactly opposite effect, by prioritising public- rather than police-initiated information, preferring specific information about crime and not generalised information about the population as a whole, and invoking local rather than central command; but that would require a greater flow of information from the public. Whatever the rhetoric, Treasury-led efficiency drives have caused forces from 1993 onward to discourage that flow; community patrol was cut back, forces said they would not investigate low-loss burglaries and would no longer respond to burglar alarms, the public was urged not to use the 999 service, but 'non urgent numbers' (or the internet) delivering an indifferent service, and so on. Meanwhile community consultative meetings go unattended. The message is that the public is not interested in policy, but in getting their problems dealt with. When they are, information flows.

Stress, isolation and internal divisions

Technology and disaffiliation are not the only factors obstructing the police/public relationship. It is widely acknowledged that policing is a stressful occupation. The police have customarily dealt with this by various kinds of denial, one of which is a particularly emphatic form of black humour. Venting frustration after a troublesome shift, officers claim 'policing is the only job where you have to wash your hands *before* you go to the toilet'. The police organisation was tardy relative to other public services in formally acknowledging the personal difficulties the job can cause and making allowance for them. In recent years it has put in place the kind of provision one expects in a profession that looks to its employees' interests. There remains evidence that some who would benefit from taking advantage of the provision of counselling, temporary leaves of absence, transfer to other duties, and the like, fail to do so because they feel a stigma is attached. One of the main causes of stress can simply be where officers spend all of their time, on duty or off, in the company of other police. This circumstance was one that was actively promoted in the past, and that can still feature where police are provided with accommodation by the force.

Intra-force rivalries and divisions mean there is less unanimity of purpose than outsiders may assume. While sincere efforts have been made, the evidence of relations between regular officers and the Police Community Support Officers introduced early in the 21st century suggest that strong internal divisions endure. During the 1990s, awareness of the malign aspects of occupational culture spread from the research world into more widespread awareness. While academic concerns included the effect of enculturated practices and views on the delivery of policing services, the most general concern was over sexist and racist attitudes. In 1993 the newly appointed Commissioner Paul Condon told a conference at Hendon police college that racial issues presented the greatest challenges to the police ('Met chief promises to help fight racism', *Guardian*, 1 March 1993). Police had a pivotal role, not least in acting against racially motivated attacks and those who used racial hatred for political ends. The police had to be '"equally intolerant of our own colleagues who fail to reach the required standards"'. It was '"totally and completely wrong"' to take the view that prejudiced views and behaviour were present in the police because the composition of forces reflected that of wider society.

While not doubting Condon's sincerity, his force was falling far short of these ideals. Two weeks after the speech, the Met had to be forced by an employment appeal tribunal to release internal grievance procedure documents to a complainant of Turkish origin, WPC Sarah Locker, who had accused colleagues of racial and sexual abuse, including a colleague hiding under her desk to look up her skirt, others snapping her bra, and placing of a sign saying 'Mad Turk's Telephone Room' next to her desk. Her complaint had, however, been about the force denying her promotion to detective duty in favour of men with a less illustrious and experienced record ('Force told to free papers', *Guardian*, 11 March 1993).

A survey current at the time suggested that 6% of female police had suffered serious sexual abuse by male colleagues; earlier work by the same team found widespread sexual harassment, with 48% of female police reporting inappropriate touching and 92% hearing suggestive jokes ('Sexual assaults "rife in police"', *Guardian*, 12 December 1993). Home Office research suggested that 90% of female officers had experienced sexual harassment at work and that many felt they were denied opportunities to enter specialist squads ('Police to debate sexual harassment', *Guardian*, 20 February 1993). In 1993 a chief superintendent who referred to female delegates at a domestic violence conference as 'a bunch of lezzies [lesbians]' was immediately dismissed – the most senior officer to be sacked for such an offence. He was reinstated on appeal in 1994, having denied the remark and maintained that other comments had been decontextualised ('Met chief reinstates "lezzies" policeman', *Guardian*, 30 April 1994). The Inspectorate found widespread sexual harassment in Cleveland Police in 1994, including cases involving senior officers ('Police slated for sexual harassment', *Guardian*, 5 May 1994).

Complaints of racial discrimination by police rose sharply in the early 90s; there were 49 in 1991, 73 in 1992, but 291 in 1993. Disciplinary action was taken in 4% of cases ('Sharp rise in claims of race bias by police', *Guardian*, 29 March 1994). The Police Complaints Authority chairman attributed part of the rise to less willingness to tolerate racial prejudice, but it was difficult to prove whether a stop and search had been racially motivated. From 1994 the ethnic origin of all complainants has been recorded. These troubles should be seen against the context of the ethnic and racial composition of police forces. Ethnic minority recruitment, already low, slowed further in 2001. Two years after the Macpherson report recommended a rapid rise in ethnic minority recruitment, the number rose by 155 in 2000 compared to 261 in 1999, against a target of 6,000 by 2009. There were big variations, with West Midlands accounting for a quarter of the year's increase and 13 forces failing to recruit any Asian or Afro-Caribbean people, or seeing a fall. Amongst forces suffering a reverse was the Met ('Decline in ethnic recruits for police', *Guardian*, 24 February 2001). Clear-up rates on race crime also varied heavily, with the Met showing the worst rate at one in four. In 1976 there were 96 ethnic minority officers in the Met, and in 1983 there were 232, under 1%, at a time when London's ethnic minorities were 11% of its population. By 2003 some 5.2% of Met officers were from ethnic minorities. The Met announced in 2004 that it wished to fast-track ethnic minority applicants into training ahead of white candidates. The Met believed that without positive discrimination – illegal under the 1976 Race Relations Act – there was no hope of meeting the government target of 25% of officers from ethnic minorities by 2009.

The Commission for Racial Equality (CRE) believed they should be able to exempt an institution from the Act if it would make it more representative ('Met plan to fast-track black recruits', *Guardian*, 17 April 2004).

Internal divisions over race, ethnicity and gender are corrosive. There are three elements of career progression relevant here: recruitment, utilisation, and retention. Research on the circumstances of ethnic minority police has been rather sparse. There is a particular absence of the kind of statistically based study that would permit systematic analysis of what many minority officers feel is a promotion and career advancement system that favours whites, and of course, the same has been argued in respect of female police, where Britain now has its first female chief constable, but less elevated peers regularly speak of ongoing obstacles. While there is an 'objective' element to the promotion process in the form of the Objective Structured Performance Related Examinations (OSPRE) test, advancement in the police relates to breadth of experience in different 'functions', and in specific functions at that, with experience of detective work being particularly important. Both minority people and women have argued that they are kept from the functions needed to secure advancement. There appears to be an element of typecasting. For example, where women do feature as detectives, it is often in child protection, and ethnic minority officers tend to find themselves assigned to areas with high proportions of ethnic minority residents. However, systematic evidence is lacking and what we know about the circumstances relating to such internal divisions is derived from qualitative research and from studies in the US. Prominent among the former are a series of studies by Holdaway (for example, Holdaway and Barron, 1997) that establish two significant things: first, there is abundant evidence of discriminatory behaviour, and although much of it is relatively trivial, in aggregate it can be damaging. Secondly, ethnic minority officers are generally hostile to the idea of quotas, either for recruitment or for advancement. They want to advance on their merits. The Home Office has long taken the same view, although progressively more emphatic targets are being set and from 2004 onward there has been open discussion of quotas.

The ethnic composition, and to an extent the gender composition, of Police Community Support Officers (PCSOs) has been much more balanced than among the regular force. In London 35% of PCSOs are from ethnic minority backgrounds, compared to 6.6% of all officers, and 30% are female, compared to 18.4% (*Guardian*, 13 July 2004). While this is welcome, ethnic minority police in particular do not feel that forces should only address their minority recruitment problems by the PCSO route and that more is needed to secure more ethnic minority regular officers. What we know about the effects of quotas for minority and female recruitment and advancement is largely based on the US experience. Many major US city forces operate on a quota basis by ethnic group and, in effect, provide a separate career advancement path for them once recruited. There are also ethnically based patrol-officers' benevolent associations (unions). Historically-white police departments have slowly become integrated over the last three decades as a result. The latest research is, though, pessimistic about the depth of change. Bolton and Feagin (2004) report that deep divisions remain; the forces may nominally be integrated, but, from within, the picture is more like the 'separate but equal development' associated with segregation. African-American officers drawn from 16 different law enforcement agencies told Bolton and Feagin of their anger at their continuing daily experience of racism, both from colleagues and from citizens. Respondents reported ongoing racial barriers in recruitment, training and promotion. The picture of ongoing discrimination is deepened by reported lack of trust from white citizens and castigation by fellow blacks on the basis of perceived betrayal. A British Asian woman who was obliged to leave the police after sustaining a serious injury '"got more abuse while on patrol from my own community than I did from white officers"' ('Comradeship won over Asian woman', *Guardian*, 12 August 1994). It seems that, even where there is formal 'integration', significant cultural barriers remain and that quotas in themselves do not decrease the stress in being other than the stereotypical white male officer. Where there are ethnic minority police chiefs in the US, this does send important signals (Fielding 1999), just as the appointment of the first female chief constable did in Britain, but in terms of stress and isolation the experience of the generality of officers is more important.

British ethnic minority officers emulated US peers in the 90s by forming a 'Black Police Association'; interestingly, the Asian WPC mentioned above opposed the initiative on the basis that how one got on in the police was a matter of personal qualities, not ethnicity. The association was founded in the Met in September 1994 to tackle within-force racism and the high wastage rate of ethnic minority officers ('Black police officers form ethnic force', *Guardian*, 12 August 1994), and was originally called the Black and Asian Police Association. It was fully approved by the Met, but denounced as potentially divisive by the Met branch of the Federation (*Guardian*, 22 September 1994). The BPA appeared to have little effect on recruitment; there were several years during the 90s when fewer ethnic minority people (and women) were recruited than the previous year, and the Inspectorate found 'unacceptable levels' of prejudice, sexual harassment, and racist and sexist behaviour within the police, with discriminatory selection for desirable specialist functions and pigeonholing; one example was where female detectives were regularly assigned work in child protection ('Minorities shy away from police career', *Guardian*, 14 July 1994). In late 1994 the Met introduced a revised equal opportunities policy including advertising aimed at ethnic and sexual minorities, improved personnel practices, and with an intention to preempt the formal grievance procedure (*Guardian*, 10 December 1994). Forces began incorporating sexual orientation into their equal opportunities policies in the 90s; by 1993, 10 had done so. In 1993 it emerged that gay officers had formed their own organisation (*Guardian*, 20 January 1993). In 1995 Lancashire became the first county to appoint a female chief constable, Pauline Clare. She had joined the force as a cadet aged 17, was a butcher's daughter, and had taken a psychology degree in her spare time. She had become an assistant chief constable in Merseyside three months before Alison Halford, also an assistant chief, resigned, complaining of sexual discrimination. Clare had a strong background in the community relations branch, but unlike many females who find their promotion path difficult, she had experience of a very wide range of police functions (*Guardian*, 15 June 1995). Halford called for civilians to be considered for top police posts so as to challenge discrimination against women (*Guardian*, 9 November 1992). Some 139 serving and prospective women officers lodged complaints with the Equal Opportunities Commission involving 33 police forces between January 1990 and June 1992, and of entrants to the service in 1977, 78% of females had resigned by 1993 compared to 53% of men (*Guardian*, 26 February 1993). Cases of sexual harassment remain current, including those against very senior officers, such as the deputy chief constable of Surrey, suspended in 1999 on charges of assault and harassment against a female employee (*Guardian*, 9 January 1999).

Returning to our three elements of career progression, in the UK limited numbers of black or Asian officers are recruited, those who are recruited appear to be differently deployed in terms of role and rank compared to whites, and ethnic minority officers resign at higher rates than whites. Recruitment of female officers has significantly improved, but the evidence on deployment and retention is less positive. While it has long been recognised that policing is stressful, it appears that for many the major stressors are internal. Ethnic minorities, females and graduates had higher resignation rates. Most resigners from police forces were dissatisfied with management and paperwork, and felt undervalued. Among females, domestic responsibilities were most often cited. Forces in the Southeast had highest rates; Met resigners cited wanting to leave London and others in the Southeast were concerned over pay (Home Office, 2004b).

Stress became a recognised problem in the police after the 1983 Home Office Memorandum on efficiency, economy and effectiveness. Traumatic stress symptoms include difficulty in establishing and sustaining close relationships, poor sleep, poor concentration and poor memory, all problems which may impair subsequent performance and be particularly marked in conflictual policing of the sort regularly encountered in public order work (Bonifacio, 1982). Among the symptoms of stress are anxiety, depression and irritation, headaches, tension, heavy smoking, heart disease, suicide, alcoholism, compulsive work patterns, marital discord, hypertension, sexual dysfunction, and emotional exhaustion (Maslach and Jackson, 1981; Bonifacio, 1982). In response, there have been positive if somewhat isolated developments. In 1994, there was a nod to family-friendly policies when the Home Office abolished the rule preventing police working part-time (Home Office News Release 20/94, 28 January 1994). Officers now have access to a confidential independent counselling service, but there is stigma attached to using such services, and worry that doing so will be entered on personnel records may inhibit take-up. The seminal 1983 report on police stress concluded that poor management produced more widespread and long-term stress than operational duties. Increasing stress-related problems have had a large impact on rising sick-leave figures. The incidence of sickness has held steady since 1991 at about 12 days per year or around 5.6% of police working days. In 1997 just over 1.5 million working days were lost to sickness, equating to about 6,600 officers absent each day, equivalent to the whole police establishment for Wales, at a cost of £210 million per year (HMIC, 1997a). In some forces days lost were up to 18.6 (Merseyside). Assaults on police decreased from 19,150 in 1991 to 14,840 in 1995, but began rising again in 1996, by 4%, to 15,488. A third of injuries suffered by police are to the head ('Survey shows police training muddle', *Independent*, 18 October 1997). The Inspectorate's report into officer safety found weaknesses in police first-aid training and confusion about the use of protective techniques and equipment.

The percentage of sick leave accounted for by assaults in the 1990s ranged from 1% in Essex to 6% in Northumbria. Musculoskeletal conditions provide the greatest cause of sickness absence and medical retirement; force physiotherapists reported an increase in such injuries as soon as the new police batons were introduced. Stress is the second main cause of medical retirement. Officers taking early retirement on medical grounds more than doubled, to 1,326, in the period from 1980 to 1985, a time of major public order disturbances. In 1995–96 some 46% of all retirements were on medical grounds, having peaked at 59% in 1991; there were 2,002 in England and Wales in 2000, against 2,466 normal retirements. It is well-established that most assaults on police are by 17–25-year-old males, the majority having criminal records; in one study 80% percent had records, 60% were recidivists, 18% had over 30 convictions and 40% knew the officer concerned ('Police "need training" to face violence', *Guardian*, 27 December 1990). In the research area, unemployment was then 13%, but 60% of assailants were unemployed; the report suggests police were convenient scapegoats. There is also indirectly assaultive behaviour; West Midlands Police answered 468,000 emergency calls in 1996, of which 4,000 were abusive (*Independent*, 19 April 1997).

Bearing all this in mind, the kind of stress reported by Manolias and Hyatt-Williams (1988) may be more widespread than their focus on post-shooting trauma suggests. After interviewing 25 officers who had shot someone, the study recommended immediate and long-term support for officers and their families, including counselling by mental health specialists (Manolias and Hyatt-Williams, 1988). Some two-thirds of those interviewed had a marked emotional reaction after the shooting; there were three cases of 'severe post-trauma stress disorder'. Some senior officers were unsupportive and some colleagues expressed their support clumsily and/or inappropriately, for example, by bloodthirsty remarks. It is not being suggested that the particular incidents in which these officers were involved could have been avoided or dealt with short of force. The point is that policing by force is extremely stressful and alternatives that can reduce resort to it should be prioritised.

Intelligence-led, problem-oriented and partnership policing

A major part of the turn towards proactive policing styles has been under the banner of 'intelligence-led policing' (ILP). Tilley (2003) identifies commonalities between ILP, community policing and 'problem-oriented policing' (Goldstein, 1990). We have already noted the links between ILP and surveillance and other modern technologies. Well-founded ILP can give advance information, allow response options to be considered, and enable the best option to be deployed in a well-planned way. In a public order context, a further step can be to allude to the option that is likely to be deployed when negotiating with representatives of those on whom one has intelligence. This enables a pre-emptive approach in a 'two-pronged' strategy whose other part is conventional action backed by the threat of force (King and Brearley, 1996). From a police perspective, the appeal of ILP is that information can be used to achieve objectives rather than merely to set them (Chatterton, 1991: 8).

A similar premise lies behind problem-oriented policing (POP). Davies (2003) offers the example of a rural carpark used by ramblers. On the ramblers leaving for their hike, vandals smash car windows and empty cars of their contents. A traditional response might be for a constable to lie in wait and arrest the offenders, but this assumes others will not take their place. A POP approach was to build picnic tables beside the carpark and license snack vans. This secured 'natural surveillance'. In the example, crime in the carpark fell 48% in a year. An urban example involved a takeaway pizza parlour where drunken revellers gathered late at night, with predictable public disorder consequences. The conventional response would be to deploy an officer as a visible deterrent and to make arrests. Such deployment could not be maintained indefinitely. Analysis of the problem suggested that the crowd built up because the parlour could not cope with the rush of customers at closing time. Police had hotlines from drinking venues installed so the parlour could have orders ready when customers arrived. Crowds no longer built up and disorder fell. As the examples suggest, the principle is not to make arrests, but to solve problems. Unfortunately the appeal of POP was compromised by Goldstein's corollary, the inauspiciously misnamed 'zero tolerance policing'. Goldstein meant by this that police would take action of some kind in relation to minor social and physical problems, such as broken streetlamps or unruly behaviour that, although legal, disturbed others. Unfortunately the more red-blooded audiences construed it as 'getting tough' on minor offenders and the attention that should have been given POP fell instead on a mis-rendering of 'zero tolerance'. In some analyses zero tolerance achieves the opposite of what it intends, by undermining police legitimacy and increasing disaffiliation that provokes offending (Paternoster et al, 1997; Bowling, 1999; Karmen, 2000). The power of a slogan is shown by the fact that the Cleveland senior officer, Ray Mallon, who did most to popularise the jackboot version of zero tolerance, became so popular that he subsequently took office as mayor.

The jackboot version of zero tolerance flatly contradicts the core principle of POP, to seek solutions rather than fill gaols. As a crime reduction philosophy, POP makes liberal use of target-hardening techniques as well as looking at routine crime and disorder from the perspective of perpetrators and the circumstances that come together to promote social problems. When New Labour took office in 1997 the police service was detecting fewer crimes, and the criminal justice system was marked by delay and high recidivism rates. James Morgan, a management consultant, had prepared for the previous administration a report (Home Office, 1991a) addressing these problems. The report emphasised partnership work between police and local authorities.

Crawford (2000: 202) observed that 'the relationship between government and governed is now one in which we are all reconfigured ... as "partners against crime" in a new corporate approach ... involving a fundamental re-articulation of individual and group responsibilities and professional "expertise" as well as state paternalism and monopoly of control'. New Labour heeded Morgan, and research that rebutted the effectiveness of harsh law enforcement, and endorsed early intervention where youths displayed signs of being at risk to offend, along with situational crime prevention. The Crime and Disorder Act 1998 promoted inter-agency work with a partnership approach. The outcome was a legal requirement to set up 'crime and disorder reduction partnerships'; there were 376 by 1998. Police were required to partner local social work, education, housing and health services. They had to consult local communities on their priorities and take advice on tactics to deal with them. From 1999 there was a three-year investment of £250 million in crime reduction, which then rose to £400 million with a major investment in CCTV. However, government did not enact Morgan's recommendation that each Crime and Disorder Reduction Partnership (CDRP) receive money from the crime reduction programme; CDRPs were to fund partnerships from existing police and local authority budgets. This receives less emphasis in the academic literature, which is more concerned with friction between the partners, but is the first thing that CDRP practitioners say when asked what constrained their effectiveness. The resource problem meant that the crime audits that began in 1999 and were to spearhead determination of local priorities – an initiative relating the ILP of 'grand policing' to the everyday policing of communities – were either methodologically flawed or simply not done. Some 117 of 376 CDRPs failed to deliver their first audit at all; of those that did, only 38% had data on truancy, 27% on drug treatment, and 27% had social services data on offenders (Davies, 2003).

These early problems were compounded when ministers began to assign the £400 million investment to their own priorities, including burglary, prostitution and school management. This meant that CDRPs where such things were not a problem received no earmarked funds; 'a rural CDRP which was most concerned with traffic speeding through its villages would get nothing unless it could find some sex workers to help' (Davies, 2003). Moreover, the money went direct to individual agencies rather than via CDRPs, and funding had to be bid for, an activity for which some CDRPs were ill-equipped. Some CDRPs continued without funding, others gained it via the police, but had to tackle police priorities rather than their own. Treasury pressures also subverted a premise the CDRP programme inherited from POP – careful and deliberate analysis. The Treasury required results within a year; a CDRP that did not spend its budget in-year lost what was unspent. In 2000 the government required all CDRPs to set five-year targets for vehicle crime, domestic burglary and robberies; local priorities were sidelined. Once means had been found to perform crime audits properly, 87% of CDRPs had put domestic violence as top priority, an issue ignored by government's priorities; only 8% had identified robbery as a priority. Likewise the Home Office countermanded local targets. CDRPs set vehicle crime reduction targets from 2% to 25%; the Home Office imposed 30%. The Whitehall targets were set for five years, so CDRPs could not adjust priorities to changing circumstances. Latterly, the regional governments of England and Wales have been required to appoint 'regional crime directors' to write business plans, collect data and conduct audits. CDRPs became part of a regional government apparatus that looks more readily toward London than local communities. CDRPs were initially premised on strong functional links with police Basic Command Units (BCUs), but police reorganisations meant some BCUs related to several CDRPs; by 2000 only 120 BCUs matched the area of their local CDRP. Boundary misalignment also marked the CDRP/Drug Action Team (DAT) interface, while in Wales DATs were abolished as soon as they began operating. None of the 54 probation areas in England and Wales at the inception of CDRPs had matching boundaries, and the 2001 reorganisation into 42 areas aggravated this. Health and education boundary changes tell the same story. Indicative of official disenchantment with partnership was the refusal in 2000 to extend the Crime and Disorder Act to require partnership work not only with local authorities, but with central government departments.

If CDRPs were subject to ministerial interference, civil service rigidity and Treasury caprice, the story on POP reflects ill on the police. HMIC (1998) found that in 32% of POP initiatives there was no evidence that the diagnosed problem actually existed, that there was evidence of proper analysis in only 27%, and that only 7% even claimed to have succeeded. The assessment was that police needed time to learn problem evaluation, and needed targetted training that offered more than apocryphal examples such as the rural monument (it was Oakham Castle, Leicestershire) whose windows were constantly smashed until police had the idea of removing nearby rubble so there was nothing to throw. Instead, there were 'action team' initiatives, such as that on reducing burglary. Police were asked to bid for funding either for projects using innovative tactics or for projects taking a more traditional approach. Home Office researchers wanted to focus funding on the innovations, but senior officials divided funding equally, which gave each project a £100,000 budget, too little to be effective. The researchers who evaluated the £30 million investment in POP, Karen Bullock and Nick Tilley (2003), indicated that 'the conclusions are not encouraging'. The problems were familiar. Projects were given insufficient time to realise their potential, and there had been premature closure around problem-definition. The police were employing more analysts for problem-solving, but, against the context of the FMI (Financial Management Initiative), they were not spending their effort on addressing long-term problems by long-term solutions, but on satisfying short-term performance indicator requirements.

Moreover, target hardening had failed because the most vulnerable households were least likely to accept help: 'the victims were alienated from officialdom and suspicious; ... the houses were owned by absentee landlords who could not care less about protecting their tenants; the victims lived chaotic lives in short-term housing and had moved before the offer (of equipment) was made' (Davies, 2003). Hardening the most co-operative households diverted all the burglary onto the most vulnerable. The most successful schemes had worked bottom-up, using community knowledge; the least successful were imposed by police on their own, and though they could see there were problems they reacted by spending the funding before it was clawed back. The message is that the first step in such initiatives must be to know the community better. A one-line statement on the Home Office website in 2003 announced that the £400 million crime reduction programme, intended as a ten-year initiative, had ceased in March 2002, after three years. It was replaced by the 'safer communities' initiative. Its budget was £20 million. As to CDRPs, their budget was £84 million per year to 2006, a substantial cut in that £25 million has been diverted to police BCUs. If BCU commanders ponder whether to spend the money on POP, they might consider that the real challenge for POP is not protecting monuments or ramblers' cars, but dealing with the routine crime and disorder on large estates and town centres that a government disillusioned with crime reduction now addresses by 'anti-social behaviour orders' offering a fast-track to gaol.

Against POP, enthusiasm for intelligence-led policing is undiminished. Formal support for ILP is commonplace on the basis that 'good quality intelligence is the life blood of modern policing' (HMIC, 1997b: 1), and the Inspectorate endorses ILP as a more cost effective form of policing potential disorder than waiting for it to happen and then deploying. That may be so, but ILP also raises problems of ethics (Reiner, 2000b; Maguire, 2000; Tilley, 2003) and problems of delivering on the promises (Innes *et al*, 2004). In Reiner's judgment, 'the development of "intelligence led", risk-oriented, inter-agency and "partnership" policing methods has accentuated the breadth and depth of pre-emptive surveillance and analysis in all police forces' (Reiner, 2000b: 76); but when we turn to service delivery, the evidence is that while ILP has supplemented established responses to public order situations, a pragmatic approach based on homely assessments of risk and the resources available continues to prevail, response remains largely reactive outside major public order incidents where there are formal organisers with whom to engage, and when things go wrong paramilitary policing remains the backstop (O'Malley, 1992; James, 2004).

The case of the policing of New Travellers illustrates some of these themes. James (2004) found that police regard policing the travelling community primarily as a social service rather than criminal matter (as indeed was the emphasis until the current Criminal Justice and Public Order Act; Bancroft, 2000). The social service aspect of their work has received little emphasis in recent years, encouraged by legislation, such as the Police and Magistrates Act 1994, which measures their performance in dealing with crime, and by the law and order rhetoric of politicians and media. The fact remains that, because the police are a 24-hour service, social welfare matters still account for a substantial share of their work. Indeed, in the US and UK only about 25% of officer time is spent dealing with crime (Bayley and Shearing, 1996). Social service work requires police to interact with social welfare organisations, including social services departments, the health service, council housing departments and local authorities. Community policing, and dealing with groups such as New Travellers, requires particularly close liaison. It is, in fact, rare for police dealings with travellers to become legal undertakings.

The formalisation of partnership work, furthered by the National Intelligence Model and a general drive for 'joined-up government', requires police to engage more fully with social welfare concerns and mandates them to work with social agencies that have very different working practices and occupational ideologies. The police sense of mission and their instinctive preference for action runs at odds with agencies that are less well-resourced, deal in deeper, longer-term responses to social problems, and work more closely to local government requirements. It also forms a tension with the pressure to focus on crime and produce narrowly measurable 'results' based on detection rates and response times. The tension may account for the modest impact of partnership work; there have been some undoubted improvements, but frontline public order policing has not been much affected. For example, in the event that a local authority uses s 77 of the Criminal Justice and Public Order Act (CJPOA) to move travellers on for unlawful camping, police will seek to regain control themselves. Use of the sections of the CJPOA that relate to police-based eviction measures can also be frustrating and ineffective, but the police are loath to see the local authority acting without reference to them (James, 2004). Partnership research generally suggests that police are keen to retain the control that can be lost in inter-agency working (Barton, 2002). They may take both problem and preferred solution to partnership meetings 'and pass it off as a sort of *fait accomplis*' (Barton, 2002: 114). There is longstanding evidence that police tend to take the lead in partnership forums (Blagg *et al*, 1988; Crawford, 1998).

In Crawford and Jones' (1996) analysis partnership practice is invested in to varying degrees relating to respective agencies' attempts to protect their organisational identity. Those agencies most protective of that identity engage in partnership practice in a way that does not affect their own working practices. The police, in particular, seek to maintain their autonomy. Crawford and Jones label agencies with such an orientation as working in a 'multi-agency' format rather than an 'inter-agency' one. In the latter, working practices align over time and agencies lose some of their self-contained character. We need not seek far for the strength of the police value on autonomy. It can be traced to the doctrine of constabulary independence. This is not to suggest that partnership work is easy for any agency. Partnership descends onto a public services management ethos and organisational structure that means the practical application of inter-agency work will generally occur in a patchy way (Liddle and Gelsthorpe, 1994; Gilling, 2000) and its impact is most likely to be felt in interstitial areas, the responsibility for which is hard to establish, rather than in the core work of a given agency. Police participation in partnership work is thus from a bounded perspective seeking to protect their independence, autonomy and occupational culture.

Thus, while ILP's appeal may rest on being able to resolve situations simply by knowing about them, without the need for direct action, the fact is that the way intelligence is enacted is still generally by the long-standing tools of operational policing rather than by partnership means. ILP little affects the twin prongs of negotiation and forceful intervention. That ILP is interpreted on the ground as little different to traditional evidence-gathering is apparent in the policing of travellers. Police dealing with them take details of vehicles on traveller sites, and record names and descriptions of individuals, with a view to the CJPOA stipulation against travellers returning to the same land within three months. Infiltration of sites may also be used, often by posing as council employees. Video and photographs somewhat update the practice, but the details taken are better read as evidence-gathering with a view to breach of the Act than as ILP for proactive purposes. The information gathered is not generally relayed to other forces in an ILP-type communication exchange, but simply filed in case the same people show up within three months. While the ethics of ILP may preoccupy researchers, the constraints on police practice of it in a routine public order context are largely practical. Sophisticated surveillance technologies, and the training to use them, are expensive, and the marginal groups that feature in disruptions of routine social order are not perceived as a priority.

Further, the focus of human service agencies is often on each other rather than the community. Their focus is organisational. It seems not to occur to the proponents of such approaches that the agglomeration of social agencies may seem threatening to people who already distrust and feel cowed by 'them', the state bureaucracy which grudgingly dispenses resources and capriciously grabs them back, as in New Labour's turn in 2005 to frequent testing of the long-term disabled to see if they have miraculously recovered sufficiently to have their disability benefit cut, or the wrapping-in of fire and rescue services to a role in crime reduction, and joint training with police (*Guildford Times*, 11 December 2003). There may be advantages for the *agencies* in exchanging information, but if intervention is not to be seen as intrusion the overtures must be low-key, local and highly specific to individual agents and citizens, not orchestrated and uniform. For example, a police/probation collaboration involved young offenders on community service orders providing practical assistance to police, and organisations connected with police, at community events, repairing facilities and helping with parking (*Surrey Advertiser*, 14 November 1997). The police can do rather well in such collaborations because of their preference for brisk action and their access to resources; but the traits that can make police effective partners also make it hard to gauge effectiveness. Co-ordinated programmes are centrally mounted, but their implementation is patchy and evaluation seldom systematic. Before-and-after comparisons are defeated by the police preference for immediate action and their willingness to regard any positive development as an outcome of the initiative rather than other factors.

The focus of partnership policing on the residue of policing that lies outside core business means that partnership work generally addresses the most intractable problems, the problems least likely to be susceptible to 'Action Man'-type interventions, and the problems that all the partner agencies are apt to construe as someone else's responsibility. These constraints suggest that the return on two of the chief innovations of recent years, intelligence-led policing, and partnership policing, may be more in terms of PR than impact on service delivery.

The preventative potential of community policing

Problem definition in concert with the community, attempts to reduce fear of crime, and partnership work, are policies informed by a belief that making citizens the first line of defence in high-crime neighbourhoods can overcome multiple inner-city deprivations. It is to this that Bowling and Foster (2002: 990) attribute the emphasis on community policing following the 1980s riots; '[d]eveloping closer contacts and reducing the gulf between police and public in these areas became a priority'. Both academic and political analyses see community policing (CP) as the essential response to police/public divisions. Thus Bayley and Shearing (1996: 604) see it as a prerequisite for policing by consent, especially in high-crime areas (Bowling and Foster, 2002) and the Patten Report (Patten, 1999) deemed CP 'the core function' of the reconstructed Police Service of Northern Ireland. There is little doubt that, construed as long-term beat assignment with regular patrol, the public favours the CP approach. Surrey Police's 'geographical policing' system, which attempted in the 1990s to deliver community policing by relief officers, failed to persuade its public. Area liaison meetings revealed that the 'beat bobby' was preferred (*Guildford Times*, 29 August 1992). Residents wanted long-term beat assignment so children became familiar with and respected their police; but CP faces many obstacles, including problems of definition, interpretation, implementation, and evaluation. There is no agreed definition of community policing. Conceptualisations range from Neighbourhood Watch schemes through fixing 'broken windows' and on to 'problem-oriented policing' and 'zero tolerance'. The evidence is that CP has proved particularly problematic in just those high deprivation, high crime and social problem areas where it is believed it has most to contribute (Bowling and Foster, 2002).

It is important to be realistic about what policing can do to impact on communities whose troubles arise from multiple deprivation, and to be aware of the latent effects of police initiatives. Informal social control, such as in Neighbourhood Watch (NW), can heighten fear of crime, with residents leaving meetings more afraid (Bennett, 1991a). This may certainly happen where police publish general warnings, as when Surrey Police warned in 2005 that burglaries in homes and business rise across the county between 19 January and 4 February every year ('Police crime alert', *Surrey Advertiser*, 5 February 2005). Research suggests that NW schemes do not reduce crime rates, and lack of interest prevents them working in poorer areas; programmes have no consistent effect on crime or incivility levels.

NW schemes emerged in the context of public policy concerned with risk management and alleviating fear of crime with a view to community cohesion. About 27% of UK households belonged to a scheme in 2000

(Home Office, 2001). Most schemes are police dominated and rely for their public input on a few enthusiasts. The relationship between perceived and actual risk is not straightforward and, paradoxically, those least at risk, such as the affluent and the elderly, may feel the most fearful. NW schemes tend to emerge and reach the participation threshold set by the police in high-income residential areas, areas having low relative crime vulnerability. The affluent may have low actual risk, but can best afford preventive measures like burglar alarms and can muster the social resources to ameliorate perceived risk. Membership correlates with income more than with risk. Owner-occupied households and those with above-average annual income are most likely to belong; areas with low burglary rates have a higher membership (32% in UK) than high rate areas (13%; Home Office, 2001). Where respondents said that in their area 'people try to help each other and do things together' membership stood at 37%, but at only 19% where respondents said that in their area 'people go their own way' (Home Office, 2001).

While the avowed orientation is to the public 'acting as the eyes and ears of the police', an underlying purpose is to reduce fear of crime by giving citizens a sense of control. There is modest evidence that participation gives rise to feeling better protected as a result of efforts such as installing security equipment, but little evidence of an overall impact on levels of fear (Bennett, 1987, 1990). Schemes can reinforce fear by raising awareness of crime risk, personal knowledge of recent victims, and concern about the neighbourhood's future, prompting intentions to leave (Hough, 1994). When logistic regression techniques are used to control other variables affecting fear, membership is found to have no significant effect on fear levels (Home Office, 2001). More influential is the level of perceived disorder; where this is high so is fear of burglary (Budd and Sims, 2001). There is evidence that members are more likely to call police if witnessing vandalism, but no significant difference in members' and non-members' likelihood of calling police if witnessing an assault or theft from a vehicle.

Bennett (1987, 1990, 1991a and b) found that most schemes struggle to maintain committed participation, the information-gathering function is of limited value to police, and schemes do little to raise established levels of notification of suspicious circumstances. Another notable finding relates to Neighbourhood Watch's aim to get residents looking out for the security of each other's property. Such activity is extremely geo-local, extending to the property either side of the typical resident's own property, and the property opposite (Shapland and Vagg, 1988; Bennett, 1991b); and even this applies only to single-tenanted properties. It also competes with norms of 'civil inattention' that deter people from raising their own risk by 'getting involved'. The clearest picture from empirical evaluations of Neighbourhood Watch is that its manifest function may be less significant than its latent if modest effects on social cohesion.

Attempts to promote more strenuous frontline participation by citizens based on NW have unsurprisingly failed. When the Home Secretary introduced a nationwide scheme of 'parish constables', many councils saw the initiative fail because there were no applicants for the post of volunteer crime prevention co-ordinator (*Guildford Times*, 15 January 1994). The Home Secretary nevertheless urged NW schemes to mount civilian street-patrols, despite warnings from senior officers that this was 'legal vigilantism' ('Vigilantes urged as police strength cut', *Guardian*, 6 December 1993). The 1993 NW conference raised a number of concerns, including accountability, selection, insurance, and whether racial confrontation had been considered ('Scorned patrol', *Guardian*, 6 April 1994). The Home Secretary's speech to the conference had cited a Gallup poll finding that 46% of those polled said schemes should be able to organise and run patrols. The speech did not mention another finding, where the sample was split 44% for and 44% against citizens patrolling to prevent crime and make arrests. Security firms were quick to respond to the Home Office's 'permissive, not prescriptive' position by offering councils patrols for a fee; the Avon and Somerset chief cited one overture where the operator had a criminal record (*Guardian*, 31 March 1994). The Federation declared its 'total opposition' to NW-based patrols ('Howard rebuked over "vigilantes"', *Guardian*, 19 April 1994).

The picture is also discouraging where officers are assigned long-term to geographically based beats that they regularly patrol. Evidence for the impact of this approach on crime levels is weak. Research has examined the role of senior police administrators, line-level officers and the role and impact of community residents. The broad finding is that all are important to successful community policing and that, when empirically investigated, all are problematic in practice. There are thus organisational, operational and individual difficulties in delivering CP. Frontline officer commitment and motivation is essential, and is itself reliant on managerial support (Lurigio and Rosenbaum, 1994; Lurigio and Skogan, 1994; Fielding, 1995). Although organisational commitment and a clear focus on crime control can improve the effectiveness of community police (Fielding, 1995), the necessary conditions demand much of the organisation. Even where these obtain, CP faces the problem of demonstrating its success. The move to performance-measurement regimes based on target-setting and quantitative indicators serves CP particularly poorly. Indeed, some of CP's greatest successes are impossible to demonstrate by such measures since they involve preventing offences. There is also the problem that CP officers may 'give' arrests to other officers in order to distance themselves from interventions that have in fact been brought about by their efforts, in order to maintain their 'in' with community contacts and informants. Some of their most effective work may thus be claimed by others. Community-oriented patrol may make for effective crime prevention, but the best efforts of such work may effectively be 'invisible' to performance measurement (Fielding and Innes, 2005).

A distinction between 'community' and 'association' has been made since the work of Tonnies (1955). When Hillery (1955: 111) examined 94 different definitions of 'community' he concluded that 'most ... are in basic agreement that community consists of persons in social interaction within a geographic area and having one or more additional ties'. Its essence is locality and community sentiment (Rex, 1981: 52). An association is a 'group organised for the pursuit of an interest or a group of interests in common' (Rex, 1981: 52). Both communities and associations generate norms and institutions, but have different group dynamics, different calls on adherents' loyalties, and different degrees of inclusiveness. Change in urban 'communities' represents a shift in forms of affiliation from the generic and inclusive community to the particularistic and exclusive association. City-dwellers are more convincingly analysed as recognising and acting on the interests that *divide* them from others living in the same space. Associations cross physical boundaries (for example, members of sporting teams) while the decline of communities bound by local values has been extensively documented.

Trojanowicz and Moore (1988: 5) maintained that mass transit, mass communications and mass media have 'widened the rift between a sense of community based on geography and one based on a community of interest'. That is, contemporary society evolves towards ties of association. Geo-local ties are of declining general importance, but vary in strength by socio-economic and demographic factors, being relatively strong for older people, the poor and disadvantaged and those with mobility problems. Community policing must therefore capitalise on the most immediate and compelling focus of a community of interest: crime. Crime control problems give police their best 'in' to marshaling a mutual community of interest (among non-offenders). To carry out that mandate the police need good information and this is the core of community policing's appeal.

It may be that police have exaggerated the contemporary importance of community and underestimated the extent of sociality in associative groups. There are few signs of recovery in the heuristic value of the concept of 'the community', and empirical indications of its decline are abundant. A 1999 Royal Mail survey found that a quarter of people aged under 35 rarely or never speak to their neighbours (*Guardian*, 24 April 1999), but a third were in regular contact with people overseas. In contrast, over 70% of over-55s often chatted with neighbours and over half said neighbours were close friends. A third of under-35s could not identify their neighbours by sight, would only offer to help neighbours if it was absolutely necessary, and did not want to get to know them. A third of British adults wanted to emigrate. These do not seem promising auguries for the community integration of the future.

The declining importance of community means that, if police are to engage it in some communal mission, their own role will have to be intrusive and some will see it as sectarian. Police overtures are more likely to register with some (home-owners, business interests, the elderly) than with others. Unless the police wish to replicate in themselves the deviant, the marginal and the dispossessed there is no prospect of their embodying 'the face of the community'. The need is not to claim that the police can somehow reflect the whole community, but to determine at what threshold – higher than at present – police will use their discretion to ignore infractions regarded as tolerable by various local groups with which they wish to engage. Only when police concede that civil order will vary by locale can community policing be distinguished from any other kind of policing. Community policing relies on a realistic estimation of the friends and enemies of the police, but it does not have to pretend to a universal appeal to reach those it has neglected in the past.

Community policing practices

People do not contact the police to widen their social network, but to obtain a distinctive service. Their resentment of reactive 'fire brigade' policing is that they want a sustained involvement that will solve problems. Even when police feared attack if they entered the Toxteth riot area, regular foot patrols by community police were not attacked (*Guardian*, 22 November 1988). A law centre source said 'the community is not anti-police but wants the same policing service as any other community'. To meet local needs the community constable enforces as well as befriends. The case of the Lambeth WPC sacked because her supervisors thought her closeness to the community compromised her ability to enforce the law, was noted in Chapter 4. Similarly, a constable who had patrolled Tenterden for 23 years and emphasised a community policing approach, but had made only one arrest in the previous year, was given three months to make more arrests or face transfer ('"Start nicking villains or else" warning to country PC', *Guardian*, 29 April 1994). Subsequently transferred, he was applauded by colleagues when he marched into his new station with a suspect. A police spokesman said he would be returned to Tenterden eventually, after a month with a Police Support Unit (PSU) and a month with a crime unit. With their transient population, fragmentation and physical deterioration, apathy is a greater problem on estates than committed criminal attitudes or political disaffiliation. Even estates with the worst reputations are not uniformly so; there are high crime-rate streets adjacent to low crime, low anti-social activity streets. Older residents are as likely to disapprove of infractions as are police. Theirs is a crucial constituency. Tactics must be tailored to the group being cultivated.

Police can never be for the whole community because some of any community is committed to crime. There is most mileage in identifying the undecided, those who want more of the police resource and who can be swayed to support police if their experience is positive. The yield from careful cultivation of such people is potentially very great: research regularly shows that about 80% of crimes cleared are due to information supplied by the public (Mitchell, 1984; Simmons, 2002). One problem with focusing effort on pro-police and 'neutral' members of the public is the great difference in black and white experience. Black and minority ethnic males are much more likely than white males to have last been in contact with police as suspect or offender, particularly those in the 16–24 age group (Home Office, 2004c); but the black community cannot be treated as undifferentiated: many have close friends and/or relatives in the police, particularly since inception of the Police Community Support Officer scheme, which has recruited a much higher ratio of ethnic minority people than the regular force. The point is to identify members of such groups who are pro-police and may co-operate and to accept that their demands are as legitimate as those of any other group. Reporting crimes to police shows only very slight differences by ethnicity, with whites showing a 40% reporting rate and black/minority ethnic people a 39% rate; Asians had an elevated rate (42%) and blacks one slightly below average (37%) (Salisbury and Upson, 2004).

Despite periodic recourse to a 'war on crime' rhetoric, the police and Home Office have grown more realistic about *their* capacity to fight crime and have taken to emphasising that action can only be taken on offences the public choose to discover, notify and witness. The public education necessary to maximise public involvement will itself convey information police will find awkward. Greater public confidence will initially *increase* reported crime. Further, when given a voice the public consistently picks low-level problems as its priorities. The problems most often include dog mess, youths loitering, and parking. An instance was the elevation of parking problems above all else by residents of Ash, one of the highest crime areas of Surrey ('Public pick parking as a police priority', *Surrey Advertiser*, 27 February 2004).

The vogue for 'social' crime prevention exemplifies the potential and dangers of orchestrated rather than self-initiated informal social control. The ephemeral nature of the modern sense of community and the political element in social control militate against any radical transformation in responsibility for social control. Crime prevention programmes still reach those who have traditionally supported the police. Much crime is spontaneous, impulsive and opportunistic. Deterrence is irrelevant. Faced with this the advocates of social crime prevention have called for better internalisation of normative controls. Thus Braithwaite (2001) argued that new methods are needed to inculcate social norms: there will have to be greater reliance upon internal controls deriving from early socialisation and schooling and less reliance upon external controls such as punishment. That is one sense in which crime prevention is not for the police alone, but involves re-making contemporary sociality.

The police play a limited role in the discovery of crime. In the British Crime Survey (BCS) police knew of only 24% of incidents reported to interviewers (Home Office, 1998). Some 33% of non-reporting was because people thought police could do nothing, 22% because the police would not be interested, 11% because victims wanted to deal with it themselves; but the relation between effectiveness and public satisfaction is not direct. The BCS regularly finds that about 75% of respondents think that 'taking everything into account' the police are doing a good job. Some want to be satisfied regardless of the quality of police service, to preserve the emotional benefits of contact. The symbolic basis of public satisfaction is evident in the finding that the public evaluated police mainly by their performance as helpers or comforters, while the police evaluated themselves against their proficiency in crime-fighting (Jones, 1980; Fielding, 2001a). Officers must attune to the public's sensitivities: in an incident cited by Burns-Howell (1982), victims were dissatisfied because a detective announced he was 'off-duty in an hour' and continued to be dissatisfied despite property recovered with an arrest. Many police do not credit social service work and resent devotion of extra resources to disadvantaged areas. Deprived areas, after all, are the standard trawling ground for suspect offenders, and not all officers will see the best response as one of compensating disadvantage rather than imposing tough formal social control.

The limited role of the public and the reluctance of the police as presently organised to redefine thresholds of action to include minor offences that are currently tolerated suggests that the most plausible means of meeting demands for a locally responsive version of proactive policing is through the agency of community constables. The Police Reform Act 2002 put community policing at its heart, and recognition of the need for community engagement is encapsulated within Home Office objectives. For example, local authorities are not only statutorily obliged to participate in Crime and Disorder Reduction Partnerships, but are measured against these efforts through the Comprehensive Performance Assessment Process. A principal initiative representing this emphasis is the inception in 2002 of Police Community Support Officers. PCSOs are popular with the public; between 50% and 70% of residents responding to surveys said they felt more secure because of the introduction of PCSOs, and government committed to funding 15,000 more such posts between 2004 and 2007 ('"Plastic police" prove their worth on the beat', *Guardian*, 13 July 2004). However, they are viewed dimly by many regular officers who suspect that resources are being diverted from well-trained regular officers to novices with only a month's training and limited powers. A profile of their work suggests a focus on those things regular officers disdain: low level crime, disorder and anti-social behaviour. A PCSO told interviewers that her last working week had included passing on intelligence about counterfeit notes, checking passes at New Scotland Yard, monitoring the cordon at the scene of an attempted murder, scolding litterbugs and graffiti artists, confiscating alcohol from street drinkers, telling people riding bikes on pavements to dismount, and monitoring homeless people at Victoria Station ('"Plastic police" prove their worth on the beat', *Guardian*, 13 July 2004). The constraint on PCSO powers may also make for conflict with regular officers. PCSOs can issue fixed penalty notices, seize vehicles causing alarm or distress, request the name and address of people behaving anti-socially, ask suspects to accompany them to a police station and use 'reasonable force' to detain anyone running away, but not all have a power to detain (it is a matter for individual forces, and the maximum is 30 minutes). For example, Surrey's chief constable indicated that he wanted to keep a 'clear definition' between PCSOs and police constables; '"I'm not supportive of giving coercive powers to police support staff"', he said ('New powers are arrested', *Guildford Times*, 12 February 2005). Powers would be confined to giving warnings and issuing fixed penalty notices, as the price of a mistake if a PCSO had powers to detain suspects would be 'very high'; the force would 'end up in the civil court being sued and I do not have the appetite for that'. It may not endear PCSOs to regular officers to hear comments such as that of a shopkeeper, who observed '"they're much more like the normal police should be"' ('"Plastic police" prove their worth on the beat', *Guardian*, 13 July 2004). For Surrey's chief, though, he 'believe[d] this could leave the public confused between what is a police officer and what is a PCSO'.

The government's aims and initiatives conflict with longstanding suspicion that the community constable role is one for those who cannot make it on the reliefs or specialist squads. However, the customary hostility of relief and specialist squad officers to community constables is somewhat moderated in stations where they are given the resources to deliver reliable information that assists the work of reliefs and the CID (either by identifying culprits and criminal activities or by community constables themselves prosecuting minor cases that would otherwise fall on the CID) (Fielding, 1995). The resolution of conflict at a community level is also a benefit other branches will sometimes acknowledge. CP can follow crime across organisational boundaries. A Welsh hospital suffering theft on the wards and assaults on staff and patients opened a 'mini police station', with police posting a full-time officer to patrol the hospital, detain suspects and interview witnesses; other officers were encouraged to use the 'station' during breaks ('Crime-hit hospital gets full-time PC', *Guardian*, 24 March 1995). Community policing can achieve results by very simple means; the informational yield from enhanced community contacts need not be complex or detailed. Residents on St Saviour's estate, Retford, told community police they needed better street lighting and fencing; an 18% reduction in crime rates was achieved over three years (*Guardian*, 8 June 1996). From a police perspective, the contribution of community policing is not in school visits, Neighbourhood Watch, community development or other forms of community contact, but in crime control. To the extent that community constables orient to that central tenet of the police mandate, their work will receive support from other officers. To police, the most convincing argument for community policing is the gain in terms of information.

The impatience of most police with the community policing approach is related to the occupational perspective on crime control. Police are not only motivated to find the truth about crime and bring those responsible to justice, but to ensure that a prosecution is brought. They are 'prosecution' rather than 'investigation' oriented. They want to find a viable suspect as quickly as possible and gather maximum evidence incriminating that suspect. There are legalistic reasons for the haste and superficiality of relief policing to augment the more usual arguments about the occupational culture. An analysis starting from the legal performance required of police, rather than their attitudes or culture, better comprehends findings such as those pertaining to officers' intentional pursuit of planned tasks (Burrows and Lewis, 1988). About three-quarters of constables regularly chose particular, extra, tasks to pursue; 40% identified a crime objective (for example, investigating burglaries further to the initial response) and a third identified vehicle matters, such as checking cars belonging to disqualified drivers to see if they had moved. The ranks *did* want to work less reactively, although the relief role meant they were usually frustrated.

Officers spend almost as much time in the police station (43.1% of their time) as on the streets (Singer, 2001), and most time out of the station is spent dealing with incidents and making enquiries in reactive mode; officers only have 17% of their working time free to pursue matters they have prioritised. Most patrol is from a car and foot patrol is a rarity. For five hours a day over half the officers on a shift are in the station; they can get out more at night, with night-shift officers in the community two-thirds of their time, but at hours when fewer people are around to be encountered. There is little evidence that community beat officers spend more time on their beat than relief officers, a finding regularly repeated in over 30 years of supposed prioritisation of community policing and for precisely the same reason – 'abstractions, sickness and training mean that many reliefs are down to a bare minimum' (Singer, 2001: vi). Another consistency is the frustration officers feel at this state of affairs. They want to spend more time on patrol. In light of constables' strong desire for autonomy, the proactive brief and considerable independence of community policing could be attractive if wed to a crime control orientation.

Experience on urban housing estates shows that both organisational commitment and a clear focus on crime control can improve the effectiveness of community police (Fielding, 1995). Where community constables enjoy both autonomy and organisational support, they invest more time in dealing with incidents of comparable seriousness. In an initiative where community constables had their own inspector and office and determined for themselves their response to demands for service, the priority given to these demands was balanced against those arising from beat patrol and from meeting longer-term demands, such as motivating Neighbourhood Watch co-ordinators and managing relationships with local informants (Fielding, 1995). The organisational environment facilitated identification with a locale and developing sustained relationships with its members based on reciprocity of interest. By contrast, relief officers had a very limited definition of success which primarily referred to the avoidance of negative sanctions against them. The difficulty for community policing may lie less in establishing that it is an appropriate response to important demands on police services than in securing an organisational environment in which it can endure. The great problem is providing an index of the efforts of community constables that is as readily accessible as arrests.

Despite the emphasis on 'sector policing' in the Met and similar CP initiatives in forces outside London, the 1990s were not marked by a general and determined effort to deliver community policing, but by retrenchment in levels of routine patrol as forces attempted to adjust to the new performance measurement culture, the public sector Financial

Management Initiative, Home Office refusal to raise police establishments, and local authority reluctance to compensate central government parsimony in the face of voter sensitivity to the community charge. Home Office policy in the 21st century emphasised addressing the 'reassurance gap', the fact that public confidence and the perceived risk of criminal victimisation proved to be little affected by a declining crime rate. 'Reassurance' involved acting on the public's long-expressed wish to see a return to the 'bobby on the beat'; but budgetary constraints affected both PCSO (previously 'neighbourhood wardens', 'community wardens') and Neighbourhood Specialist Officers (NSOs – regular police). PCSOs were introduced with central government funding for the first two years only, after which they fell on police authority budgets, and NSOs were to be funded by re-designating existing posts. Consequently many forces were unable to introduce both, or either, throughout the force area ('New force takes to local streets', *Surrey Advertiser*, 10 December 2004).

There are numerous dilemmas in attempting to deliver community policing. To implement community policing on any scale requires re-thinking both the police and the community role in crime prevention, the role of consumers of police services in influencing organisational policy, the response to community divisions, and a restructuring of demand management and supervision. Reward and discipline systems have to be altered to reflect new values such as effective rather than short-term response to social problems, de-escalation of violence and many other currently unmeasured police outputs (Fielding and Innes, 2005). Extending police/public co-operation in law enforcement and order maintenance faces organisational, environmental and occupational barriers.

6. Governance, performance management and the politics of social conflict

Accountability and governance

Police accountability has been problematic since the beginning of modern policing. Although a number of adjustments have been made in the contemporary period these have emerged as a series of unco-ordinated initiatives, complicated by the increase in organisations having a policing role – reflecting the move from 'government' to 'governance'. To trace why attempts proved necessary to make good the deficiencies of accountability by reforming complaints procedures, changing the membership of police authorities, introducing codes of practice for arrest, interrogation and detention, and implementing new mechanisms for public consultation, we must examine the gaps left by the tripartite system that is formally, but increasingly nominally, the principal mechanism for making the police accountable.

The 1960 Royal Commission established the principle that the administration of each force was to be a tripartite arrangement between central and local government and the chief constable, whereas operational and law enforcement matters were the responsibility of the chief constable, answerable to the law and subject to the need to be efficient. This arrangement was not only unclear in application (Marshall, 1965: 14), but did not resolve controversies over police/public conflict. In the aftermath of the Commission, chief officers unsurprisingly exploited a situation whereby they decided what matters were no business of the police authority. Chiefs were effectively empowered to decide the powers of the police authority. In case this seems too jaded, consider that Chief Constable Anderton refused to answer his police committee's questions about the attendance of police at a labour dispute on the basis that the questions had 'political overtones' and were 'thoroughly unreasonable'. In fact, s 11 of the 1964 Police Act permitted the Home Secretary to rule on the admissibility of such questions, but the procedure was rarely used; Anderton's 'authority' never got an answer.

The two principal tokens in police chiefs' construction of their relationship with democratic oversight are the scope of the 'operational' and the spectre of 'sectarianism'. Chiefs believe that 'independent and impartial policing is so important that it should not be governed on a day-to-day basis by partisan politicians' (Oliver, 1987: 6); but local authorities – the political interest to which chiefs take exception – are charged with seeing that their respective forces are efficient. They cannot assess a force's value without taking account of force operations and policy: he who pays the piper calls the tune. If the public calls for Rachmaninov and the chief plays Radiohead, the public have a right to examine the chief's technique.

Recurrent controversies over police accountability obscure the limits of formal governance, which lie in the even murkier depths of uncertain legal doctrine. If the rightful province of police authority supervision extends to policy, but not to operations, then perfecting constitutional mechanisms cannot in itself assuage conflict over policing. Improved mechanisms may satisfy politicians, but do little to regulate the actions of police. This is because the doctrine of constabulary independence puts a chief constable on the same footing as other officers regarding the right to take independent action. This is compounded by the permissive nature of many police powers. So long as the law grants wide powers and discretion, scope for malpractice to provoke conflict over the licence given by the police mandate will continue. It is therefore misleading to separate 'administrative' and 'operational' matters, and the powers allowed the office of constable must themselves be part of the accountability debate.

Both officers and chief possess discretion, but the restriction of one to particular enforcement decisions and the responsibility of the other for general policies suggests the need for different mechanisms to regulate each and the unhelpfulness of eliding one range of discretion with the other. It is insufficient to argue that because law is the final arbiter of the rightfulness of a constable's frontline enforcement decisions, it must also be the sole line of accountability for the chief. There is more to the difference in discretion than a simple matter of scale. The ordinary constable's interpretation of discretion is highly situated and contingent, while the chief constable's is generic, planful, and takes place in a public arena. Yet when chief constables' decisions are reviewed, the review is confined to narrow interpretations of 'lawfulness'. The result is the absurdity that chief officers do not make policy and, indeed, that the law is so apt a guide that in matters of justice there is no such thing as policy at all.

The operational autonomy of chief constables has in recent years expanded to a point where they are dominant partners in accounting for strategy or policy. Police committees have stringent financial responsibilities and a legal duty to secure efficient and adequate policing, but cannot ultimately prevent chiefs incurring vast expense, inefficiently using resources or dispensing resources to other areas under mutual aid. National initiatives, such as the National Crime Squad, National Criminal Intelligence Service and Serious Organised Crime Agency, and initiatives in respect of riot training and mutual aid, exclude local authority involvement. Home Secretaries have increasingly taken powers to override police authorities. Chiefs are not obliged to provide information or respond to suggestions from local consultative committees. The tripartite system has steadily evolved to endow chiefs and central government at the expense of police authorities.

Despite the nominal responsibility of police authorities, tough action on police finances seems as much characteristic of central government as it is of police authorities. Occasionally the most severe fiscal sanctions are delivered, as when the Inspectorate several times refused Derbyshire Police its certificate of efficiency during the 1990s. The case suggested it was as much in the name of accountability to the Home Office and Inspectorate as to the public. Potential sanctions included refusal to release its central government grant and the sacking of the chief ('Police force fails new efficiency test', *Guardian*, 19 October 1993). The action prompted an unprecedented counter-report by Chief Constable John Newing, who said the Inspectorate's criticisms should be aimed at the Home Office and county council for imposing unrealistically low staffing and budgets ('Police chief rises to inefficiency attack', *Guardian*, 17 November 1993). The Inspectorate had cited failed attempts to bring the force up to strength, excessive overtime, cuts in training and a 16% rise in crime in 1992. Refusal was largely symbolic on that occasion. The certificate was refused a third time for understaffing. The chief again blamed this on underfunding, consequent on Home Office failure to raise the force establishment. Certificates of efficiency were phased out altogether in 1995. They had served since the mid-19th century as one of the earliest means to exert central government influence over local forces, accompanied by introduction of the first inspectors of constabulary, but at a time when the central/local balance was very much on the local axis.

In the context of the urban riots of the 1980s, the Financial Management Initiative of the 1990s and the 21st century extension of the 'police family', there has been a recognition that accountability is a serious problem, however determined chief officers are to stand by customary arrangements. Among the mechanisms of change have been new police complaints procedures, reconstituted police authorities, Codes of Practice under the Police and Criminal Evidence Act, and consultative committees. These and other major initiatives have made for a busy, but not entirely co-ordinated, time of change for police accountability.

Complaints

While it may be thought that the best response to complaints is to ensure that action giving rise to them does not happen in the first place, it is inevitable in an activity that is discretionary and seeks to mediate contentious matters that mistakes will be made. Tyler (1990) suggests that people are as concerned about inequality in the manner of their treatment as they are about inequality of outcome. Stops, arrests, and other interventions can be carried out aggressively or politely, in ways that display contempt or respect. The British Crime Survey found that some 20% of all those stopped by the police felt they were treated impolitely or worse (Skogan, 1990b). Ethnic minority people and youths are particularly likely to experience police interventions in such a way that they are dissatisfied with the way they are treated, irrespective of outcome. Although the name, organisation and approach of the bodies tasked with investigating complaints have changed markedly, only recently did the public gain what it long demanded – an *independent* complaints service.

Complaint case totals gradually increased up to 1994 and then began a 8-year decline (see Figure 2). There have been some sharp local perturbations, such as the halving of the Met's share of complaints totals between 1979 and 1987. Such changes can reflect changed policing, declining confidence in the system, or effort to allay grievances and dissuade people from formally complaining. Evidence for the last of these was that, despite declining totals, *serious* complaints did not decline (Maguire and Corbett, 1989). The total number of complaints (opposed to *cases*) in England and Wales fell from 32,443 in 1982, to 27,932 in 1987, mostly due to the trend in the Met. The total rose to 35,820 in 1998. There were 23,000 (equating to 15,248 cases) in the year to March 2003, 8% down on the year, the third year of falling numbers (Cotton, 2004).

On average over half of complaints concern aggressive behaviour, verbal or physical, with incivility accounting for about a quarter, and assault and oppressive conduct/harassment giving double digit figures. Officers know which situations have high risk of provoking complaint, and have sometimes told researchers they proceed in such a way that no allegation could be substantiated. Patrol officers who did not occasionally attract complaints were likely to be avoiding responsibility (Maguire and Corbett, 1989: 9). Most knew officers they would describe as 'complaint prone' – otherwise good officers who tended to lose control when provoked. Police also felt people would complain without cause because they were malicious or seeking a *quid pro quo* against charges (Bowling and Foster, 2002). While the average number of complaints per thousand officers was 178 in 2003, down 11% on the year (Cotton, 2004), the fact that the City of London figure was 95, while the Nottinghamshire figure

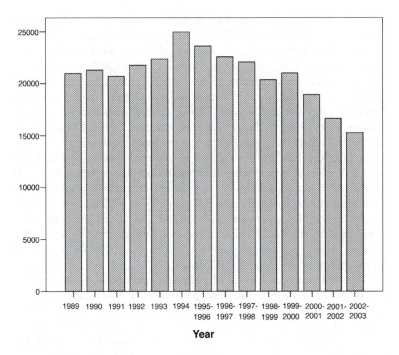

Figure 2

Complaint trend

Source: Home Office Police Complaints and Discipline figure

was 269, suggests there is a story behind the figures about the nature of police/public relations in the areas served by the respective forces. Sussex managed to reduce its figures from 305 in 2002, to 149 in 2003, a staggering 51% decline in one year.

It is widely known that most complaints are 'unsubstantiated'. During the 1990s the substantiation rate was around 2%; of substantiated cases, about 20% resulted in criminal or disciplinary hearings (Police Complaints Authority, 2000). Decisions over prosecution of officers accused of criminal offences long advantaged the police – more evidence is in practice required against a police officer than a member of the public before a prosecution will be authorised, because the Director of Public Prosecutions (DPP) takes into account the reluctance of juries to convict police officers. As a result, prosecutions against police officers were only mounted where there was overwhelming evidence. Further, for many years, if the DPP decided not to prosecute, officers were immune from internal disciplinary proceedings. Only rarely was disciplinary action taken against Met police involved in incidents that led to out-of-court settlements or damages; in 1993 it emerged that no action was taken against 80% of officers involved in cases where payments of more than £10,000 were imposed over the previous five years ('MP queries lack of action against police', *Guardian*, 15 April 1993), during which £1.9 million had been paid in out-of-court settlements and £758,000 in court awards, largely arising from civil actions alleging assault, false imprisonment or malicious prosecution. Officers against whom a criminal offence was alleged, but where there was insufficient evidence to prosecute, were in a better position than officers accused of something short of a criminal offence. Under the system where the Police Complaints Authority (PCA) supervised police complaints investigations, complainants whose cases were supervised were rarely satisfied, while those whose cases were not referred to the PCA were even less satisfied (House of Commons, 1998; Waters and Brown, 2000). The British Social Attitudes Survey repeatedly showed near-unanimous support for a genuinely independent complaints authority (Tarling and Dowds, 1997).

The contemporary history of police complaints is one of ongoing lack of public confidence, increasing numbers of civil actions taken in frustration at the deficiencies of the complaint system, costly awards against police in the civil courts, and major institutional change in response to these problems. Even the Police Federation called for a wholly independent system. After years of opposition it wanted to stop people blaming a rigged system when officers were exonerated. In 1984, 8% of all investigated complaints in London were substantiated, but not one involving harassment, racial discrimination, false evidence or perjury. The problem was not just procedure, but the strong sense of solidarity amongst police; indeed police would 'normally tell lies to prevent another officer from being disciplined or prosecuted' (Smith and Gray, 1983: 329). This underscored the need for independent investigators immune to the effects of solidarity (House of Commons, 1998). As we shall see, it took some years to achieve a system with the potential to deliver this, and, interestingly, current statistics on such things as substantiated cases of racial discrimination show little change as yet.

Initially the government ignored the highly significant union of Police Federation and National Council for Civil Liberties by setting up a PCA that still relied on investigations by the police themselves. The PCA was established by the Police and Criminal Evidence Act 1984 as an independent body to *oversee* investigation of complaints. Its function was 'supervisory'. Complaints involving death, serious injury, actual bodily harm, corruption or serious arrestable offences could be referred to the PCA. The PCA could order investigation by another force and comment on whether it was satisfied with the investigation. If a chief constable refused to bring disciplinary charges it could direct him to do so. The limits of these changes were soon apparent when the West Midlands police authority and Chief Constable asked that the report of an investigation into the shooting of a five-year-old hiding under his bed be made public. The PCA refused, claiming witnesses would withhold information, effectively backing the silence of the only witnesses, police who killed a child. A survey for the Royal Commission on Criminal Justice estimated that police malpractice serious enough to justify disciplinary proceedings occurred in an average of 100 cases a year, using the conservative index of judicial assessments that evidence should be excluded (*Guardian*, 9 December 1992).

Police authorities are the disciplinary body for senior officers, and could refer cases to the PCA, appoint the investigating officer and 'one person tribunal' from a list given by the Lord Chancellor and set the punishment. This power occasioned an unedifying manoeuvre. Because of the power, any action of the chief constable in directing and controlling the force could not be subject of a complaint. The complaints process was concerned with individual misconduct, not policies, even if the policies were misconceived. The current arrangements confirm this approach: complaints do not provide an avenue to review policy.

The Federation voted no confidence in the PCA in 1989, describing it as aggressive, interventionist and more interested in earning the goodwill of complainants then securing justice (*Guardian*, 18 May 1989). The PCA chairman thought this the 'clearest evidence possible that the PCA is performing effectively the task which Parliament gave it' (*Guardian*, 18 May 1989). The PCA periodically criticised the number of officers escaping disciplinary action by taking early retirement on medical grounds (proceedings were abandoned when officers left the service) ('"Too many" police evade censure', *Guardian*, 29 April 1993). Early retirements were frequent in high-profile cases; but the PCA also raised concern over 'tactical complaints' by people facing trial, who could say in court that complaints had been made, but afterwards would not co-operate with the investigation of them. During the 1990s there were increases in such complaints.

Modest changes marked the PCA's last years. Traditionally selected by nominations from the Public Appointments Unit, the PCA advertised publicly for members for the first time in 1995. Serving or former police officers were ineligible; the advertisement referred to a graduate with a 'senior management background' (Home Office Press Release 12/95, 20 January 1995). The 'double jeopardy rule' protecting police from internal disciplinary procedures as an alternative to criminals prosecution was abolished by new police conduct regulations in 1999 (Smith, 1999). The rule had done much to vitiate the independent element of the police complaints process between 1976 and the introduction of the PCA, because government guidelines took the view that where the DPP decided there was insufficient evidence to prosecute, the Police Complaints Board (PCB), the PCA's predecessor, was precluded from directing the chief officer to initiate disciplinary charges on grounds that the charge relied on the same evidence. An early factor in the Home Office interpretation that ensured the system operated on the double jeopardy basis from 1976 to 1999 was the statement in Sir Robert Mark's biography that creation of the PCB had caused him to resign as Commissioner, a resentment shared with his successor ('Hounding the bad cops', *Guardian*, 30 June 1999). A judicial review found the guideline wrong, in that the DPP's decision could have no bearing on deciding whether to bring discipline charges. 'Whether or not there was evidence that an offence against discipline had been committed was to be decided on the facts as detailed in the complaint investigation report' (Smith, 1999: 1223). Differences in the criminal justice and police discipline processes and the sanctions available were reason to see them as separate decisions.

In 1998, under the PCA, there were 847 substantiated complaints against police, in 1981, under the PCB, there were 1,542. Although the number of complaints increased, from 32,443 to 35,820, those substantiated fell by nearly half. The continuing police involvement in PCA investigations limited public confidence; the other recourse of the public was to civil action (re-named 'civil claims' by the Civil Procedure Rules 1998). Between 1991–92 and 1997–98 there was an over 500% increase in amounts paid out by police in civil proceedings. In 1979 there were seven cases against the Met, and under £2,000 in damages were paid in total, but by 1997 the Met faced a thousand actions and it paid out nearly £4 million damages in 2000 (Metropolitan Police, 2000). Civil actions seem less likely to directly impact on police probity and effectiveness (Bowling and Foster, 2002: 1019); a US study showed that fewer than half the officers successfully sued in civil court would alter their behaviour in any way (Hogarth, 1982: 115). Since a minority of complaints of abuse result in compensation being awarded, many are left dissatisfied and without redress. The backdrop to the move to an Independent Police Complaints Commission was not simply an increasingly litigious public. The National Criminal Intelligence Service attributed to bribery associated with the drugs trade the spread of police corruption in Britain to levels normally found only in 'unstable Third World countries' (*Daily Telegraph*, 27 September 1998). Information technology helped officers sidestep exclusion of police from 'whistleblower' rights. Dissatisfied with management response to his criticism of safety and training procedures, and threatened with disciplinary procedures for raising his concerns, the head of Surrey Police's firearms squad purchased the domain name 'surreypolice.com' and posted details of corruption cases on the website. When Surrey Police made legal moves he set up a comprehensive site detailing police corruption in all British forces. In 1999 the Surrey Chief Constable stated that the majority of complaints against police officers were not from the public, but from colleagues, reflecting a 'major cultural shift' and the influence of increased numbers of civilian staff (*Surrey Advertiser*, 26 November 1999).

The way that complaints are regarded was coloured by the general perspective police apply to the criminal justice system. In the view of senior officers, the criminal justice system had tilted too much in favour of defendants by the mid-1990s, spurring then-Commissioner Sir Paul Condon to declare the risk of 'noble cause corruption', where officers fabricate evidence against those they are convinced are guilty ('Corruption fear as police lose faith in justice system', *Guardian*, 10 March 1995). A main police concern was the judicial interpretation of the disclosure rules, where major cases had to be withdrawn to avoid identifying informers during pre-trial defence scrutiny of prosecution evidence. However, the legal picture is always a mixed one. For instance, the Court of Appeal ruled in 1991 that in appropriate circumstances trial judges are entitled to excuse police from answering questions designed to find out the location of observation posts used for surveillance purposes (*Regina v Newitt* and *Regina v Davis*, 20 December 1991). Police had argued that disclosing the location of premises used to observe drug dealing could lead to reprisals and deter others prepared to help.

The 1993 Royal Commission on Criminal Justice (RCCJ) recommended an independent Criminal Cases Review Authority to act proactively to consider alleged miscarriages of justice, and that acquittal of police in a criminal court not be a bar to disciplinary proceedings on the same facts with the sanction of dismissal (RCCJ, 1993). In parallel, the Home Secretary set new procedures by which police accused of misconduct would be handled under less formal and legalistic procedures than formerly, with a possibility of dismissal whether or not the courts decided a criminal offence occurred (Home Office News Release 197/93, 22 September 1993). While the dramatic shift to independence desired by the RCCJ took years more to achieve, in its later years the outgoing system thus ran in accord with some of the principles of the incoming one. Data published in its last year of operation show the continued disjunction between complaints made and those upheld. While 7,262 complaints were investigated in the year to March 2003, 941 were substantiated (Cotton, 2004). Over half of these involved a failure in duty, and about 20% oppressive behaviour. Disciplinary/misconduct charges were proved against 1,529 officers, of whom 115 were dismissed or required to resign, 19% up on the year. Over a quarter of complaints made were for assault, but it accounted for only 10% of substantiated complaints. The ratio reflects a longstanding fact behind the figures: public order policing routinely gives rise to citizen dissatisfaction with rough handling, but investigators tend to accept police action as having been proportionate. That is, one prime source of police/public conflict is enduring, and little affected by any investigatory system yet tried. As for complaints of racially discriminatory behaviour, there were 49 such complaints in 1991, rising 12-fold to 579 in 2000 (Police Complaints Authority, 2000: 19). Just nine such complaints were substantiated in 2003, the same number as 2002. Some may feel there is little gain on the 1984 figures noted earlier in this section.

The investigation of complaints independently of the police finally saw fruition with the inauguration in April 2004 of the Independent Police Complaints Commission (IPCC). Its statutory powers, and the respective responsibilities of the IPCC, chief constables and police authorities, were set out in the Police Reform Act 2002. The system covers all police officers and special constables, police staff, and designated contracted escort and detention officers. The IPCC can choose to manage or supervise the police investigation into a case and independently investigate the most serious, in which latter case IPCC investigators have police powers. The IPCC is also responsible for setting standards, monitoring, reviewing and inspecting the police complaints system. It has a legal duty to increase public confidence in policing. An immediate priority was for the system to be more timely, 'with a proportionate response to complaints and action that is demonstrably fair for complainants and for police officers' (IPCC, 2004: 7). Police authorities retained their role as 'appropriate authority' in the investigation of complaint and conduct matters against ACPO-rank officers; the authority for non-ACPO ranks is the chief constable.

IPCC requires police to inform the public about the system and the right to complain. 'Local resolution' was usually the most appropriate and proportionate response, and would boost confidence in local policing, settlement being via a station inspector, civilian staff manager or at Basic Command Unit (BCU) level. However, while an informal resolution option was included in the Police and Criminal Evidence Act 1984, 30% of the public were opposed to it because they did not trust the police to carry it out, felt it let off the accused too easily, and would not be a deterrent. In fact, 70% of complaints were informally resolved or withdrawn in 2003 (Cotton, 2004). For groups that may assume the police are unfair – black and minority ethnic communities, gay and lesbian communities, and the disabled – complaints of discriminatory behaviour meet the threshold for mandatory referral to the IPCC 'where a relatively minor criminal offence such as common assault is alleged accompanied by discriminatory behaviour' or where there has been abuse of authority (Cotton, 2004: 19). Innovations, such as sending flowers with an apology, are acceptable provided they could not be misconstrued as avoiding the issue. Where a force considers no action should be taken about a complaint before 'local resolution'/investigation it must seek an IPCC dispensation. It is important to remember the feelings that can be engendered by what seem to be purely administrative decisions. So sharp was the reaction to the IPCC's decision not to independently investigate the first black death in custody since it began operations, it was obliged to rescind the decision ('Police watchdog to investigate death', *Guardian*, 14 August 2004). Troublingly, the IPCC gave shortage of resources as the reason it wanted Essex Police to conduct the investigation. Its Deputy Chair said it had wanted to investigate independently from the outset, but was already investigating two shootings. Supporters of the victim's family, and an organisation representing relatives of people who died in police custody, took the view that the IPCC had had to be forced to do what it should have done in the first place and raised concern that Essex Police had been brought in despite heavy criticism of their role in similar inquiries.

Identifying four causes of complaint – unprofessional behaviour, criminal conduct, tortious action and unacceptable policy – and four functions of a complaint system – managerial, liability, restorative and accountability – Smith (2004) advocates a system differentiated by cause and function, with a tier to deal with unprofessional behaviour, another to deal with criminal conduct, and a third tier to consider complaints of unacceptable police policy. This is a useful specification of purposes that are often entangled, and conveys the way that we look to a single system to both address individual and generic problems with policing. However, it seems unlikely that government and police will so lightly concede a means for the public to influence operational policy, nor that such an upheaval will soon be contemplated against the snail's pace of institutional change that has led to the IPCC.

There is reason to be cautious about the impact of the IPCC. The adoption of an independent approach has no doubt raised public confidence, but the effect on substantiation is debatable. The fact that police investigated other police, and the requirement to prove cases 'beyond reasonable doubt' were not the only causes of low substantiation rates (Bowling and Foster, 2002: 1018). Complaints often relate to circumstances where no independent witnesses are available, so outcomes depend on the complainant's word against that of the police (Brown, 1997). Independent investigations and reducing the standard of proof to 'the balance of probabilities' may not impact much on substantiation rates (Reiner, 2000b: 187) because a number of other obstacles documented in other countries can affect investigations, including police unwillingness to testify against colleagues (Kappeller *et al*, 1994), politically driven interference (Gordon, 2001), resource problems and a lack of investigative skills (Melville, 1999). Appraisal of the effect of the new system awaits detailed research, but early reaction suggested that the public was relieved to have a system with a substantial measure of independence and that the public was watchful over the proportion of cases the IPCC elected to run for itself, 'supervision' of cases having been the approach that had failed to establish the PCA as an improvement on the previous system.

Police authorities and police committees

Police authorities have fallen a long way since the 19th century, when watch committees were the most prestigious in city corporations. Stripped of policy-making power, authority to direct officials, intervene on behalf of constituents or even discuss substantive matters from a position of responsibility, it is unsurprising that by the 1980s they were mostly 'the preserve of the inactive and the conventional' (Lustgarten, 1986: 87). Powers, composition and public profile remain significant problems. Members were latterly not among the most dynamic councillors, and authorities were marked by 'strongly pro-police orientations' (Weitzer, 1995). Contemporary evidence is that some members are barriers to change, others have little involvement, and other members have their own agenda (Home Office, 2003a: 3). Moreover, members are constrained from acting as genuine 'community leaders' because they often do not live in the area where they were responsible for community engagement. Consultation arrangements varied between areas, sometimes reflecting a 'lack of involvement or initiative by members' (Home Office, 2003a: 3). There was 'very mixed success' within and between authorities in reaching ethnic minority, disabled and other minority groups. To meet government policy for police to work more closely with community members, some police authorities have brought senior police officers into membership of new 'community safety committees' (*Surrey Advertiser*, 8 January 1999). In Surrey the six divisional commanders were each paired with an authority member to establish closer ties at district council level. While police are non-voting members, it seems a bizarre way to involve 'the community'. Official research recommended that authority members be given training so they could play a fuller part in meetings, and that authorities should set members a minimum threshold of engagement (Home Office, 2003a: 5).

Fiscal responsibility was the principal enduring concern of the authority, but more recently three-quarters of funding has been central. Moreover, police salaries and pensions are nationally negotiated and, since they account for over 85% of police expenditure, the scope of local decision-making over police finances is highly restricted. The representatives of the business community, added to membership under the new arrangements initiated in the 1990s, do not appear to have sharpened fiscal oversight or much altered external influence on policy. The obstacles to real influence have been as much a result of police skills of manipulation and councillor apathy as a consequence of inadequate constitutional mechanisms. Police authorities also have a low public profile. Recent research found a general view that the public has little say in decisions about policing and the vast majority of respondents had not even heard of police authorities; those who had did not know what they did (Home Office, 2003a). In light of police dominance of authorities it is noteworthy that respondents saw them as part of the police. Most were sceptical as to their effectiveness, largely because of their low profile. Once respondents were briefed on the nature of police authorities there was a general view that it was crucial that the police authorities be independent of police and that the way members were selected was key to this. There was scepticism about local authorities nominating members; 'there was concern that there might be a "closed shop" or "old boys' network" and that members might have too close a relationship with the police' (Home Office, 2003a: 2). Many had no interest in how well the police were performing, and those who had an interest expressed doubts about performance measures and the usefulness of statistics. Interest was confined to residents' immediate locale. Apathy, conflicting priorities, and a lack of expertise were all cited as obstacles to police authorities being a genuine vehicle for consultation and action. Nor did these perspectives come as news to police and to police authority members and staff. They knew there was little public awareness of police authorities and of their status separate from forces, and some authority members thought the authorities' role was not understood by police either. Moreover, some did not see it as necessary for police authorities to be separate from police in order to do their job effectively.

There appeared to have been little improvement in authorities and police consulting on prioritising their aims since Elliott and Nicholls (1996) identified it as essential. Some authorities did not have a consultation strategy, there was overlap between force and authority, and some authorities were not aware of what consultation steps their force was undertaking (Home Office, 2003a: 2–3). Political and geographical factors, and the strength of Crime and Disorder Reduction Partnerships (CDRPs), affected the effectiveness of multi-agency consultation. Force planning horizons and those of CDRPs were not aligned. The outcomes of consultation were not systematically fed back to the public, despite evidence of consultation sometimes having an impact on policing plans, service delivery, and police/community relations. 'Local political factors' sometimes affected authorities' effectiveness and ability to work with other agencies. Authorities needed to do more to encourage people to serve as independent members. Forces needed to respond more effectively to consultation output and to transmit it to frontline staff. It is somewhat staggering that authorities still need official advice that they should monitor what action forces are taking on issues raised via consultation (Home Office, 2003a: 5). Competition for resources, the need to balance local views with national priorities, inadequate channels for integrating consultation output with decision-making, the fact that the authority's remit does not run to operational matters, all joined consultation output quality as factors inhibiting police authority effectiveness (Home Office, 2003a: 4). This appraisal provokes substantial pessimism about present arrangements for two reasons. First, even official research such as this concluded that 'authorities cannot provide true accountability or engagement while largely invisible to the public' (Home Office, 2003a: 4) but, secondly, some stakeholders nevertheless set their face against this view and did not accept that police authorities needed to establish a genuinely separate identity with the public.

Sound accountability mechanisms are central to liberal, community-based models of policing (Kleinig, 1996: 212). Police must account for actions, explain them, and be co-operative with an external, independent authority (Savage *et al*, 2000: 50). In politics, social contract theory requires citizens to exchange some of their freedoms in return for protection from the state and it follows that 'there is a moral onus on those who limit the freedom of others to provide a justification of that limitation' (Kleinig, 1996: 13). Bowling and Foster (2002: 1015) note several features of policing that make such accountability problematic: low public confidence engendered by scandals over corruption and miscarriages of justice, an insular organisational culture, high frontline officer discretion, the breadth of the police role, and the low visibility of police decision-making, to which may be added the increasing amount of 'policing' done by non-public police agents (Loader, 1999: 333). Accountability to the law alone is insufficient despite the doctrine of constabulary independence, because it leaves the police to make choices about which laws to uphold and by what means. What is at issue is not that police should be free to make decisions, but that they should be accountable for the decisions they make. Accountability purely to politicians, such as the Home Secretary, is insufficient because politicians are attuned to the short-term and to electoral advantage, and are also heavily influenced by the media (Koch, 1998).

The year 1993 was a signal one for police accountability: the three major inquiries (Home Office, 1993a, 1993b; Royal Commission on Criminal Justice, 1993) that reported initiated a reform process that significantly modified the constitutional settlement enshrined in the tripartite system, while not sweeping away either the principles on which it was founded or the structures that expressed them. The principles and structures set in place by the 1962 Royal Commission on the Police had been triggered by two incidents that now seem remarkably mild, suggesting the commission was overdue. The first incident involved the suspension of Nottingham's Chief Constable, Captain Popkess, by his police authority for refusing to report to them a criminal investigation he had conducted concerning a local councillor. The second incident involved Met police who stopped the entertainer Brian Rix for speeding. A civil servant, a Mr Garratt, intervened on Rix's behalf and became embroiled in an argument with the arresting officer PC Edmond, leading to mutual assault allegations. When the Commissioner settled out of court in Garratt's favour there was public criticism that public money had financed the settlement and that Edmond was not disciplined.

The motivating background behind the triggering incidents was a steep rise in recorded crime, and a perceived increase in confrontational policing as the late 1950s saw the emergence of recognisably contemporary conflicts involving emerging youth cultures, racial tensions, and political demonstrations over causes such as the Suez crisis and nuclear disarmament (Walker, 2000). It was felt necessary to re-examine the constitutional position of the police, clarify accountability arrangements, and consider how complaints should be handled. The existing constitutional framework was 'a patchwork affair which reflected the gradual and uneven acceptance of the modern policing idea' (Walker, 2000: 41). Equally motivating were the gradual centralisation of power and the consolidation of police professional autonomy around the concept of constabulary independence. As discussed in Chapter 2, the First World War and the police strikes had spurred central government to promote the incorporation of chief constables and local government into an integrated network concerned with developing a joint policy framework. The Home Office Police Department and the advisory Police Council founded in the Police Act 1919 were the focus and source of this approach.

These centralising moves ran alongside, and often in tension with, the doctrine of constabulary independence that came to emphasise that police are responsible for their actions to the law and only to the law (*Regina v Metropolitan Police Commissioner, ex p Blackburn* [1968]; discussed in Chapter 7). The origin of the doctrine is murky and its derivation from a series of judgments in individual cases makes it unstable. It is in itself an inadequate doctrine in respect of the span of issues involved in police governance. As we saw earlier, the key case in the doctrine's development was the 1930 High Court decision in *Fisher v Oldham Corporation*, following Fisher's tort action claiming false imprisonment by the local constabulary. From Fisher's action – not against the officers, but against their employer – ultimately emerged the principle that a master/servant relationship did not apply, and with it the dismissal of the local authority's tortious liability. One aspect of the legal reasoning was that constables represented 'citizens in uniform' and thus had 'original authority'; another was the idea that constables were 'the specialist repository of the general peace-keeping responsibility' (Walker, 2000: 50), a public functionary serving the general public interest in civil order; but against this reasoning was the failure of the judge to appreciate that the County and Borough Police Act 1856 empowered the watch committee to give orders to officers.

Between *Fisher* and the 1962 Commission, the case was taken well beyond its specific foundations to argue a general freedom from external control, including decisions taken by chief constables (Walker, 2000: 52). Walker sees the doctrine as both harmful and positive. The harm is the emphasis that all other authorities must defer to the law as the sole basis for taking police to account, while the positive aspect is that law alone is a sufficient authority for doing so. The latter obviates direct political authority over, and interference in, policing. The trouble is that it elides the anathema of direct political control of constables with justifiable democratic influence over senior police managers (Lustgarten, 1986: 65). Government's brief is to ensure fair – meaning equal – treatment across society and across the system, and to do this it must be able to influence chiefs. Yet the fundamental good of impartiality is also threatened when considerations of extraneous political factors enter professional judgment in individual law enforcement decisions. The key issue is the 'feasibility of separating the legitimate sphere of policy decision-making from the illegitimate sphere of operational decision-making' (Walker, 2000: 59). The distinction between policy and operations is not clear, and never will be. Nor is it credible that in itself the law is capable of holding the police, of whatever rank, to account. The law is largely a *post hoc* authority, awaiting infractions and relying on citizens to cry foul.

It is not pretended that the law is not a powerful constraint on police action, but it is also a resource and the police do not approach its processes as complete outsiders. Constitutionally there is a particular difficulty in that a strict separation of executive and legislative power is not possible in a political system that puts supreme authority in

Parliament and in those who command its confidence, the executive (Walker, 2000: 61). Operationally, much law grants high discretion in the interpretation and application of law to the police, particularly in respect of public order. Since public opinion rates the seriousness of different offences quite differently, the need for police to arbitrate by setting priorities and thresholds for intervention is inescapable; but the constabulary independence idea fails to accept that the 'task of distinguishing between legitimate and illegitimate forms of political influence over policing is both positive and necessary; that, in any case, the law is not proof against illegitimate political interference, and that any positive guidance offered by the law in pursuit of the mandate is intrinsically inadequate' (Walker, 2000: 67).

These were the problems the Royal Commission faced, problems of local versus central control, and professional autonomy versus democratic governance. It is hardly surprising that the 'system' the Commission produced was 'under-specified', or that the vagueness was in some ways functional to permit flexibility to respond to events; but flexibility cannot accommodate fundamental disagreement and inherent institutional conflicts of interest. Under the Police Act 1964 the police authorities, with elected members outnumbering magistrates, could not direct chiefs. Centralisation was endorsed through new powers for the inspectorate, and the Home Secretary could call for reports from chiefs on policing matters, issues of collaboration and amalgamation of forces. Constabulary independence was little affected bar a requirement that each force should be 'under the direction and control' of its chief. Police authorities retained their remit – personnel matters, a duty to provide and equip an adequate force, consultation of the public, and giving advice to chiefs; but neither the Royal Commission nor the legislation fully specified the statutory responsibilities of the partners in the tripartite system. Moreover, both were backwards-looking and failed to anticipate the impact on government of monetarist economics and new approaches to public sector management, making ongoing conflict and confusion inevitable.

By the time of the re-election of a Conservative government in 1991 the police were increasingly anxious of the new managerialism and their anxiety was soon confirmed by the new government's police reform agenda. The Sheehy Inquiry (Home Office, 1993a) and the Core and Ancillary Tasks review (Home Office, 1993b) were key expressions of this agenda, and the Police and Magistrates' Courts Act 1994 and the Police Act 1996 its principal instruments. These provide the contemporary framework of police governance. The extent of mooted change – and its limits – are apparent from the Core and Ancillary Tasks Review. Senior police, including the ACPO President and the Deputy Commissioner of the Met, warned that the review seriously threatened the service role of the police ('Top policeman attacks "alienating" Howard bill', *Guardian*, 18 October 1994). 'Government accountants' were running the risk of removing all non-confrontational tasks from police, and public trust would inevitably be lost. Sir John Smith believed that '"the result is to increase the police's enforcement role by criminalising issues previously regarded as subject of civil law enforcement procedures or even matters of conscience"'. It is interesting to compare the duties identified as 'ancillary' by ACPO and by the review. ACPO nominated fingerprint and DNA forensics; summonsing defendants; warning witnesses of court dates; executing warrants; disclosing criminal records; impounding stray dogs; dealing with lost property; enforcing litter and animal diseases laws; parking law enforcement; and licensing of taxis, sex shops and betting shops. The review identified 20 areas, including response to absconding from children's homes; school liaison; dealing with stray dogs, lost property and noise pollution; licensing of gaming, explosives and liquor; a large number of traffic matters; and 'a more effective approach to policing public events' (Home Office News Release 205/94, 25 October 1994). The review's head, Ingrid Posen, a civil servant, made clear there would be no public consultation until after final recommendations were with the Home Secretary.

In 1995 the Home Secretary confirmed 'an amicable retreat' from plans to privatise much police work. Instead, 26 peripheral tasks, including immigration escorts, serving court summonses, licensing work, and dealing with lost property and stray dogs, would be transferred to local authorities or business ('Retreat over privatised police work', *Guardian*, 28 June 1995). Civilian gaolers would receive powers of arrest and detention over detained immigrants, to which the Federation objected. Reference to improving public order policing disappeared. Instead, the Home Secretary's statement emphasised the rounded nature of the police role: '"policing requires the police to undertake a wide range of tasks which are a service to the community and require the consent and active participation of the public"'. The Criminal Justice and Public Order Act 1994 bore out some of Smith's pessimism. It obliged police to divert effort from community policing to dealing with ravers, squatters, travellers, hunt saboteurs and gypsies as criminals. Also ignored was Smith's warning that allowing the Home Secretary to set national objectives was 'constitutionally and operationally naive' and a threat to community policing as it violated the principle of local determination of priorities.

As Smith's observation implied, accountability has impact beyond the purely constitutional. Equally, developments such as the managerialism informing the Sheehy inquiry have effects on accountability. Sheehy proposed reduction of the rank structure, fixed-term appointments, lower starting pay, performance-related pay, and abolition of many overtime payments and allowances. Before the 1993 Trade Union Congress (TUC) conference the Federation placed a half-page attack on Sheehy in the paper of the 'Democratic Left', formerly the Communist Party, and other 'left' publications. As well as attacking Sheehy, the Federation pointed out that police are unable to take industrial action and that Sheehy had recommended it become only a consultative body in negotiations over police pay and conditions ('Police woo trade unions over Sheehy', *Guardian*, 3 September 1993). The Federation was not alone; ACPO also made clear that Sheehy's proposals on pay and conditions would damage the ethos of the Service ('Police chiefs reject key proposals from Sheehy', *Guardian*, 19 July 1993), and former Home Secretary and Prime Minister Callaghan featured in Federation adverts attacking Sheehy. Reaction to the rather obviously inflammatory nature of the recommendations, with a 23,000 strong police rally at Wembley and the Police Federation, Superintendents' Association and ultimately ACPO and the Inspectorate united in opposition ('Police chief sees risk in reform delay', *Guardian*, 2 July 1993), overshadowed the more radical White Paper on Police Reform, which focused on governance and was inspired not by constitutional considerations in themselves, but addressed and evaluated them for their effect in bringing about better policing and greater public safety. The Paper recognised that under-specification was the problem in the post-1964 system, but was narrow in its solution. It sought to make internally coherent each of the tripartite parties' governance role, to ensure that the performance of each was 'transparently' accountable, and to garner a co-operative rather than conflictual relationship between them; but the goal was not a better-founded normative framework, but more effective service delivery, like Sheehy, construed on private sector lines. This tilted the balance to central government. Combining economic market principles with the politics of centralisation came about because, in the absence of a conventional market in policing, 'the fashioning of a common police product and the supply of methods of assessing its quality and cost-effectiveness necessarily presupposed a high degree of central decision-making and standard setting' (Walker, 2000: 102).

Among the specifics of the reformed framework, all three parties were given a more explicit strategic role in policy formation, with chiefs granted more day-to-day autonomy in managing the force, but also guided toward more concern with strategy rather than detailed management on the ground. Chiefs would set key objectives informed by national performance indicators. The Audit Commission would have a greater role, working in tandem with an Inspectorate advising chiefs through 'thematic inspections'. The Home Secretary gained new powers to require reports from police authorities and to intervene if they were not operating effectively, but lost detailed financial control over staffing levels; and the central contribution to police expenditure became cash-limited. The sharpest change impacted on police authorities, with the move from their former concern with the detail of force provisioning to a strategic policy role. They had to establish local priorities, a costed plan, and set the force's overall budget; but the local plans had to fit into an overall national framework, while satisfying a public now construed both as 'customers' and as 'active citizens' who must play their part. Civilian staff became employees of the chief constable rather than of the police authority, joining officers in a 'unitary management structure' (Home Office, 1993b: para. 3.8). The philosophy was intended to percolate down, with the 'Basic Command Unit' (the former 'divisions') functioning under its local commander and more closely tied to the inhabitants of its 'sector'. There was to be devolution of managerial authority, and responsibility, down from politicians to professionals and from senior to middle ranks.

Accountability was partly addressed within these moves by the new local objective-setting and performance indicators. Vertically, the local command units were answerable to the chief, who answered to the police authority in terms of the local objectives and plan, which in turn answered to the Home Secretary who represented the national framework of objectives and performance indicators. Work to engender co-operation was served by the plan dialogue and new 'partnerships' with local agencies. Police authorities were reconstituted, with fewer local authority members, more Home Office appointees from the 'general community' (often the business community) and the chair was a Home Office appointee. Senior officers were particularly hostile to the provision for salaried police authority chairs appointed by the Home Secretary, not least because the incumbent, Michael Howard, was a reactionary who prioritised locking up more offenders ahead of addressing the causes of crime ('Police bill "risks local crime fight"', *Guardian*, 17 January 1994). When fighting to secure control of the new police authorities Howard even suggested involving Lord-Lieutenants alongside a corporate headhunter to select the Home Office appointees, a suggestion undermined by news that 12 out of 51 Lord-Lieutenants were Conservative peers or former Conservative MPs, 12 were retired Field-Marshals or Admirals, eight held knighthoods, most had attended Eton and all were male ('Whitelaw tilts at Police Bill', *Guardian*, 18 January 1994). Those puzzled why Howard was so attached to wresting control from local authorities speculated a connection with the fact that Conservatives controlled only five of the 41 police authorities ('Howard strives to quell Lords revolt', *Guardian*, 20 January 1994). In the event, authorities were given power to appoint their own chair and flexibility in the overall number of members (Home Office News Release 21/94, 2 February 1994), and plans to allow the Home Secretary to appoint a third of authority members were dropped ('Howard in new U-turn on Police Bill', *Guardian*, 16 February 1994). Local councillors retained a (bare) majority, and the independent members were not, as planned, appointed by the Home Secretary.

When it came to legislating the changes, much of Sheehy was also dropped. There was to be no performance-related pay, fixed contracts were restricted to ACPO ranks, the starting salary stood as before, and the rank of chief inspector was retained. However, policy options are the business of government and remain embedded in the civil service mind. In 2001 it was reported that the Prime Minister and Home Secretary wanted to see fast-track promotion to secure entrants direct from other professions to middle management of the police ('Blair to shake up police culture', *Guardian*, 17 February 2001). Entrants would skip the traditional initial two years on the beat, which remained even in the established accelerated promotion scheme for graduates. The Federation opposed the idea and no more was heard.

Legally, the Home Secretary added to responsibility for force efficiency a responsibility for force effectiveness. The central government prong of the tripartite system thus holds responsibility for strategic policy-making, oversight of police authorities, oversight of chief constables, budgetary powers, the responsibilities of the Inspectorate, detailed regulation, central services, and alteration of force areas. Strategic policy-making through this framework in the 1990s and into the 21st century was characterised by the principles of the Crime and Disorder Act 1998, with its emphasis on multi-agency strategies for preventing and reducing crime. The Home Secretary can direct police authorities to establish performance targets to achieve the national objectives. The Home Secretary's battery of new powers over police authorities consolidated that office's status as 'senior partner' in the policy function. When considered alongside the 'informational' role the Home Secretary has with respect to chief constables (as well as long-standing personnel and budgetary powers) and the enhanced role of the Inspectorate, which is in effect appointed by the Home Secretary, one might suggest that central government and the relevant minister holds senior partner status for much more than strategic policy.

The Police and Magistrates Court Act 1994 added the Met to the Inspectorate's brief, a requirement parallel to the Home Secretary's to look at effectiveness as well as efficiency, and special inspections where the Home Secretary is doubtful about effectiveness and efficiency (Home

Office News Release 302/94, 14 December 1994). The Inspectorate, under a Labour amendment to the Police Act 1996, has a role in the Best Value initiative, and this gives it oversight of police authorities' compliance with the requirement to effect continuous improvement in delivering its functions. The Inspectorate thus takes a role over two of the tripartite parties (Walker, 2000: 114–15). At local authority level the 1997 Labour victory and a referendum in 1998 led to London getting its own police authority, although the Home Secretary retained special responsibility for the Met's national and international functions. As to chief constables, the new framework stressed the complex interdependence of the role with the other tripartite parties, and has extended personnel and financial powers acquired from the police authorities, including powers over civilian staff. While such powers are real, it is undeniable that, where before chiefs had recourse to constabulary independence, the new emphasis on interdependence and the obligation to orientate to the police authority's plan significantly confines the chief's autonomy.

In Jones and Newburn's (1997) judgment, and that of other authorities (Loveday, 1998; Johnston, 2000), the restructured tripartite system has not effected as far-reaching changes as anticipated. The Home Office used its new powers over objectives to consolidate its existing capacity. The objectives and performance indicators grew steadily sharper after initial over-generalised ones, and all police forces gradually became more drawn in to their application. Similarly, police authorities were slow to develop their new role, and there is little evidence of the new 'independent members' making much difference, although they have helped to depoliticise police authorities (Walker, 2000: 140). Certainly the selection panels for the independent members were packed with senior management types and Conservatives ('BT to help police mean business', *Guardian*, 9 August 1994), and Michael Howard's choice as chair of the first Met Police Committee was a bank chairman with no police experience, who did not live in London (*Guardian*, 5 December 1994). Jones and Newburn (1997) perceived a typology of police authorities – the 'rubber stampers' with minimal involvement in the policing plan, the re-drafters who got involved in the consultation process, and the 'junior partners' who had greatest involvement in the plan process. Thus, even at the most vigorous end of the spectrum the police authority is subordinate to the chief. Further, police authorities still seem most concerned with internal managerial and organisational objectives rather than larger strategic issues. Generating their own data to balance that controlled by police remained a minority activity. It seems that the police authorities have benefited least from the new framework, while the chiefs have gained most. The picture is one of enhanced managerial control.

Command of police forces was for much of modern policing's history informed by a military model. Chief constables were either drawn from the military or emerged from policing's 'officer class'. Post-Second World War, the product of Trenchard's officer class steadily retired and chief officers increasingly were men who had risen from the ranks. By the 1990s, Reiner (1992: 56–57) observed that most chiefs came from manual working-class or routine non-manual origins, as did the generality of police, but had risen to the top 'by dint of merit rather than social pedigree' and combined 'street wisdom with intellectual potential'. His comprehensive study of chiefs suggested a group who blended 'the best characteristics of the traditional British bobby with the managerial skills of the efficient bureaucrat' (Reiner, 1992: vii). The balance is important in understanding the instinctive preferences and approaches of chief officers. Particularly important in the context of accountability is the strong, even aggressive, insistence on the special insight that police experience affords, relative to the other partners, in accountability mechanisms, tripartite or otherwise.

New Labour administrations have adjusted the post-1994 mechanism rather than sweep it away, and retained the managerialist, business-model set in train by the Conservatives. This has altered the sphere in which chiefs operate. A main mechanism was the investment in a real, rather than presentational, partnership approach. Hence the importance of chiefs' ingrained insistence on being pre-eminent, especially in operational decisions. Since such arguments register ill with other parties to the accountability mechanism, it behoved chiefs to spread the ambit of 'operational' decisions as wide as they possibly could. Reiner (1992: 251) observed that the chiefs' idea of a good police authority is 'one which acts as a sounding-board for local opinion but which does not ultimately question the chief's decisions'. As one chief told Reiner, '"this tripartite arrangement is based on the fact that you are a reasonable individual, they (police authority) are reasonable, and the Home Office is reasonable. And we will work together. I am accountable to the police committee, unless they were making a political decision about an operational matter, which the tripartite set-up obviates happening"' (Reiner, 1992: 251). In 2005 the Conservative opposition announced it favoured replacing police authorities with directly-elected 'police commissioners' (The 'Today Programme', BBC Radio 4, 10 February 2005). The Home Office view was that this could lead to a focus on a few high profile issues rather than addressing the needs of the whole community.

While the Home Office has powers to sanction chiefs, the source of chiefs' general inclination to abide by Home Office guidance is not so much because of its legitimacy derived from the electoral process, but because they see it as expressing 'the consensus of expert professional policing opinion' (Reiner, 1992: 271). ACPO and Her Majesty's Inspectorate (HMI) both interact with the Home Office, after all, so there is a consensual process of policy formulation. Only when this breaks down are chiefs reluctantly guided by the sanctions the Home Office has on its side. Home Office circulars are, then, regarded as virtually mandatory. Moreover, chiefs gave Reiner (1992: 274) numerous instances of central government intervention in specific operational matters, 'usually in important public order conflicts', classically labour disputes. Reiner's judgment was that 'the line of accountability for chief constables is tilted increasingly towards the centre' (1992: 285).

While Reiner (2000b: 189) characterised the situation under the 1964 tripartite arrangements as one where police authorities 'paid the piper but did not call any tunes', the revised arrangements under the Police and Magistrates' Courts Act 1994 little changed the picture because of 'differing power dynamics between the police authority and the chief constable, and an understandable reluctance on the part of those without specialist knowledge to make decisions about operational matters' (Bowling and Foster, 2002), leaving power to concentrate further in the hands of chiefs (Jones and Newburn, 1996; Savage *et al*, 2000). Related to this, but also to Home Office and Audit Commission policy, is the shift away from political to managerial accountability (Savage *et al*, 2000: 26–30), reflected in the setting of national policing objectives and performance targets, and standardisation of recruitment, equipment and training. The reigning metaphor is one of 'customers' (the public) purchasing services rather than responsiveness to elected bodies and principles of equity.

If policing has partly been refashioned on a business enterprise model, the process reflects the demerits as well as gains of such an approach when applied to the delivery of public sector services. A major problem is that of finding meaningful and convincing performance measures. Many police services remain ineluctable, and it cannot be said after some years of operation under the new framework that the performance culture is yet deeply embedded in any thoughtful way. Indeed, some of the more simple-minded performance measures, such as answering station phones within a certain number of rings, have plainly distorted police effort in rather meaningless directions. Moreover, for all its technocratic neutrality, the performance culture approach cannot avoid the major and unresolved political questions about priorities and tradeoffs. The perennial local/central tensions have not gone away, even if they have been obscured by management-speak. When initiatives are not 'owned', the canny turn to the achievement of a mock compliance behind which they can carry on by their own lights. The effective invisibility of much operational work and the failure to identify performance measures that address the qualitative factors that outweigh in the public mind measures like instantly answering station phones leave much scope for tactical play. It is even possible that under this construction of accountability the explosion of useless or insignificant, if precise, information leaves the system less accountable and transparent than before. This is particularly likely if the public (*qua* consumer/voter) sees the audit culture as too readily manipulable by politicians, with the reining in of police authorities leaving only the remote central state and the chief constable, as chief executive officer (CEO), holding real power. Nor has the new framework done much to resolve the potential conflicts between the tripartite parties. It could hardly be otherwise where the principal instrument was largely to encourage a spirit of co-operation. The overall picture is one where none of the parties are entirely confident of their position or their relations with the others. This is not a strong basis to engender a robust culture of co-operation or of accountability.

Codes of Practice

If citizens cannot look to constitutional protections for accountability they must look to the law. This is a mechanism of last resort, though, because it necessarily relates to individual cases rather than general policy. The Codes of Practice under the Police and Criminal Evidence Act 1984 that replaced the Judges' Rules have a broader scope, covering detention, treatment and questioning of suspects, identification and search and seizure. They have substantially evolved since implementation. The Codes seek to closely regulate police performance, and include many restrictions on police powers. However, breach does not occasion criminal proceedings, but internal disciplinary action. The Codes primarily attempt to regulate routine exercise of powers rather than provide legal recourse for malpractice. An important instance is the treatment of the legal prerequisite for stop and search, 'reasonable suspicion', which is subject to substantial explanation, including instructions warning officers against stops and searches based on racism or hostility to 'street people'. Skin colour cannot in itself be reasonable grounds, nor carrying a particular item, nor mode of dress, hairstyle, nor a previous conviction for unlawful possession. A further intended safeguard is the device of making a specific senior officer personally responsible for decisions concerning the welfare of suspects or prolongation of detention. The Home Office first revised the Codes in 1989. Guidance on reasonable suspicion and stops was shortened, but retained reference to not acting simply on the basis of stereotype. Officers searching premises must issue a notice of their authority and the occupiers' rights. More information about access to legal advice was to be given those held in custody, and interrogators have to show those detained the interview record. Following the Macpherson Inquiry, new procedures were implemented in the conduct and recording of street stops/searches, with written records of stops being issued to subjects, although few seem to welcome the time that preparing them adds to the encounter (Miller *et al*, 2002).

The key issue is practical application and enforcement. It hinges on the willingness of middle-ranking officers to take the Codes seriously and monitor their use. Breach is more readily detectable at some stages of the process than others; it is less effective regarding behaviour on the street. Even where supervision is more readily undertaken, such as during detention and questioning, much depends on the attitude and diligence of custody and review officers. Disciplinary proceedings in relation to, for example, right of access to lawyers or nature of the caution given, are discretionary (their breach 'shall not of itself render them liable to any criminal or civil proceedings': s 67.10 of the Police and Criminal Evidence Act (PCEA) 1986) and, while this is necessary to condone trivial infractions and those resulting from poor training and misunderstanding, the discretion is open to misuse if senior officers are complacent or collusive (Lustgarten, 1986: 129–30; Lustgarten, 2002). No firm exclusionary rule on evidence unlawfully obtained stiffens the safeguards.

The 1993 Royal Commission on Criminal Justice found a widespread practice of interrogation of suspects prior to arrival at police stations, where custody suite procedures apply; 31% of suspects were questioned before arrest to establish whether a crime was committed and 8% were interviewed outside the police station. While relevant law distinguished 'questioning' (done 'to obtain an explanation of the facts' and not constituting an interview, therefore carrying no obligation to be recorded) and 'interviewing' (done to establish involvement in an offence, with recording compulsory), the distinction appeared not to be fully understood (Moston and Stephenson, 1993).

The case of the 'Cardiff Three', wrongfully convicted of murdering a prostitute, drew attention to lapses between PCEA provisions and the conduct of interrogations. The Court of Appeal was 'horrified' by the tape recording of the interview of one suspect, who they judged had effectively been brainwashed into confessing. He had been 'bullied and hectored', and one detective's 'pace, force and menace' was 'impossible to convey on the printed page' ('Wrongful conviction due to "human error"', *Guardian*, 17 December 1992). The suspect, who bordered on being mentally handicapped, had denied involvement 300 times, but the officers had made clear they would keep asking until he agreed their version of events. The Inspectorate warned police to stick to PCEA rules after the Appeal Court judge said the case was one of 'human error' rather than failure of the rules. Random samples of interviews should be made by supervisors, and officers using bad techniques should have remedial training (*Guardian*, 12 December 1992).

Evidence that is unfairly obtained is not normally inadmissible. The exclusionary rule in the Act is confined to cases where the prosecution fail to rebut oppression or circumstances rendering the confession unreliable. The courts *could* be stricter – there is a discretion to exclude evidence unfairly obtained – but it is little used. Similarly, many consent to 'voluntary' searches although the 2003 Codes of Practice bar such searches. Guidance says that suspicion informing a stop should be no less than that required to arrest for the offence suspected. Where no one is present except the citizen and officer concerned, the disciplinary process can only be set in motion by a formal complaint, making enforcement of the Code reliant on the effectiveness of the complaints system.

Revised Codes were issued in 1994, covering the use of stop and search powers, searches of premises, and the treatment, questioning and identification of suspects (Home Office News Release 153/94, 18 August 1994). Police gained a power to stop and search people and vehicles in the street without reasonable suspicion where they believe violence is imminent or to protect against terrorism. Detailed guidance was issued on the conduct of intimate and strip searches, and on taking non-intimate (DNA) samples. A new form of the police caution permitted inferences to be drawn from a suspect's silence. The proposed wording initially was 'You do not have to say anything. But if you do not mention now something which you later use in your defence, the Court may decide that your failure to mention it now strengthens the case against you. A record will be made of anything you say and it may be given in evidence if you are brought to trial'. The caution was regarded as 'wordy' by the Federation, and the Law Society forecast an extra £46 million in additional legal advice costs and longer trials as a result of the wording. Lawyers would use the lengthy wording to argue their clients were confused and misled by it ('New police caution alarms legal experts', *Independent*, 20 August 1994), and thus inferences about silence could not be drawn. The Law Society thought most police would be unable to explain what it meant if asked by suspects. Research found that 42% of A level students could not understand it. The average IQ of suspects in police stations being 82, and most A level students scoring above the average of 100, problems were likely (*Guardian*, 7 December 1994). The caution was cut to 37 words when the revised Codes went before Parliament: 'You do not have to say anything. But it may harm your defence if you do not mention when questioned something which you later rely on in court. Anything you do say may be given in evidence'

('Relief all round as rewritten police caution cut to 37 words', *Guardian*, 1 February 1995).

While legal attention focussed on fine-tuning the Codes, and are further discussed in Chapter 7, the increases in recorded stops after implementation, as police became more comfortable with the accounting required, and the high levels of unrecorded stops observed in inner-city policing (Fielding *et al*, 1992; Fielding, 2001b), suggest the limitations of the Codes. As a mechanism of accountability they share with the complaints process the problems of being *post hoc*, subject to interpretation, and focused on individual cases.

Local consultative arrangements

Independent consultation was long thought of as obstructive and unhelpful by police, but in recent years senior officers have come to regard it as a means to gather information about crime and disorder not available from other sources, as well as having a role in oversight of policing arrangements (Bowling *et al*, 2004). It offers a means to build public confidence and trust and, where there is real public engagement, to challenge narrow police thinking. The breakdown of police/public consultation was cited as a contributory factor in the 1980s riots (Warren and Tredinnick, 1982: 16). Subsequently s 106 of the PCEA 1984 required all police authorities to make arrangements to obtain 'the views of people in that area about matters concerning policing of that area' and 'their cooperation with the police in preventing crime'. However s 106 did not *require* new or formal machinery, and, particularly in non-urban areas, no provision beyond the customary attendance at parish council meetings was made. Arrangements were consolidated in s 96 of the Police Act 1996. Consultative arrangements have latterly come under the aegis of Crime and Disorder Reduction Partnerships. The situation is one of substantial variability in arrangements, reflecting research-based recommendations that police forces and authorities compile their own aims for consultation reflecting local circumstances (Elliott and Nicholls, 1996: 66). There is generally considerable joint working between police authorities and police forces on consultation. Indeed some authorities empower their forces to undertake the majority of consultation (Home Office, 2003a).

When the committees were introduced, local government was hostile to them, seeing them as undermining the campaign for full accountability or as implying problems with police where there were none. The main problem is representativeness. In Islington, the inaugural public meeting to receive nominations was attended by 16 people, mostly tenants' association representatives. No ethnic minority representatives came. In the end the Council had to nominate members. In prosperous Sutton, the Council unilaterally decided who the community representatives would be, with a third of places for the Chamber of Commerce. In Hillingdon, the Council opted for five councillors, three council officers and four police, with community organisations barred from attendance and the meetings held secretly. Widespread apathy and disengagement means that 'the few who are involved tend to be repeatedly consulted by agencies, resulting in "overload" and "fatigue"' (Home Office, 2003a: 3), this particularly being a problem for voluntary organisations; such problems affected half the police authorities researched. Responsiveness to consultation was not encouraged by the fact that feedback on the outcome of consultations was piecemeal.

As implemented, statutory consultation falls foul of satisfying the demand for accountability without relinquishing control. The fact that the traditional Police Community Consultation Group-type public meeting remains the principal consultation mechanism means that the problems early identified with them still mark the process; one official assessment noted that 'it has long been recognised that these meetings fail to attract a representative audience and to generate a meaningful output on strategic issues' (Home Office, 2003a: 3). Independent assessments also deem Police Community Consultation Groups (PCCGs) 'ineffective [and] unrepresentative' (Bowling and Foster, 2002) and as having neither 'the information nor independence to critically evaluate police proposals' (Loveday, 2000: 218). PCCGs are a poor vehicle for change for a reason familiar from other accountability arrangements – they do not relate to 'the principal areas of police activity' (CRE, 1991: 30). A tract influential on the initial development of PCCGs declared 't]here may be a requirement to explain a course of action ... but this does not mean that the persons to whom a course of action has been explained have the power to reject or amend the course of action' (Warren and Tredinnick, 1982: 13). This was no advance on the chief constables' position that they are prepared to give reasons, but that is all. Three-quarters of police authorities still run PCCGs 'despite none considering them to be very effective' (Home Office, 2003a: 3). The dilemma was well put by police testimony to the Scarman Inquiry.

> [H]ow can you tell community leaders ... that you are about to mount a saturation operation which will undoubtedly antagonise a large number of citizens going about their lawful business, and which in addition requires secrecy for its effectiveness ... and then not call it off when community leaders tell you that a general disturbance is likely? (Quoted in Cowell and Lea, 1982: 148)

Consultation may be statutory, but it remains advisory, and the options of saturation tactics, secret operations, timing and deployment remain with police. It is hardly surprising that latterly there has been a large increase in use of other consultative mechanisms, such as market research; consultative mechanisms fail particularly to reach groups, such as ethnic minorities and people with disabilities (Jones and Newburn, 2001; Newburn and Jones, 2002). There are dangers of meetings being 'hijacked' by individuals with special interests, but the problem is more often public apathy (Home Office, 2003a: 5).

The evidence of ongoing public concern about the composition of police authorities, which at least include elected representatives of the community, suggests that the openness of PCCGs to skewed membership as a result of their more *ad hoc* arrangements is likely to prompt strong reservations about their decisions (Home Office, 2003a: 2). Official rather than ordinary representatives continue to dominate, extending the role of established interests rather than enfranchising the marginal. Police dominate proceedings, providing administrative services and sometimes venues. Individual cases and allegations against officers, cannot be discussed, although these may be the matters preoccupying residents. Other matters require police approval before they can be discussed at PCCG meetings, including the deployment of officers and method of operations. Particularly in suburban, rural and prosperous areas the committees are moribund, the membership apathetic, the discussion trivial; there is nothing to discuss and no significant business is put before committees.

The principal problem confronted by most local consultative committees remains that of engaging public participation, particularly amongst young people. The December 1998 meeting of the Isle of Wight police liaison committee attracted just 16 people (from a population of 130,000), most of whom were councillors, magistrates and representatives of youth and community services (*Isle of Wight County Press*, 11 December 1998). The youngest was middle-aged. No young person had ever attended any of the meetings. It seems perverse to focus precious resources on meetings that operate under heavy constraints and that few attend when it is already clear what communities want. Reinstatement of community policing is invariably welcomed, an instance being the reception given 'designated neighbourhood specialist officers' protected from other duties (*Guildford Times*, 24 August 2002). When Warwickshire's 1990s 'Back to the Future' initiative enabled community officers to work from their home villages, using their own home as offices, residents were delighted, particularly as the initiative addressed minor, but longstanding, public order problems (*Guardian*, 24 March 1993).

Where police venture into interaction with the community it is usually on their own terms, and this is reinforced by low public awareness of police/public consultation mechanisms and a consensus that the public has no say in decisions about policing (Home Office, 2003a: 2). Like police authorities, PCCGs are heavily reliant on police for information, which can be selected to persuade committees to the police view. Community input is seldom sought on genuine decisions over policy, and proceedings sometimes have the character of no more than consensual impression-management. If enhanced accountability is a means to ameliorate police/public conflict the answer does not lie here. Problems beyond the reach of police authorities, with their long history, cannot be solved by making statutory a body of uncertain membership and no powers.

An alternative to this unhappy circumstance is the overstepping of constitutional propriety. In 2005, police in the Holy Trinity district of Guildford 'pledged' that 'priorities set by the residents ... will become the top concerns for the police' (*Surrey Advertiser*, 14 January 2005). While this showed welcome responsiveness, the mechanism may be less welcome. 'The community has been asked to attend a public meeting where they will be asked to vote on the single issue that concerns them most [and] the police have promised that the issue with the highest number of votes will then become their main focus in the area' (*Surrey Advertiser*, 14 January 2005). The Police Community Support Officers (PCSOs) who organised the meeting said '"[w]e we have adopted this new way of policing which allows residents to decide what issues we concentrate on in the community."' Priorities would be reviewed at subsequent meetings. As students of politics know, direct democracy is vulnerable to problems of representativeness; those with a particular interest can organise people to pack out meetings, and such meetings are inherently discriminatory because the elderly, the overworked and those with mobility problems have difficulty attending. Further, the articulation of strongly-held, but competing, views in such a forum could be divisive and raise innate conflicts not reconcilable by police interventions, or expectations not achievable with the resources available. While the Crime and Disorder Act 1998 requires local authorities and police to consult the public, the fact is that consultation is not the same as accountability (Bayley and Shearing, 1996). Honing existing mechanisms and creating new ones is not an adequate means to make good the deficit in legal and political accountability.

Measuring and managing performance

Delivery of public services has been profoundly reconfigured in the last 30 years by the routine use of performance indicators and targets, and some read these as an alternative accountability mechanism. During much of the 1980s, the police were largely protected from the performance measurement regime imposed on public services, such as education and health. However, as Loader and Mulcahy (2003) chart in their 'de-sacralization' thesis, since the 1990s performance indicators and measures have become integrated into the routines of policing and have reconfigured the structures of police governance. They have also exposed long-standing dilemmas, as illustrated by the case of the Met as an early adopter of performance measurement. Ahead of other forces, the Met in 1993 introduced response time targets, with officers expected to arrive within 12 minutes of urgent requests for service 75% of the time, respond to non-urgent requests within eighteen minutes 90% of the time, answer 999 phone calls within 15 seconds 80% of the time, to assist callers without delay 75% of the time, and to achieve public satisfaction with 90% of crime victims and 80% of callers at police stations ('London police to get response targets', *Guardian*, 30 August 1993). Response figures were published quarterly. However, the targets sat uneasily against a policy shift to focus on 'prolific offenders' even if it meant no longer responding to some types of minor crime ('Police to be told to ignore minor crimes', *Guardian*, 20 September 1993).

The conviction that elaborated performance measures were necessary to monitor and evaluate service delivery, and that police performance should be responsive to performance indicators, was not so much due to public calls for reform as it was a result of the application of private-sector management principles to the public sector. The key programme was the Financial Management Initiative. Pressure for 'effectiveness and efficiency' using market-led business techniques informed Home Office Circular 114/83, 'Manpower, Effectiveness and Efficiency in the Police Service'. Among new management strategies was 'Policing by Objectives', giving 'value for money'. Under the Police and Magistrates Court Act 1994, the Home Office set national objectives. Police authorities had to set performance targets to achieve the objectives. The then-Home Secretary Michael Howard set the first key objectives for the police service for the financial year 1994–95, including to 'maintain and if possible increase the number of detections for violent crime', to raise the detection rate for burglary, to work in partnership with local agencies against local crime problems, to provide reassurance via high visibility policing, and to promptly respond to emergency calls (Home Office News Release 282/93, 3 December 1993). Performance indicators were specified for each objective. Emphasis on crime prevention, local consultation and inter-agency working, increased. Home Office Circular 8/84 encouraged all agencies to participate in crime prevention and Circular 44/90 profiled successful partnership working. This approach was sustained by New Labour in the Crime and Disorder Act 1998. Along with the emphasis on partnership, the Act imposed a requirement for

'Best Value' and strict performance measures using crime clear-up rates.

However, the new orientation to intelligence-led, risk-oriented and inter-agency 'partnership' policing has eroded the adequacy of the measures tracking police performance. None of the new emphases is adequately addressed by established measures, none has an unproblematically direct or straightforward relation to crime rates and none of the policy initiatives has been accompanied by equally determined efforts to put in place systematic tests of their effect. Performance indicators for the police service cover six areas: call management, crime management, traffic management, public order management/police visibility on patrol, community policing management and resources/costs. Each measure in each area is owned ('required') either by Her Majesty's Inspectorate of Constabulary (HMIC), ACPO or the Audit Commission (no indicator is shown as required by the public). Each measure is represented by an 'indicator' and expressed as a 'data requirement' from a 'source'. For example, within the 'call management' performance indicator, there are several items relating to emergency calls, one of which sets a local target time for answering the call and another of which is 'the percentage of 999 calls answered within that target'. The indicator is 'required' by the Audit Commission, the data requirement is 'total calls answered within target' and the source is an HMIC data table. The performance of each force can then be compared in terms of adherence to its locally determined target time, and no doubt forces internally compare adherence by their different BCUs. Call management is entirely represented by quantitative indicators. Each suite of performance indicators is supported by a commentary. It is here that the performance management regime acknowledges the complexities that cannot be captured by a stopwatch. For example, the commentary notes that 'the indicators do not take account of the nature or seriousness of incidents, which need to be borne in mind when making comparisons between forces and over time' and that 'speed of response, although important, is but one measure of police service delivery'. It answers its own conundrum by saying the problem is fixed by the requirement that forces conduct public satisfaction surveys. However, research methodologists have for the last 50 years shown that such surveys are incapable of giving more than a broad-brush picture lacking in precisely the detail that is necessary to understand things as complex as satisfaction with public services (Deutscher, 1973), and the only official criteria for assessing the quality of the surveys are 'sample size' and 'percentage satisfaction'.

While response times, clear-up rates and other measures generated by the criminal justice system can trace the outline of police activities it is also recognised that awareness of the measures can lead to a dysfunctional level of orientation to them. Officers focus on optimising activities indexed by the measures. If there is a performance indicator (PI) for answering the phone, officers will sit by the phone. Personnel resources being finite, this is at the cost of activities less directly measured. Authoritative proof of this came in the multiple-method study of public and police attitudes in London (FitzGerald *et al*, 2002). Those behind performance measure regimes are not unaware of the limitations of purely count-based measures. Indeed, the Home Office sought advice on devising measures for community policing some 20 years ago (the author was among those approached). The National Policing Plan 2003–2006 lays down new clusters or 'domains' of measures: citizen focus, reducing crime, promoting public safety, investigating crime, resource usage. These 'performance monitors' are explicitly designed as multi-dimensional and as providing a sophisticated means to make force comparisons; but there is no indication that the information 'behind' the measures will show any gain on the purely quantitative data, notably those generated by the police themselves, that invest the current performance indicators.

Despite numerous critical assessments of the short time-horizon, reactive, and narrowly result-oriented perspective of the police in routine 'relief' mode, the limits of a performance measure understanding of police work do not escape officers. They have, after all, been trained in the importance of discretion and socialised into recognised ways of exercising it. The reciprocal of a broad mandate and legal empowerment is that officers work with substantial practical autonomy. This feeds awareness of the extent of their activity that remains uncaptured by performance measures. Such lacunae trouble officers who rightly seek credit for more subtle and long-sighted work, and deny the organisation an accurate view of what its officers are doing. Legally the distinguishing feature of the police amongst state institutions is their ability legitimately to use physical force to regulate social order (Bittner, 1974). The thrust of Bittner's argument is that, while the police role is wide-ranging, everything they do falls into place when one recognises force as the distinguishing feature of their office. However, physical force is, empirically, a minor means of resolving the general run of circumstances with which the police deal, and explanation of a large share of police work is little-advanced by reference to the forceful authority officers ultimately enjoy. The kinds of demand potentially calling for force are well-covered by straightforward (if contested) measures, such as arrest rates, clearance rates and crime pattern analysis (Innes, Fielding and Cope, 2004). Similarly, there are measures such, as response times (of various kinds), to gauge what the police do in their 'emergency function'; but such occurrences are relatively rare and, set against overall time on the job, they are not the empirical core of police work. Neither the legal powers of the police nor the emergency function account for policing in empirical terms. Measures are needed that capture the breadth of police work and do so in ways the police and public find meaningful. Without these, performance measurement remains a highly misleading mechanism of police accountability.

7. Tomorrow's headlines today |

Media and polity

Whatever the social scientific reality of the police role in social conflict, both political institutions and mass media have recurrent needs to present the 'reality' in certain ways to achieve instrumental, ideological and rhetorical ends. Recognising this, the police have increasingly sought to control their image in the media. Many observers have remarked on the moves to take the public platform on the part of senior officers that emerged in the 1970s and from which police have never looked back (Reiner, 2003).

The 'information explosion' accompanying the internet, mobile telephony able to deliver media pages to phone screens, and satellite TV, has not transformed the police move to control information. Rather than a few outlets relaying stories that could substantially vary according to the journalists 'in' with police contacts, the 21st century audience has thousands of outlets relaying exactly the same story. There is little point in journalists being police 'accredited' when stories are ghostwritten at New Scotland Yard or the Home Office; we are no longer in the age of the 'scoop', but the age of the press release. If proof were needed that the police have got wise to impression management one only has to reflect that it is the essence of one of the major emphases of contemporary policing, 'reassurance policing' (Fielding *et al*, 2002), which is concerned not with the reality of the crime rate, but the public perception of the crime rate.

Worries over the media generally do not go far behind the scenes of news production, but concentrate on the effects of reportage. News coverage of spectacular challenges to order, such as riots and terrorist attacks, plays a key role in fuelling fears about social breakdown and mobilising support for tough responses. A more subtle media effect is the negative tenor of reports on inner-city areas, so those without direct contact are prompted to see them as problems. We must appreciate how much these effects are due to the practicalities of news production rather than distortion and political manipulation. Police and government sources get more cover than community leaders and others able to speak to conditions in dispriviledged areas because they are easy to contact, skilled at uttering juicy quotes, and feed the journalist's ego at being conduits from elite to mass. Local people and community representatives are hard to contact, often inhibited, and may be concerned about identifying themselves. Similarly, following public order incidents police injuries may appear greater than injuries to others because officers must report injury, and totals are kept conveniently and centrally. Injured participants may avoid treatment in case of identification, so there is no reliable injury list. Footage of major public order incidents is usually from behind or beside police lines. Police policy encourages this and photographers know it is the safest position. This encourages people to see the event through police eyes. If footage were shot from behind demonstrators the view would be of a paramilitary phalanx. The first image reinforces demands for more riot equipment while the second prompts reflection on how things have become so bad that it takes police in riot gear to control people.

A notable thing about 21st century protests and demonstrations is the use of digital video (and similarly equipped mobile phones) by protest organisers and participants so there is a record independent of police, as in the autumn 2004 Westminster protest at the parliamentary vote on hunting with hounds, where independent footage enabled organisers to claim their people had not initiated the violence. Video is also *de rigueur* for campaigning journalism. An undercover BBC journalist who joined Greater Manchester police in 2003 to investigate racism filmed serious instances, but was arrested. Police claimed he could be liable to charges of using deception to obtain pecuniary advantage. However, he had deliberately kept his police pay in a separate account with a view to post-investigation repayment ('BBC man arrested on undercover job as police recruit', *Guardian*, 16 August 2003). The footage showed an officer wearing a Ku Klux Klan hood and saying he would like to 'bury' an Asian under a train and that Stephen Lawrence had 'deserved it', that his parents were a 'pair of spongers', and that Hitler had the 'right idea' (*Guardian*, 5 March 2005). No officers were sacked as a result of the footage, but 10 resigned after the programme. Following an Independent Police Complaints Commission (IPCC) investigation, 12 officers were disciplined and the IPCC recommended a review of recruitment procedure to identify 'unacceptable personality traits' and for selection panels for police trainers to include independent members. While this speaks to the affordances of new technology, where alternative footage exists the issue is whether it will be taken up by the media. The existence of independent recordings of events such as the May Day protests and the demonstrations against the policies of the G8 countries on international aid and development had to compete with the official line that the demonstrations represented violent anarchist confrontations. The independent recordings often indicated the good-natured manner of the protestors in the face of brusque handling by riot police, but coverage by major networks was constrained by corporate considerations and editorial policy informed by the need for 'balance'. In the US the rise of the 'neo-conservative' and Christian fundamentalist interest has become a blatant inhibitor on open reporting, but all media organisations are subject in some measure to interests other than simply reporting all the news that's fit to print.

Even without such pressures the media continually face the problem of quickly telling a 'story' that makes sense. Protests and riots easily solve the problem of creating interest, having the classic ingredients of a good story: dramatic and violent action, many participants, political implications; but it is harder to examine the original incident that triggered rioting and harder still the accumulation of resentment over policing. A senior newsman complained of the Brixton coverage that no one had adequately explained why the riots were happening (Murdoch, 1984: 80). Fear of the crowd and of rebellious youth fuels superficial analyses. The image of predatory delinquent gangs crystallised when the London Hooligans were reputedly formed by Patrick O'Hooligan, a Lambeth street fighter of the 1900s. The term was generalised to apply to almost any outbreak of public disorder in which youth were involved or adults behaved like adolescents. Rioting is sometimes depicted in such terms, as an outbreak of adolescent hooliganism, and we know that in the 1980s riots 'copying other areas' was the second most popular reason given by rioters in Handsworth and 50% of them first learned of the riots through the media – 31% via TV (Southgate 1982); but reporting cannot cause disturbances where the conditions do not already exist. The point is that it is necessary to explore the interaction between reporting and social ruptures rather than look for simple causation. Such is also the message of recent revisions of the established view that the period since 1945 has been marked by the dramatic 'demystification' of the police (Loader and Mulcahy, 2003). Combining analysis of official representations of policing and oral history interviews with police policy-makers and the public, Loader and Mulcahy find the symbolic and political significance of policing has stronger commonalities with previous periods than may be supposed. It seems that, while the 'golden age of policing' was more tarnished than we imagine, the public still responds to 'postmodern risk society' by first looking to the police.

The constable's authority

Law and order is fundamentally political. To sometime critics like Jack Straw MP, senior police were increasingly engaging in general political controversy in the 1980s, and 'the more they become involved in politics the less their case for seeking immunity from the democratic process' (quoted in Oliver, 1987: 73). It was not a view that endured until Straw's tenancy at the Home Office. The higher profile of senior officers, that Straw as Home Secretary did nothing to discourage, is another consequence of more open public debate about law enforcement and order maintenance. If the public is sufficiently mature to receive the opinions of police chiefs on contemporary society, then the police should be able to handle the public's opinion about the service it pays for. It does not take a politics degree to grasp that if the expression of conflict is suppressed the conflict does not go away, but takes other forms. The fact that such an essential tenet of democracy arouses in police a suspicion of 'sectarian' interference betrays the grip of an occupational culture with an insider/outsider barrier of awesome strength.

Police are extremely protective over their role in constructing law's daily administration. 'Operational' matters are seen broadly, extending to any choice the police make in interpreting the law. Yet in routine policing, the scope for alternative interpretations cannot escape even the dimmest constable. It is as if the lesson of discretion was not the selectiveness and contingency of police decision-making, but the minor corollary that, until challenged, a police decision bears the force of law. Yet it is that very selectiveness which supports the 'swift, situated, contexted judgment' that bolsters the notion that the constable's authority is original. The woeful case of *Fisher v Oldham Corporation* had effects beyond the 'original authority' debate, not only establishing that constables were not police authority servants, but were 'free from democratic control exercised by both local and central government' (Lustgarten, 1986: 60).

Legal authority is not the only cement to the constable's independence. The late Lord Scarman himself drew an analogy to judges. This position only stands if we accept that the legal matters the police handle are contentious, require impartial judgment, and are defined in detail. Not all police interventions involve contention between parties; there is no complaint nor evidence from non-police sources in various public order and traffic offences. Neither is the law always clear: it is notoriously difficult in assessing the likelihood of disorder and exercising powers of search. While these ambiguities could foreseeably be reconciled in the case of ordinary constables, equivalent clarification cannot be made to fit chiefs. Charged with a duty to enforce all the law against all known infractions, chiefs face two insurmountable obstacles. First, offences are under-reported, as victim surveys have established beyond doubt. Secondly, reported offences receive a response rationed by resources. The task of the chief constable cannot be reduced to that of simply dealing with all offences as they occur. Yet chiefs have long argued that their ultimate accountability to law excuses any deficiency of the formal accountability system.

When the law fails to guide, other factors must plainly be in play. In that respect, operational matters are intrinsically outside the bounds of constabulary independence. For a number of years following their introduction it was apparent that mobile phones endangered life if used when driving. Drivers are in fact four times more likely to be involved in a collision if they are using a mobile phone. Despite this, police argued that driver behaviour could be adequately regulated by existing laws on driving without due care and attention, and on dangerous driving. The matter could be left to discretion, and the discretion was theirs. Following the change in law in 2003, police found themselves issuing a rapidly increasing number of fixed penalty notices against drivers using mobile phones; 675 were issued in Surrey in the first six months (*Guildford Times*, 24 July 2004). A tougher approach was announced, with police using unmarked cars to catch yapping drivers, and prosecution rather than cautioning took place. Before the ban, police privately conceded that they did not want to see drivers barred from using mobile phones because they themselves regularly drove with one hand while using their police radio. The difficulty with the high-discretion approach is that the 'common sense' that mediates enforcement can become 'a cloak for conscious or unconscious discrimination on the basis of political opinion, personal appearance, demeanour, social status or race' (Lustgarten, 1986: 15). Helpfully, constables' 'original authority' is there to excuse it.

Law affords avenues for heightened police responsiveness to local priorities if police wish it. An instance was the tougher policies against racial harassment instituted by Tower Hamlets police some years before race hate laws were tightened. The local commander lowered the arrest threshold for racial attacks by treating minor assaults as actual bodily harm (ABH) rather than common assault. ABH carries a maximum of five years imprisonment and is an arrestable offence, but need only be unlawful touching and bruising. The move was not a narrowly legal decision, but implicitly political. It was followed by the Commissioner prioritising response to racial attacks. The doctrine of constabulary independence can be a means to achieve policing sensitive to the circumstances of different social groups without transforming accountability arrangements. It took many years of victimisation and lobbying before the police changed policy, and almost any other system of accountability would have been more responsive, but the 'legal mandate' is not the straitjacket it seems.

Whatever its value to police, and its occasional use as a source of brave policy innovation, operational independence finds only ambiguous expression in statute: its clearest form is in case law, namely Lord Denning's pronouncement in the first *Blackburn* case.

> I hold it to be the duty of the Commissioner of Police, as it is of every chief constable, to enforce the law of the land. He must take steps so to post his men that crimes may be detected; and that honest citizens may go about their affairs in peace. He must decide whether or no suspected persons are to be prosecuted ... but in all these things he is not servant of anyone, save of the law itself. No Minister of the Crown can tell him that he must, or must not, keep observation on this place or that; or that he must, or must not, prosecute this man or that one. Nor can any police authority tell him so. The responsibility for law enforcement lies on him. He is answerable to the law and to the law alone. (*R v Metropolitan Police Commissioner ex p Blackburn* [1968] All ER 769)

Of this passage Lustgarten observes, 'seldom have so many errors of law and logic been compressed into one paragraph' (1986: 64). The last four sentences of the passage quoted rest on the *Fisher* and *Perpetual Trustee* cases having nothing to do with chief constables or the kinds of policy decision taken by them. Denning may not be definitive, but we need to sketch in the substance of the *Blackburn* case.

Mr Blackburn was aggrieved that police were doing little against illegal gaming in casinos. He discovered the Commissioner had a policy requiring authorisation before observation inside clubs. He sought a mandamus against the Commissioner, seeking assistance in moving against the clubs. He failed but appealed.

> Seeking mandamus, he had to show absence of alternative remedy against the commissioner. Citing neither statute nor case law, merely relatively recent statements by civil servants or junior ministers, he contended that the chief officer was responsible to no political authority. Therefore he had to be responsible to the law, ie, to the courts: otherwise he would be responsible to no-one – a constitutional abomination. (Lustgarten, 1986: 63)

The only way Blackburn could maintain the police were above the law was to argue they were above all democratic institutions, because if the public were dissatisfied they could complain to the Home Secretary, who could instruct the chief. The Court of Appeal's conclusions 'rest upon acceptance of Mr Blackburn's argument that political controls normally governing public officials do not apply to the police'. As Marshall (1965), Lustgarten (1986) and Walker (2000) have argued, this ignores the checks and balances formally integral to the tripartite system. Denning also ignored the fact that the Commissioner is the chief officer most susceptible to ministerial control. Nor is the 'responsibility to law' adequately specified. Chiefs have a wide discretion in areas where courts would not interfere. This includes some policy decisions, but not others, for example whether not to prosecute for under-age sex would be left to the chief, but not a decision not to prosecute for theft of goods below a certain value. Yet the Court gave no criteria for determining where the chief's 'responsibility' was his solely or where it was judicially reviewable: what was said plainly reflected the personal opinions of the judges.

> [W]hy ... their peculiar perceptions of the behaviour of those 50 years younger than themselves (one commented that under-age sex would not be reviewed because these days many boys needed protecting from the girls), or even their view of the utility of a statute Parliament chose to retain after more than one review of the law, should command greater authority than the judgment of those responsible to the electorate, was never discussed. (Lustgarten, 1986: 66)

The 'definitive' case law prop securing constabulary independence for chief officers is tainted with factual error, historical error, logical error and crude value judgments.

The autonomy granted chief officers means their personal attitudes are a factor in the style of policing in their force. Reiner, who interviewed 40 chief constables, discerned a preoccupation with rising crime and a moral theory presuming a breakdown of family, religious and school controls; their dominant mental set was one of crisis (1992). As we have seen, when views coincide with government policy, chiefs take a different perspective on their independence from government and the avoidance of sectionalism; in the 1984–85 coal dispute, their action complicit with the government agenda 'bordered on zeal' (McCabe and Wallington, 1988: 134). That chief constables cannot in practice cloak themselves from policy review is also apparent *in extremis*. A chief who adopts controversial policies and resists advice and guidance can jeopardise the public co-operation necessary to control crime. This would threaten efficiency, and be grounds for dismissal. If a police authority seeks to remove a chief, referral is to the Home Secretary. Conflict in the 1980s and 1990s between chief constables and police authorities with Labour majorities suggests that if the chief can count on the Home Secretary's support the police authority can be ignored. Even authorities that passed motions of censure did not seek compulsory retirement, anticipating it would not be forthcoming. As sometime Merseyside Chief Kenneth Oxford declared: 'I have every Christian virtue except resignation'.

While chiefs backed by the Home Secretary can resist police authority censure, chiefs not in tune with a Home Secretary are vulnerable, even when backed by their police authority. In 2004 the Home Secretary sought to remove Humberside's chief constable following the failure of his force to provide Cambridgeshire Police with information about the criminal record of Ian Huntley, who obtained work as a school caretaker at Soham without the school knowing of his criminal record, and subsequently killed two young pupils, Jessica Chapman and Holly Wells.

The Humberside force had interpreted data protection laws in a way that limited what would be provided in response to requests. Under a protocol agreed in 2003 between Home Office, police, and local authorities, once the chief had been suspended, the case for his removal would be investigated by an independent inquiry before any final decision. The Humberside police authority refused to suspend the chief, who wished to see through changes to correct the deficiencies exposed after the child murders. Following a High Court injunction the chief was suspended ('Blunkett wins police chief battle', *Guardian*, 10 July 2004). The Police Reform Act 2002 makes clear that the Home Secretary has power to order a police authority to suspend and ultimately to dismiss their chief constable. The Bichard Report into the Soham murders provoked conflict between government and police authorities over the powers; Home Office lawyers accused the police authority of making a spectacle of itself by refusing to comply with its express legal duty; police authority lawyers argued that the Home Secretary's assessment of public confidence in the chief should purely have been on the basis of opinion in the force area rather than elsewhere. Local people were best able to judge if the force was 'effective and efficient'. Significantly, this argument was rejected by the judge on the basis that it would be wrong only to consider the impact of an ineffective force on public confidence in its own locale. Eventually the situation was resolved by compromise, which allowed the chief to return to work with an undertaking that he would retire early. This left the force and the county's residents with a chief who did not have the confidence of the Home Secretary and a police authority with diminished authority and influence (Sharp, 2005). It also signalled further erosion of local control, since the judge construed efficiency as a criterion for other than local determination. The chief may have taken some comfort in outlasting the Home Secretary, who was soon forced out of office in a sex scandal. Commentators said that the ruling had forever changed the relationship between police authorities and Home Secretary over who runs policing. The case said more about the limited powers of the police authority than it did about the relative power of the two dominant parties to the tripartite arrangement. It also contradicted the Home Office emphasis on local determination of priorities and local accountability.

Localism

The 1960 Royal Commission cited 'the local character of the office of constable', pre-Tudor in origin, as first in its list of long-standing principles of policing. Also listed was 'the subjection of police forces to a degree of local democratic supervision', established by 19th century legislation. Debating the 1964 legislation, the Home Secretary listed as legitimate matters for police authorities the allocation of officers between crime prevention and traffic policing, and between different areas; but it could not 'bombard' chiefs with questions about specific officers' actions on particular beats. The contrast suggests the poles between which 'operational' matters run, but as we have seen these have been subject to considerable revision. The meaning of 'operational' has gradually moved from being the converse of 'policy' to embracing it, with chiefs claiming ownership of both. Thus in 1985, the South Yorkshire chief declared that 'one of the purposes of the Police Act 1964 is to maintain a distinction between operational matters ... and administrative and financial responsibilities'. The latter was the province of police authorities, the rest was for chiefs. The trend to embody the chief as corporate CEO, associated with the managerialism that gathered pace in the 1990s, has undermined the distinction.

The line between 'policy' and 'operations' is indistinct. With respect to 'intelligence-led policing', whether information is mainly derived from secondary analysis of computerised databases, heavy use of informers, or the use of community contacts and partnership work is a matter of policy, but also relates to finances, as the different approaches have different costs, and also relates to 'operational' decisions because the different approaches involve different kinds of interaction with the public. Much of chiefs' reluctance to share responsibility around the policy/operational interface is their belief that because they must uphold the law without favour, they must not be influenced by the sectional interests of local politicians. Interestingly, they did not perceive as sectarian the magistrates who, until the Police Act 1996, selected from their own number those to serve on the police authority, and may be thought to have tended to the police view (under Sched 2 of the Act, magistrates were reduced to three, against nine councillors, and are chosen by a local selection panel independent of the judiciary). Plainly, the police are instinctively uncomfortable about 'politics', whether founded in a fervent regard for constitutional propriety or protection of a privileged degree of occupational autonomy. Oliver declared that 'traditional methods of policing in the UK are so important that they should not be controlled, either directly or indirectly, by the normal processes of democracy at local government level' (Oliver, 1987: 237). The 'normal' state referred to is a situation of partisan contest. Instead of 'normal' processes being desirable because they are the mechanism for citizen access and influence, they are distrusted because they represent party politics.

Yet, while local government became highly political in the Thatcher years, and more recent times have seen concern at its greater orientation to party politics, the two moments are not at all the same. The Thatcher period saw local politics as the only part of the political system susceptible to the Opposition influence, and engaged the public as seldom before, while the contemporary politicisation of local government has been accompanied by widespread public disengagement; but local issues do not go away, they merely vent through different channels, and what may be perceived as an urge toward more 'direct democracy' confronts a political mechanism once again out of kilter with the public. Where police reject 'sectarian' control on grounds that it contradicts the 'equality before the law' that they must uphold, it is on the basis that it would lead to different applications of the law in different locales. However there is more to it. Chiefs know how difficult it is to control subordinates. We do not hear much about the threat to the 'fundamental principle' of equality that is posed everywhere in the country every day by the exercise of police discretion.

There is compelling evidence that policing can be partial in respect both of preference for particular types of enforcement and targeting of particular types of suspects, only the preferences expressed are those of the police rather than the people. One example is the use of mobile patrols rather than community policing, another is the concentration of street stops on young males. It is absurd to suggest that policing is uniform throughout the country: I cannot behave at 11 pm on a suburban street as I may at that hour in the town centre, nor do the standards applicable to central London apply to rural villages. Chiefs confound responsiveness to the public with sectarianism. The demand is not for accountability to politicians, but to people. The public simply wants policing appropriate to the problems they see locally. This requires selectivity, not uniformity, and involves choices ordinary police negotiate daily.

Under the 'responsibilisation' approach of the 1990s, official thinking was increasingly about the limits of police impact on crime and the necessity of partnership with social agencies and public. As an early commentary on this said, [t]he police process those crimes which the public choose to discover, report and solve. They try to educate the public to understand the limits of police effectiveness, by encouraging us to take over responsibility for certain tasks ourselves' (*Guardian*, 18 July 1988). The new emphasis is on a partnership in crime prevention, which extends both the public and the police role through Neighbourhood Watch, paying informers through Crimestoppers, working on the public conscience through 'Crimewatch', and co-ordination with numerous other agencies and private organisations. It extends into the school, family and workplace in a way earlier societies would have found intolerable. Much public order work is already the province of private security guarding private space.

Such initiatives shift police from 'simple protectors of the community' to key players in the reconstruction of the moral order. Overactive preventative approaches involve a reversal of the foundational common law principles behind the relationship between police and community. This is founded on the idea that securing order is the precedent condition for crime control and that neither order nor law enforcement can be secured without public consent. Peel's single-minded belief that the main task was 'crime prevention' was not embraced even by Sir Richard Mayne, whose instructions in 1829 to the new Metropolitan Police endorsed 'the prevention of crime ... the protection of life and property, the preservation of public tranquillity' (Lustgarten, 1986: 22). The most sustained review of this doctrine in contemporary times was that in Scarman's Inquiry into the Brixton riots. When Scarman cited Mayne approvingly he added an important caveat. Recognising these roles could conflict, he maintained that preservation of public tranquillity had to come first (1981, paras 4.56–4.57). If a drive for crime control supported by the majority were to threaten consent by curbing the interests of the minority, and the police had to resort to coercion on behalf of the majority, it would ultimately curb the rights of the majority as well as the minority. Once one accepts that law enforcement is subordinate to securing civil order, the argument that police can withhold negotiation over their exercise of discretion becomes untenable. Order maintenance being prime in the forms of policing requiring the exercise of discretion, the issue of external influence on policy regulating its exercise must be negotiated.

Negotiating demands for particular priorities to be met would make some of the hard choices that police confront better understood, and could extend support for the police. A Police Community Consultation Group (PCCG) demanding extra patrols in a high burglary residential area may need to be shown how this would affect town centre public order. Such discussions do take place, but the PCCG is a forum without decision-making powers, and we have already seen that as a vehicle for localism the police authorities have been steadily undermined. The interesting thing is that the arrangements implemented in the 90s, that could be construed as seeking to enable just such debate over choices, have been interpreted in police authority practice as a managerialist exercise in preparing a formal annual plan. Accountability arrangements have resulted in, and been fed by, substantial public disengagement.

State, government and the police institution

Even if achieving a democratic control of policing would spearhead a reconstruction of declining communities as political entities in which the disaffiliated could be re-engaged, conflict will endure. Postmodern critical theory has moved away from concentration on social class, but the critique of the state as 'neutral' remains essential. The liberal-democratic idea that the state is a neutral arbiter implies that it seeks balance and the benefit of society as a whole. Central to the liberal-democratic view is the idea that the elected government controls state institutions, and 'government' and 'state' are used interchangeably. However, government is more accurately seen as one institution comprising the state, bearing executive authority, but itself limited in respect of other state institutions. Latterly the concept of 'governance' has extended this perspective to quasi- and non-state institutions. A jostling to advance specific institutional interests is more plausible than a monolith, but means that conflict is regular and endemic.

Monolithic assumptions are readily rebutted by evidence of conflict in government/police relations. In 1989, Avon and Somerset Police refused to fund further inquiries into the convictions of those charged with the Guildford pub bombings because the Home Office had not reimbursed it for work already done, and sued the Home Office. The force said it was a constitutional issue: continuing with the inquiry could leave the force without resources for local policing (*Guardian*, 10 April 1989). The long march to the 'extended policing family' of the 21st century, from the Home Secretary's 1989 declaration that he was very comfortable with private sector policing and had no intention of regulating it, on to the furious debates over the 1993 Sheehy proposals, the implementation of Council-run 'estate patrol' schemes, and the emergence of 'neighbourhood wardens' and Police Community Support Officers in 2003, has been consistently accompanied by dire warnings from the Federation, chief officers, and sometimes both. Yet the diffusion of interests represented by the governance perspective has to negotiate the fact that one party, central government, has been steadily increasing its authority. It is not so much that the diffusion of social control to other agencies reduces central government's dominion as that it adds to that of the other agencies. Regulation extends to the previously unregulated while the state advances its power over the areas it has long claimed.

The sustained impetus to centralisation certainly has strands that make constitutional accountability a less important constraint. The growth in policing services and operations requires regional and national organisation. Mounting operations against organised crime and terrorism are a further impetus. Another is the privatisation agenda; new agencies like the Forensic Science Service require a national 'customer base' for financial viability. Reiner has shown that chief constables have become a cohesive power-elite whose promotional progress depends on the Home Office. The power lies in the nexus of Home Office and senior officer interests (Reiner, 1992). Until recently the Home Secretary was London's 'police authority', circumstances tending to chief officer control. Relinquishing this curious arrangement was steadfastly resisted until public demand was overwhelming. The reason goes to the heart of central government's relation with the police. A 1928 article by Sir Edward Troup, a Home Office official, stated that:

> [t]he central government should have complete control of the police in the seat of government. It would be intolerable that the legislature or executive should be at the mercy of a police force controlled by a municipal authority which might come into violent conflict with the national authority. (Troup, 1928)

This bizarre anxiety is the sort of consideration those who must see to the preservation of the state find highly compelling. Not until the Police Act 1996 and the Greater London Authority Act 1999 did London get its own Metropolitan Police Authority; Troup was finally seen off in a provision that the Home Secretary had to heed representations on Commissioner and Deputy Commissioner appointments made by the Mayor, the first being left-winger Ken Livingstone, although the posts formally remain Crown appointments made on the Home Secretary's recommendation.

The Inspectorate occupies a significant position between central government, chief constables, and police authorities. It develops and promotes policy, 'advises' chiefs, co-ordinates with the efficiency oversight of the Audit Commission and plays a large role in headhunting the rising generation of police leaders. The Inspectorate shapes and co-ordinates police practice, but the policies it promotes are ultimately those of the Home Office. It has shown itself capable of pushing chiefs to adopt priorities they have resisted, such as the privatisation agenda. The Inspectorate can also be a line of communication to chiefs in respect of covert messages. During the miner's strike it was the Inspectorate that made clear that government would provide resources to ensure that the picketing was 'adequately' policed. The Inspectorate's relations with police authorities are more distant. Like ACPO, the Inspectorate impacts on authorities indirectly via policies, but in the form that these are interpreted by the chief.

If a government chose to take emergency powers it could have a national police force overnight. The Home Secretary may, by order under the Police Act 1996, abolish any force except the Met and City of London forces, and alter the size of police areas, except that of the City force. Short of this, the training of chiefs and their inheritance of doctrines of maintaining police neutrality and independence, have so far militated against a national force. More important is their sense of being a separate power bloc, exemplified by ACPO's rise. Formally, ACPO is a simple professional association, with no statutory basis nor legal accountability;

but its effective power is great, both in respect of policy formation and more directly. ACPO wrote the public order tactics manual, which it would not show to its own constables, and was the mouthpiece of the Home Office in public order training. ACPO officers convene the committees providing the interface between Regional Crime Squads and the Special Branch, and its president commands the Mutual Aid Centre which effectively comprises a national force at precisely the times when police actions will be most contentious.

Despite the formalisation of mutual aid arrangements by the Police Act 1996, it remains questionable how police authorities can discharge their legal responsibility for the adequacy and efficiency of the force under mutual aid circumstances. Each police authority is explicitly denied a voice in deciding whether aid should be requested or granted. During the coal dispute this obliged authorities to pay for interventions despite supporting those on strike. Reported crime rose and detection rates fell during the coal dispute. Training and community policing programmes were curtailed. The elision of police and government through mutual aid was clearly established in the minds of many, particularly as the government increasingly brazenly depicted itself as having broken the miners. Concerning the tripartite arrangement, chiefs maintain that, whatever the formalities, what matters is the cordial, co-operative and trusting way in which it is actually operated. It is curious that the 1996 legislation, which finally responded to concern over mutual aid in the coal dispute, focused purely on the formal arrangements – doing little more than confirm custom and practice – without elaborating means to prevent mutual aid again being hijacked by the government interest. We now know that chiefs' identification with the government interest in the coal dispute meant they were 'getting messages they wanted to hear'.

There remains a question that example does not answer, namely, the police response when they get 'messages they do not want to hear'. In fact, many did not want consultative committees and none relished the Financial Management Initiative, but all complied, after a fashion. It would be dangerous to conclude that the police will act independently. The government holds the sanction of withdrawing budget as a means of securing a policy; but as long as police serve the general purpose of maintaining social stability the government can be unconcerned with any periodic resistance.

In other western European states, law and order is the responsibility of the executive, and the police are the government's mechanism of law enforcement. According to the English perspective, law and order is the responsibility of the citizenry and police are citizens with special competence who act on behalf of other citizens. The US has followed the same path; but there are important differences in safeguards. In the US, federal law enforcement officials can prosecute deficient local police, a particularly important power in respect of racial discrimination. Federal constitutional rights enable a 'constitutional tort', where a civil action for damages can be mounted for denial of rights by public officials. English common law rights pertinent to police malpractice are restricted to false imprisonment, assault and trespass. The Fourth Amendment to the US Constitution requires that arrests and searches be warranted by 'probable cause', a more stringent criterion than England's 'reasonable suspicion'. Further, the English judiciary has steadfastly refused to adopt an exclusionary rule where police unlawfully obtain evidence. If the relation between police, state and government is regulated by an imperfect system of accountability, the public's recourse is chiefly to the law, but it is a law lacking important safeguards.

Privatisation, organisational change and the diffusion of policing

Policing is expensive. The cost of Law and Order and Protective Services (LOPS), which includes criminal justice, prisons/probation, police, immigration, civil defense, and the fire and security services, tripled between 1963 and 1983, doubling its share of gross domestic product (GDP) to 2% and increasing its share of public spending from 2.6% to 4% (Brewer *et al*, 1988: 11–12), and between 1999 and 2003 rose by 39% to £24.9 billion (Wallbank, 2004). Prior to a 9% increase during 2002/03, a rise of 12% occurred in the previous year, up from the 7–8% rises in the late 1990s. The share of overall government services accounted for by LOPS rose from 5.7% to 6.2% in 2003/04, and was set to rise at rates of 7–11% to £39.4 billion by 2008. Spending plans for 2005/06 designated £10 billion for policing. If efficiency gains were its only motivation the privatisation drive that increasingly accompanies these spiraling costs would be abandoned. There were early signs it was a mixed blessing, and doubts remain. In 1987/88, a total of 2,160 civilians were taken on, but only 1,236 police consequently redeployed (ACPO, 1990). Initial savings from employing civilians on low pay had faded, with higher salaries necessary to staunch a civilian wastage of up to 28%. In 2004 Her Majesty's Inspectorate of Constabulary (HMIC) still could not tell if civilianisation was saving money or freeing regular officers for core work; 'it is currently very difficult to demonstrate clear links between variations in staffing mix, resource allocation decisions and operational performance' (HMIC, 2004: 14).

Cost savings and efficiency are therefore not the whole story behind the changes in how policing is delivered. The changes strike a chord with analytic approaches that regard policing from the perspective of governance rather than purely that of criminology. Policing is seen as about the provision of security more than law enforcement and crime control. This opens the way for the delivery of policing through a plurality of formal/informal and public/private means (Johnston, 2002). The way that society delivers social control varies significantly over time, including the balance between private and public provision. The police were formerly responsible for weights and measures, animals, shops and even fire and ambulance services. In the recent past in Britain and North America there has been an increase in private provision. The growth of private policing is not purely due to new ideologies of governance and management, but also to the growth of mass private property such as airports and shopping malls. Resource constraints limit public police capacity to address emergent needs in such settings and owners of such space also prefer to control how they are policed. Private policing largely goes about social control not by statutory powers, but by invoking rights of property ownership, so change in the source of social control also changes its form. Private security enjoys the power to exclude; 'citizens may only be allowed access to the "public/private places" in which they live, work and play if they accede, voluntarily, to random searches, routine surveillance, or the disclosure of personal information' (Johnston, 2002: 141). McMullan's (1987) study of policing in the 16th and 17th centuries suggests that the increasingly private provision of security is actually similar to the situation before the foundation of the modern police in 1829, so that the public system of policing of the mid-19th to late 20th century was an exception rather than the rule.

Boundaries between the police and other public sector agencies are therefore not static. For over 20 years official privatisation policy has increasingly been applied to order maintenance and crime prevention, shifting boundaries between formal and informal processes of social control, and between public and private organisations. Taking the long view does not mean we should ignore motivations behind re-inventing established boundaries. These changes alter responsibility for crime prevention and order maintenance, diffuse blame when crime rises and detection falls, and can save money where functions can be thrust onto voluntary bodies or private security companies paid by residents or council budgets instead.

In relation to crime prevention, recent approaches depend on two assumptions – that crime prevention strategies can reduce crime and that local agencies can carry out the desired policies; but there are serious obstacles to situational and social approaches to crime reduction. For example, physical barriers to entry only help reduce crime in disadvantaged estates if accompanied by other measures. Entryphones are effective deterrents to burglary mainly when used in conjunction with caretakers (Farr and Osborn, 1997). Indeed, reliance on technology can be counterproductive. Foster reports that a CCTV scheme in a high-crime estate 'ended up facilitating crime rather than preventing it by providing offenders living in the tower blocks with visual access (through mini TV screens in their flats) revealing who was entering and leaving the building' (Foster, 2002: 185). It had been assumed that offenders all lived outside the blocks; resident criminals used the CCTV to identify when flats were vacant and they could safely break in. Where stable communities in good relation with police are lacking, 'formal estate management control and informal community controls are as, if not more, important than security hardware' (Shaw, 1986: 93). Moreover, there is no evidence of redeployment of resources towards areas not covered by CCTV or that patrol officers change their routes to take account of it (Goold, 2005). Further, while caretakers can reduce vandalism, doorstaff can reduce burglary, and attendants can reduce car crime, people are expensive. Target-hardening may be too expensive except for large businesses and may displace crime onto smaller businesses or the poor.

While police managers talk about an 'extended police family', the public police confront a reduced dominion. Early initiatives included Sealink replacing, on cost grounds, harbour police with private guards. Under the obscure Harbours Act 1847, the new guards at Harwich gained the status of constables, with the same rights, including powers to stop and search, and arrest, but without the burden of police regulations or vetting procedures. The introduction of electronic house arrest for remand prisoners saw Securicor employees gain an absolute right to enter prisoners' homes, a right even constables lack (*Guardian*, 15 August 1989). Security firms now run immigrant detention centres. Other early examples include Bromley Council's use of security guards to patrol council estates and Wandsworth's private park patrol. A private security firm was hired at Wyke Regis, Dorset, to patrol streets half-hourly after dark; patrols were linked to the police station ('Village patrols to replace police', *Guardian*, 3 June 1993). Britain's first council-funded community policing was in Sedgefield, where 11 ex-soldiers and security guards patrolled neighbourhoods. Patrol cars, walkie-talkies and an electronic map were provided, along with a fortnight's training and a uniform. Their role was to 'watch and report' (*Guardian*, 28 September 1993) rather than try to make arrests without police powers. Durham police announced they would have preferred the £175,000 budget was spent on 'real policing'. Sedgefield's scheme had a prime advantage – universality. Neighbourhoods served by private schemes raise the problem of those who decline to subscribe becoming obvious targets ('Pounding to a new beat', *Guardian*, 16 April 1994). In 1995 ACPO backed expansion of local authority contract patrols, but rejected proposals for a 'designated patrol officer' with lesser powers and training than regular officers ('Police chiefs back council funding plan', *Guardian*, 6 July 1995).

Contracting out of the prison escort service saw an initial cut of 140 police and prison officers jobs in 1993, with a further 1,700 scheduled to go when contracting out was fully implemented ('Police and prison jobs "lost to Group 4"', *Guardian*, 15 July 1993), despite previous government claims that the officers would be freed for more skilled jobs. A leaked Home Office letter to a chief constable made clear this had never been the intention. The privatisation germ was not confined to government during the 90s, however; forces with vacant posts due to budget constraints, such as West Yorkshire, took on private sector work. West Yorkshire announced plans to compete in the burglar alarm installation trade and in providing escorts and security patrols, using civilian staff ('Police planning secure income', *Guardian*, 27 April 1993). South Wales police considered running a private security service for housing estates. Most forces in fact already operated across the private/public divide; like many others, West Yorkshire was already raising revenue from training other forces at its police college and from policing entertainment and sporting events.

Commercial sponsorship of policing was conceded in 1994, with police authorities permitted to accept gifts of money, loans or property if they enabled police to 'deliver something extra', in exchange for which the sponsor could expect publicity (*Guardian*, 12 July 1994). The issue was prompted by the gift of a van as a 'scene of crime vehicle' by an off-license chain; the van's commercial logo had subsequently to be shrunk after protests from anti-drink driving campaigners. In 1996 a pilot scheme in Hertfordshire handed undercover surveillance of suspected professional criminals to civilian observers ('Force Intelligence Developers'). Car thieves, burglars and car dealers were targeted. The Force Intelligence Developers (FIDs) had no powers of arrest, but could give evidence in court. Roles such as these often involve appointing retired officers, as with the 35 'civilian investigative assistants' appointed by Surrey police in 2002 to do paperwork and prepare court files. A third of regular Surrey officers had less than three years experience and the new staff could provide mentoring as well as their primary role (*Surrey Advertiser*, 23 August 2002). Although put forward as assistants to detectives, a main activity of the 'investigation officers' was communicating with victims, a sensitive frontline role ('New force takes to local streets', *Surrey Advertiser*, 10 December 2004).

The Police Reform Act 2002 enabled civilian staff to fill frontline roles including Community Support Officers, detention officers, escort officers, and investigators. It gave chiefs the power to accredit non-police employees such as neighbourhood wardens and private security staff.

Surrey was an early adopter of 'community safety wardens', who eventually became Police Community Support Officers (PCSOs). The wardens were based in areas with significant social problems. Their objectives were community development, deterring anti-social behaviour, reducing crime and fear of crime, and environmental improvements ('Safety wardens on a mission', *Surrey Advertiser*, 22 November 2002). The central aspect of the work was patrol as a means of providing a contact point. The basis on which PCSOs were introduced was one where costs were initially subsidised by the Home Office, but fell on police authorities after two years. This, and the initial lack of definition of their powers, led to considerable controversy. A representative instance was a scheme in Surrey where Conservative councillors made an election pledge to add two officers to Guildford's complement with borough council funding, but once elected instead offered two PCSOs. PCSOs cost around £50,000 per year, some £20,000 less than full police officers (*Surrey Advertiser*, 20 July 2003). However, local police advised that the PCSOs would free up regular officers for intelligence-led work. The appointments went ahead (*Surrey Advertiser*, 17 October 2003), but doubts about job security continued (*Surrey Advertiser*, 28 November 2003). Police authorities remained concerned over temporary government funding.

Also a concern was 'the lack of integration of officers and police staff [civilians], and the existence of a "them and us" culture' (HMIC, 2004: 12). Despite good relations in longstanding teams, 'many police staff, including those at very senior levels, still consider themselves to be "the biggest minority group in the Service"' (HMIC, 2004: 12). There were tensions in mixed supervisory relations, especially where civilians supervised officers, and the innovation with PCSOs, whose incumbents were more diverse in ethnic and gender terms than regular officers, posed a danger that minority staff could increasingly be concentrated in the lower paid job of PCSO. These initiatives, prominently informed by the new 'reassurance' emphasis on frontline policing and the extension of the 'policing family', had their downside. The Crime Fighting Fund (CFF) that had driven up officer numbers made it hard for managers to get the right mix for effective service delivery; Basic Command Unit (BCU) commanders were constrained by the need to maintain officer numbers to satisfy CFF requirements. There was also difficulty in seeing the benefits of civilianisation because 'the release of officers to operational duties was taken as given and not adequately monitored' (HMIC, 2004: 15). Across-force comparison for benchmarking purposes was obstructed by different structures, job titles and grading; even within the same force different terms were used. A number of ex-officers had established agencies supplying retired officers back to their former force, raising 'potential integrity issues' and the sedimentation of obsolete approaches and procedures. The separate development of PCSOs, neighbourhood wardens and accredited private security staff created substantial duplication in training and standards frameworks.

If there is proliferation on the public police side, there is ambiguity on the private side. The private security *industry* (which provides crime prevention devices and security guards) is to be differentiated from the private security *sector*, which includes, in addition, bodyguards, private detectives, security consultants and in-house security (Newburn, 1995). The distinction makes estimating numbers and turnover slippery. By the late 1980s the security industry's turnover equaled the government's law and order budget; by the mid-1990s there were at least 7,842 private security businesses in the UK, with over 162,000 personnel, roughly equaling numbers of public police (Newburn, 1994). In the US, private security guards outnumbered public police by a ratio of 2:1 by 2000 (Johnston, 2000), but in the UK the growth has not been as rapid and most of it actually occurred in the 1950s and 1960s (Jones and Newburn, 2002). In terms of bounding the new 'extended policing family' we may be guided by Jones and Newburn's (1998: 18–19) definition of the ambit of policing: '[t]hose organised forms of order maintenance, peacekeeping, rule or law enforcement, crime investigation and prevention and other forms of investigation and associated information-brokering – which may involve a conscious exercise of power – undertaken by individuals or organisations, where such activities are viewed by them and/or others as a central or key defining part of their purpose'. The definition supports Jones and Newburn's 'multi-dimensional' construction of policing, which varies in its sectoral location, the type of space in which the practice is typically located, the legal powers held by its practitioners, the functional range and remit, and its geographical level of operation. The best estimate of the size of the private sector of UK policing on the basis of dividing policing organisations into public and private depending on the source of funding and status of the employees put it at 0.3 million staff in 2000, mostly engaged in guarding services and supplying security equipment. However, it should be noted that both the revival of the parks police (for example, Wandsworth) and the increase of uniformed personnel without formal police powers (for example, the Sedgefield Community Force) were public sector innovations.

As the 'multi-dimensional' idea suggests, it becomes harder to distinguish private versus public. For example, public sector policing is not confined to public space, nor does private policing happen only in private. Organisations like the parks police and the private security companies trade on 'legal uncertainty, lack of public awareness and the symbolic authority of uniformed force to apply a generous working definition of their powers' (Walker, 2000: 267). The conclusion of the multi-dimensional model is that an expanding policing sector means we should not overstate the differences between public and private policing. If estimating employees and turnover is difficult, so must it also be for citizens to know whether on a given occasion they are being dealt with by government using sworn officers, a private company using civilian employees, a private company using public police, or by government employing citizen volunteers (Bayley and Shearing, 1996).

Official enthusiasm for private security has not been matched by an effort to control the industry. Regulation and accountability have been contentious enough regarding the public police; government has until lately not even tried with the private variety (Loader, 2000). The system that successive Home Secretaries refused to regulate had no statutory licensing, code of practice, professional guidelines, means of checking prospective employees' criminal records, complaints procedure or accountability mechanism. Many companies remain outside the industry's voluntary association. These are conditions ripe for inequities in the distribution of security and risk; indeed, one might argue from the kinds of institutions comprising mass private space that they are by definition aimed at the better off. For government to hide behind the private nature of the industry is to dodge its ethical responsibility to secure the equitable treatment of all of its citizens (Bayley and Shearing, 1996). Concern is not confined to academic commentators. ACPO has regularly warned of rogues from the outset of the privatisation period, reporting in 1988 that over half the 600 'cowboy' firms were run by or employed people with criminal records. The evidence of contemporary scandals, such as that leading to the suspension of a large group of private security staff in 2005 for racial abuse of those they were guarding at immigration centres, suggests that the 'rogue' perspective wrongly casts a generic problem as an individual one ('Detention under Cover: the Real Story', BBC 1 television, 2 March 2005). Describing motives expressed by private guards as ranging from 'an unrefined sense of civic duty to a thirst for power and a simple desire to make money', Pilkington (1989) quoted a Birmingham patrol as saying '"it makes you feel like you've earned your money if you get a nicking, and if people hear you've caught a villain it's good for business"'. Tenants' leaders on estates with private schemes have made it plain they want 'heavier patrols and more arrests', and for guards to have full police powers. The dangers are obvious; the links between tenants' associations and racist organisations are well known, and paying twice for policing keeps the issue of crime before the public, exaggerating fear of crime. The Adam Smith Institute suggested police could be financed through an insurance-based system (*Guardian*, 28 February 1989), with unclear consequences for the non-subscribing poor. Residents would decide what laws should be enforced, as private police do not have to enforce criminal law, only private regulations. Against such a context some forecast a situation where public police focus on proactive 'bandit catching' and paramilitary public order policing, and community policing and crime prevention falls largely to private companies, voluntary groups and local authorities (Loader, 1997). However, current developments, with the implementation of PCSOs and the granting of certain formal powers to 'accredited' private security employees, suggests a more familiar mixed picture. The public may learn nostalgia for the relatively brief historical moment when it was clear enough who authorised policing, who provided it, and who decided how it should be done.

Faced by the longstanding under-regulation of private security in the UK relative to other European states, the Home Affairs Select Committee criticised the industry in 1995 and recommended legislation to license providers and regulate standards and training in the manned-guarding field. In 1999 the government introduced a White Paper proposing a hybrid of statutory control and self-regulation. A national licensing system would aim to eradicate the 'opportunities for abuse ... and evidence of criminality' within private security provision. Voluntarism remains a feature, as with the industry's self-regulating codes of practice, and some of the industry is not covered at all. The approach reflected the fact that government is limited in what it could ask for when seeking a system entirely funded by the industry itself (Walker, 2000: 270–71). The Private Security Industry Act 2001 established the Security Industry Authority (SIA). It set up an 'Approved Contractor Database' containing information concerning companies and individuals who had voluntarily registered. It was hoped that enabling the public to identify unregistered security providers would encourage the reputable to register and enable those with complaints, such as victims of violence by door supervisors (bouncers), to pursue them with the industry. The SIA regulates door supervisors by criminal record checks, excluding those with 'unacceptable criminal histories', but not those who have completed two crime-free years since their most recent sentence, five years for serious offences. Unlicensed door supervisors are committing a criminal offence, as are companies offering their services and premises at which they work. Licensing is contingent on attending a 4–5 day training course. Violations of the scheme's provisions result in fines or, for serious breaches, imprisonment.

It is noteworthy that the most clearly regulatory element of the new system is directed at individuals rather than directly at companies. These provisions replaced voluntary schemes run by local authorities in response to the levels of violence associated with door supervisors who increasingly play a routine public order role previously performed by police. Measures applicable to other major elements of the industry's work, notably guarding, are not marked by similar firmness. Indeed, if 'accredited', those performing guarding functions gain some formal police powers. In the context of immigration detention centres and private sector prisons, private security employees held such powers ahead of the setting up of the SIA. The precedent was not encouraging. In 2005 the GSL private security firm suspended 15 staff from frontline duties following a television expose that revealed them racially and physically abusing asylum-seekers and immigrant detainees in their care at a facility in Cambridge and at Heathrow Airport. The staff were filmed kicking detainees out of bed, and discussing how they committed assaults on their charges in lifts where there was no CCTV coverage ('Detention under Cover: the Real Story', BBC 1 television, 2 March 2005). These circumstances bespeak the dynamics of collective deviance in facilities such as Guantanamo Bay and Abu Ghraib rather than the actions of the occasional 'rogue'. It has to be questioned whether a 'light touch' regulatory regime is adequate to protect the public from private policing.

Under our increasingly overlapping multi-dimensional system we thus no longer have the police, but 'policing', and have traded government for 'governance'. These trends find sharpest expression in the growth of patrols alternative to the public police. The governance model here is supervision by, and co-operation with, the police, with local authorities and police having joint accountability for warden schemes, and accountability to the public either as employer or via the terms of contract with private firms. Yet slippage is already apparent. The Highways Agency (HA) – a semi-privatised body, not a government department – set about appointing 'traffic officers' in 2005 (*Guildford Times*, 22 January 2005), with 100 due to operate on the M25 alone. The HA officers have powers to stop and direct traffic, and failure to comply with their commands leads to a £1,000 fine or points on driving licences. Their control centre is jointly staffed with police. Their patrol cars are equipped with red and amber lights and are painted to resemble police cars. HA officer uniforms resemble police attire. Anyone can apply. Initially, recruits 'undertake duties on the hard shoulder to learn the aspects of the job', presumably how to leap out at traffic barrelling past. By 2006, some 160 officers would cover Sussex, Kent and Hampshire, one of seven operational regions, with a set-up cost of £70 million and annual operating costs of £50 million. The scheme was piloted in Birmingham, where one incident involved a police chase, at the end of which HA officers guarded the suspect's car while officers took him to the station, saving 20 minutes of police time. Perhaps the best index of the effectiveness of all the new private, public and hybrid provision is that on

30 September 2004 public police numbers stood at 136,797, the highest in history.

The challenge of public order used to tighten routine control

Whether it is the form of 'crisis' marked by the sharp junctures which bespeak the volatility of unstable exploitative relations or that marked by grinding subservience, Spenglerian decline and pessimism at the power of Leviathan, critical analyses based on capital's crisis have not come to fruition in contemporary times. Such analyses, given new life by the confrontations of the Thatcher era, now seem unduly apocalyptic. Conflict has often marked the police/public relation at interpersonal, inter-organisational and intra-organisational levels, just as has co-operativeness and tolerance occasioned by an acceptance of multi-cultural diversity and the convergence of perspectives associated with globalisation. It seems contradictory to argue from the enduring character of conflict to final domination by the state (or any other interest). It makes our present moment history's end.

Conflict entailed by the production of social order is a constant stimulus to political schisms, of course, and the spectre of mass disorder and terrorism has given rise to law granting exceptional latitude to police. Under public order law, disorderly conduct occurs when behaviour or language is judged 'likely' to distress or alarm another person; no victim need be produced and defendants face the awesome problem of proving their actions could not have had this result (such 'offences' would be laughed out of American courts). Most such cases are conducted by summary trial and magistrates are generally inclined to accept police versions (and to have the low threshold of outrage to imagine that, for example, yelling 'fuck' nowadays will necessarily distress or alarm). All that must be proved is a contingent or even hypothetical set of facts because the offence hinges on the likelihood of a breach of the peace, not its actuality.

While such latitude marks routine public order interventions, the pressure on civil rights from disorder is most apparent in the circumstances of Northern Ireland. The Prevention of Terrorism (Temporary Provisions) Act 1974 (PTA) went through Parliament in a day in response to a bombing campaign; the Home Secretary himself described the powers as 'draconian' and 'unprecedented'. The suppression of political activity by the PTA has perhaps been of less significance than its precedent for extraordinary police powers. The process critics feared, in which the PTA legitimates the removal of inconvenient obstacles to prosecution across the board, was neatly apparent when the abolition of the right of silence in 'terrorist' cases was a rehearsal for its extension to all trials. Undermining such rights subtly prompts presumption of guilt. The Terrorism Act 2000 was introduced to cover Irish, domestic and international terrorism, and replaced the PTA as a legislative counter to the changing nature of the terrorist threat, being applicable to any terrorist act committed not only in UK, but worldwide. The Anti-Terrorism Crime and Security Act 2001 was emergency legislation rushed through Parliament following '9/11', tightening aviation security, allowing the administrative detention of foreigners suspected of terrorist links, increasing powers of financial seizure and introducing extra controls on nuclear, biological and chemical substances.

Following the end of the Cold War and de-escalation of the Northern Ireland conflict, MI5 sought new roles against drug trafficking, money laundering, computer crime and animal rights militancy. The impetus of organisational survival has long been remarked in the field of social control (Becker, 1963), and boundary disputes about overlapping jurisdiction are a prime consequence. Interestingly, chief constables fought their corner against MI5 encroachment by emphasising the threat to accountability. Security legislation gave MI5 the capacity to gather information for the purpose of criminal proceedings, but did not define 'national security', 'terrorism', or 'serious crime'. MI5 was challenging the grey areas on the basis that organised crime could threaten national security and that a small number of animal rights activists were planting bombs ('Police concern at new role for MI5', *Guardian*, 28 February 1995). The 1995 National Criminal Intelligence Service (NCIS) annual report called for new powers and legislation to clarify the organisation's role in light of MI5's encroachment. NCIS officers were restricted to static surveillance and were frustrated at having to watch known criminals disappear. Undercover officers and technical aids were lacking. High flyers recruited at NCIS's foundation were giving up to return to their forces. MI5's opening was indeed the lack of an operational arm within the NCIS, which the government eventually addressed by its legislation for a Serious Organised Crime Agency (SOCA), commencing operations in 2006 (*Guardian*, 14 August 2004). SOCA is amalgamated from the National Crime Squad, the NCIS, Special Branch, the Serious Fraud Office and the investigative arms of Customs and the Immigration Service. There will also be input from the security services. Its focus is on drug and people trafficking, tagged 'level 3 crime', with a by-product in freeing police officers to deal with level 1 local crime and level 2 cross-country crime. Like NCIS, SOCA would still concentrate on intelligence and analysis, avoiding 'parachuting' elite agents into specific cases. Much effort would involve accountants tracking crime proceeds. Powers were planned to set up a new 'supergrass system' with heavy use of plea-bargaining to persuade those with information to turn Queen's Evidence. Responsibility for combatting terrorism remains with Scotland Yard's anti-terrorist squad. SOCA's established strength would number 5,000 agents; its first director, Bill Hughes, was the director of the National Crime Squad, and its first chairman, Sir Stephen Lander, was former head of MI5. It was widely recognised that Sir Stephen's appointment was a device to promote the co-operation of the security services.

Rare but dramatic events often spur calls for radical change, and a spate of gun killings of innocent bystanders and shopkeepers in 2003 led to renewed calls for arming the police ('Gun panic sets in', *Guardian*, 11 October 2003). Gun crime accounted for 0.4% of recorded crime at the time (0.3% in London) and most involved acquaintances or fellow criminals. Random shootings are rare and the number of incidents in London had actually fallen 16% in the year to October 2003. Police estimated that about 160 handguns enter the UK annually for criminal use. Attention later turned to the illegitimate restoration of deactivated weapons, there being few other avenues by which to tighten regulation, in that Britain has the toughest gun laws in the world.

Calls to arm police following prominent gun crimes are as predictable as those to augment police powers following terrorist attacks. The Police and Criminal Evidence Act (PCEA) 1986 extended detention powers formerly available only in exceptional cases to all cases, despite the evidence of the Jellicoe review of terrorism legislation that its detention provisions had been abused (invoking the provisions had become routine and most suspects were released without charge). If a senior officer reasonably believes someone has committed a serious arrestable offence they can be held completely *incommunicado* for up to 36 hours. Police have the further right to hold the person for 96 hours for questioning where the custody officer has reasonable grounds to believe it necessary to secure or obtain evidence relating to an offence and magistrates agree. The Act gave police for the first time a general right to detain for questioning. The Act gives police 96 hours to get a confession; access to legal advice can be denied suspects if an officer of superintendent rank or higher believes it will lead to interference with evidence, hinder recovery of property or tip off confederates (Walker and Ward, 1994: 269). There are also exceptions for drug trafficking and terrorist offences.

A suspect able to maintain silence against determined questioning for 96 hours must be rare indeed. As to access to legal advice, '[w]hile direct denial of rights is rare, it has been found that a variety of ploys ... by the police can dissuade suspects from taking advantage of this legal right' (Walker and Ward, 1994: 270–71). Proportions of suspects requesting legal advice vary greatly (in Bournemouth 41%, 14% in Bootle; Walker and Ward, 1994), suggesting variable police diligence. While the most rarely used powers applied in the initial period after introduction of the Codes of Practice were detention over 36 hours and the taking of 'intimate samples' (Brown, 1989), in recent years the former has grown and the latter has become commonplace. Since detainees may initially be held up to six hours, many are released just before that, instead of the couple of hours' detention that was usual before PCEA. The rules may also be a less effective safeguard because of underfunding, as criminal legal aid is poorly paid and legal advisers can be of doubtful quality (Walker and Ward, 1994). Average detention periods have fallen only marginally and those persons suspected of minor offences now suffer longer delays due to formal processing. For those suspected of minor offences, who comprise the majority of suspects, going to the station is now more daunting.

There are also concerns over the practical degree to which the required separation of the custody officer and investigating officers is maintained. This is essential to protect suspects' interests. 'Whether this concept is sustainable in reality is a moot point. Quite apart from the loyalties and pressures that membership of the same force might create, the custody officer may find it difficult on occasion to curb a natural desire to assist the investigation by asking questions or using his own personal knowledge of the suspect' (Walker and Ward, 1994: 264–65). While the increasing challenges of terrorism and organised crime have been used to justify the acquisition of technological and legal resources that can potentially be used to repress civil rights, it is noteworthy that the main motivation for legislation like PCEA was to resolve ongoing concern about abuse of police powers.

No such niceties accompany more recent initiatives. Legislation introduced new measures against 'yobbish behaviour' early in the 21st century. More powers were given to close disorderly drinking venues and ban drinking in declared 'dry zones', with police free to arrest drinkers, and to confiscate alcohol. Undercover 'sting operations' by children seeking to purchase alcohol were legalised, and a legal duty imposed on bar staff to ask for proof of age along with a legal power to refuse to serve drunks ('More clout for police', *Guardian*, 20 January 2001). The age range covered by curfews was raised, and police as well as local authorities could apply to courts for curfew orders. There was encouragement to use the anti-social behaviour orders (ASBOs) introduced in 1998 legislation; ASBOs rose sharply from 2003 onward. By 2005 it was apparent that many were being breached, with people then being imprisoned, including people suffering addictions, such as the man addicted to fuel sniffing whose ASBO barred him from filling stations, a suicidal woman banned from riverbanks and bridges, and a prostitute banned from carrying condoms (*Guardian*, 12 March 2005).Other enhanced police powers include retention of DNA samples and fingerprints where charges are dropped or there is an acquittal, and where samples are given voluntarily. The right to object to videotaping of a police interview was withdrawn, and courts were obliged to give reasons if they granted bail against police advice. Confidentiality of tax records was removed for *any* criminal investigation. The government's much-maligned belief in 'joined-up thinking' was at least apparent in the repression context. Plans to enable landlords to 'demote' disruptive tenants to an 'on trial introductory tenancy' were considered in 2001, and to fast-track cases where an injunction had been breached, as where anti-social behaviour had escalated and eviction was the only realistic response (*Guildford Times*, 6 July 2001).

Meanwhile, minor public order offenses, such as public urination, rampant following the rise of superpubs and clubs, was subject of innovation when police pioneered a 'waterbus', a portable water bowser towed by a police car and equipped with mops and disinfectant. Those caught *in flagrante* are issued with a 'yellow card' – another police innovation – and told they can clean up or be arrested (*Surrey Advertiser*, 9 August 2004). 'Penalty Notices for Disorder' (PNDs) were introduced in 2001, under which offenders are fined up to £80 for misdemeanours like drunkenness or littering; penalties rise 50% if unpaid within three weeks. The fact of payment is legally an admission of guilt. Police can add DNA details, fingerprints and photographs of those fined to the Police National Computer (PNC), representing a 'semi-criminal class' with no formal record, yet deemed to be offenders. The fines are applied to offences that formerly were often informally cautioned (Garside, 2005). Some 57,607 PNDs were issued in 2004, 50% for drunk and disorderly and 39% for 'causing harassment, alarm or distress'.

After the last British citizens were released from US anti-terrorist custody at Guantanamo Bay, the issue of terrorist suspects held without trial in UK came to a head. Government set about supplementing the 2001 anti-terrorism legislation, which was the subject of criticism as its detention without trial provisions applied only to foreign nationals, with a new law applying to both foreign and domestic suspects. The Home Secretary sought the power to impose 'control orders' ranging from house arrest to using curfews and electronic tagging. Controlees would be barred from contacting family or colleagues, or using the phone or Internet. It would be a violation to go shopping or enter one's garden. Interestingly, when MPs of all parties attacked the powers it was argued that their imposition when the Home Secretary had grounds for 'reasonably suspecting' terrorist involvement was a 'very low threshold' to apply (Ian Macdonald MP, 'World at One', BBC Radio 4, 26 January 2005). It was also said that the power was incompatible with Art 5 of the

European Convention on Human Rights (ECHR) and against fundamental constitutional principles. MPs and lawyers saw such action as acceptable in war and during the clear threat from Irish republicanism, but detention of British citizens without trial was not acceptable outside such times.

It was puzzling, if not for the doctrine of 'democratic accountability', that the power resided in a politician rather than a special judge, as in France and Spain, which have escaped ECHR censure despite having powers to hold for up to five years without trial under 'judicial detention'. The Opposition argued that telephone intercept evidence should be admissible in court (the UK and Ireland being among very few countries where it is not) and that where there was concern over protecting sources, the security service interest could be protected by having a private hearing before a special judge and security-checked lawyers. The judge would decide what evidence could safely go before a court and it should usually be possible to then hold a jury trial. The government would not budge on telephone intercept evidence in terrorist cases, but indicated it would consider it for criminal trials (*Guardian*, 5 March 2005). It also conceded the involvement of judges, and for the legislation to be annually reviewable; but it refused to concede a stiffer 'balance of probabilities' evidential criterion. That is, reasonable suspicion was sufficient grounds to detain British citizens without trial, and the refusal on intercept evidence further meant suspects had no right to see the evidence on which they would be held on a politician's say-so. Former Home Secretary Kenneth Clarke observed that politicians tended to get 'in awe' of the security services but that 'they are not infallible' and before imposing executive detention without judicial review a system better able to protect civil liberties should be tried. As with the doubts over 'reasonable suspicion', it is interesting how the Opposition appears to help politicians understand how ordinary people regard what in office the politicians depict as robust and sacred doctrines.

Institutionalised conflict

Forms of conflict embedded in our social and institutional structure have a pervasive, routinised effect which is insidious rather than cataclysmic. It is impossible to know their precise impact on the disaffiliation of sections of the public from the polity, but the fact that they do have some role was apparent in the widespread participation in the urban riots of the 1980s. But characteristics such as racial disadvantage, unemployment, environmental and household deprivation, political exclusion and powerlessness, and hostility to the police, endure both in areas that have not rioted and in those that did at some point, but not at other points.

Riots have not been a major feature of British life since the 1980s, yet the New Labour years featured continuing resentment of immigrants (in the guise of 'asylum-seekers'), increasing Islamophobia, and a greater concentration of wealth in the hands of a small economic elite than when the party took office. The wealthiest 1% of the population doubled their wealth in New Labour's first six years while the share of national wealth of the bottom half fell from 10% to 5% (Office of National Statistics). We must seek the roots of urban unrest in social injustice, but social injustice is endemic. The explanation of the ruptures of social order reflecting the divisions at the heart of society does not straightforwardly lie in the measurable variables of deprivation and discrimination that index the phenomenon of injustice, but in their impact on subjective experience at particular times and places. The argument contradicts the idea that specific events are 'merely' the particular trigger that manifests deeper problems. The trigger and the circumstances surrounding it become a fruitful locus of explanation, because the deeper problems are always present.

One source of those immediate circumstances is perceived bias and selective enforcement. Research regularly shows that working-class and black youths are less likely than middle-class and white youths to be cautioned than arrested for the same offence. Bias need not be explicit: in housing and employment, implicit stereotyping underlies unequal treatment and institutionalises racism. The problems of racial disadvantage and urban deprivation are hardly revelations, but policies to address these well-known problems are dogged by half-heartedness and incrementalism, and even when engagement is sincere and strong it addresses processes, such as the operation of discretion in criminal justice matters, and in employment and tenancy decisions, that are often difficult to review or to attribute with certainty to discrimination. When one considers the extent of the research effort involved in determining whether police stop and search practices are disproportionate to the share of crime committed by ethnic minority people, the conclusion of which remains debatable, a definitive account of the specific mechanisms of discrimination in the criminal justice system seems elusive. Initially, researchers were reluctant to see that the disproportion in risks of being stopped and searched bore any implications for propensity to offend, reflecting entirely on police decision-making. The perspective reflected the kind of empirical evidence initially available; if the ethnic proportion of stops exceeded an ethnic group's share of the population the practice had to be discriminatory. However, as noted in Chapter 1, later research drew attention to the description of suspects given by complainants and witnesses when calling the police, and suggests police have a role in moderating public reports that are apt to over-identify crime with minority ethnicity. Contemporary research takes account of demographic factors such as the age distribution and generational effects; crudely, crime is associated particularly with the 16–24 age group, and crime rates will peak when the proportion of a given ethnic group who fall in this age group is highest. An analysis that weighs the propensity issue, as well as police decision-making, provides better means to respond to crime by other minority ethnic groups when the 'bulge' in their own 16–24 age group works through. It is a matter of understanding the processes that account for 'propensity'. To identify ethnic differentials in propensity is only 'racist' if they are seen as innate, as where a preponderance of black men amongst perpetrators of street crime is held to indicate a racial characteristic rather than to speak to the circumstances of the group.

However, it is foolish to deny the endurance of the kind of division that uses differential propensity to warrant the exercise of prejudice. The 'war on terror' following '9/11' was held responsible for an increase to record levels of racist crime in 2003–04 (see Figure 3). Prosecutions of racially-aggravated offences increased by 2,500 since race hate laws were introduced in 1999, with increases of over 20% in 2002–03 and 2003–04. Leaders of the UK Muslim and Asian communities suggested a link between the war on terror and the rise in racist incidents. There had also been a sharp rise in numbers of young Asian men stopped by police. Prosecutions of religiously aggravated crime more than doubled in 2003–04, with Muslims the victims in half of all cases. Typically the race hate element of a crime was verbal abuse. There was also inter-racial religious hate crime. While the Crown Prosecution Service (CPS) dealt with 4,728 racially aggravated cases in 2003–04, and prosecuted 3,616 of them, some cases were not prosecuted because of difficulty getting witnesses to give evidence in court; such problems accounted for 26% of dropped charges.

In 2002 the CPS had been criticised for wrongly reducing charges in over one in four racist incidents, with crimes regularly downgraded to remove the race element, and in other cases prosecutors accepted defendants' guilty pleas to the offence minus the racial aggravation. Public order was the predominant offence having a race/religious hate element, followed by assault, criminal damage and harassment. The overall conviction rate on religiously aggravated charges was 77% and on all charges 86%. The Director or Public Prosecutions (DPP) agreed in 2004 that the war on terror had fed Islamophobia and exacerbated social conflict and decisions. 'Terrorism is creating divisions between our diverse societies ... This is a period of heightened security around the issue of terrorism and that's a position that has to be managed. It would be dangerous for us to alienate whole communities' ('Risk in race crimes due to war on terror', *Independent*, 18 January 2005).

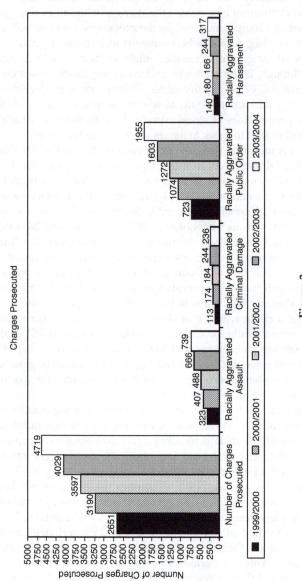

Figure 3

Racist crime trends

Source: Crown Prosecution Service RIMS Annual Report 2003–04

If differential propensity to offend does not bespeak universal ethnic characteristics, but widespread, if particularised, disadvantage, the reaction of majority communities constitutes an alternative and depressing universal. There is always an opening for politicians willing to exploit the potency of 'alien' status. Sparked by ethnic tensions aggravated by racist politicians and an inept police response, some of the worst rioting seen in mainland Britain erupted in Bradford during 7 and 8 July 2001, with repeated attacks involving the throwing of missiles and petrol bombs; 326 officers were injured out of the over 1,000 involved. West Yorkshire police had to seek help from eight forces under mutual aid. The riots involved 452 recorded crimes and £7.5 million damage. Of the 369 arrests, 260 were charged; 88% were Asian, 10% white/European and 2% Afro-Caribbean. Some 86% were from Bradford, 3% from outside the area. Some 183 were charged with riot, the most serious public order offence, and 44 with violent disorder; 191 were gaoled, including one person who received a sentence of 12 years for arson and another who received nine years for throwing petrol bombs.

Following the Bradford riots, the government convened a 'community cohesion panel'. Its report in 2004 spoke of tensions caused by 'immigration', and of a pace of change too great for some areas. It was exploited by Michael Howard's Conservative party. Howard's policy was for annual quotas for immigrants, including asylum-seekers, a point system for work permits, a stop to 'sham marriages', and Britain's withdrawal from the Geneva Convention on Refugees (measures that would have kept Howard himself out of Britain when his family fled the Nazis). While the terms of debate related to 'asylum-seekers', the reality of immigration suggested the old demonology. The rate of immigration showed a net gain rising from 50,000 in 1997 to 151,000 in 2003 (Office of National Statistics figures for legal immigration) with the majority from India, Pakistan, Malaysia, Bangladesh, Ghana and Nigeria, rather than from the EU, despite the concentration of early 21st century debate on the impact of the East European 'accession' states on UK immigration. If 'ethnic tensions' caused the Bradford riots and the ongoing rightwing press campaigns to control immigration, the tensions were with Britain's former colonial populations at least as much as with asylum-seekers and European 'economic migrants'. While only 10% of respondents to the British Social Attitudes Survey saw immigration as top current issue in 2000, some 25–33% saw it as such in 2005, and three-quarters saw a need to 'curb immigration' (John Curtice, 'World at One', BBC Radio 4, 24 January 2005).

An effective response to institutionalised disadvantage relies on means to promote the fair exercise of discretion. Since the need for discretion is inescapable, the answer must be to regulate and monitor it.

Most significant in the institutionalisation of sectionally-biased policing has been the police discretion to define events in low visibility situations. Staffing levels mean the bulk of police/public encounters are overseen by no one, since only one officer is present. In exercising 'reasonable suspicion', police must be able to refer not to intuition, hint or subjective suspicion, but to objective facts in the light of which their action appears reasonable (Walker and Ward, 1994). A range of grounds can thus be adduced, but must be 'individual to the person whose conduct is being considered and not amount to stereotyping' (Walker and Ward, 1994: 257). There must be some 'objective' basis, such as a description of an article being carried, carrying an article at an unusual time or where there have been burglaries, or a person acting in a certain way.

The framework regulating stop and search is a complex of legislation, provisions set out in statutory instruments, case law, and less formal guidance and policy. In the 1980s the emphasis in the exercise of suspicion was based on 'fact' rather than 'mere suspicion'. Between 1991 and 1999 the relevant Code of Practice, Code A, was revised four times. It moved to emphasise 'objective' decision-making and the need for reasonable grounds to be more case specific, taking account of situational context. Rather than the 1980s evidential yardstick, it was about officers as detached decision-makers, with the effect of increasing officer latitude to regard some groups as more suspicious (Sanders and Young, 2000). For example, membership of a group marked by 'habitual behaviour', such as knife-carrying, constituted reasonable grounds, as would wearing clothes, jewellery or tattoos distinctive of gang membership. Influenced by the Macpherson Inquiry, the 2003 issue of the Code reinforced emphasis on exercise of powers without unlawful discrimination. Officers should draw on a 'range of factors' external to 'the facts' at hand, particularly 'accurate and current intelligence'. The emphasis on a factual basis, albeit an enhanced one, reverted somewhat to the 1980s approach. Lustgarten (2002: 618) argues that the ongoing lack of clarity that searches without reasonable suspicion are illegal, backed by disciplinary action, means that current provisions still do not address the 'running sore' of reasonable suspicion. Although the 2003 codes said that 'generalisations' were invalid grounds, the references to habitual behaviour remain unrevised. Moreover, there are few cases to guide interpretation, and those that hinge on defining reasonable suspicion reach different conclusions on similar material facts. In essence, the Codes of Practice have less affected what officers do than how they account for it. Courts have been unable to check the abuse of reasonable suspicion, both because they can only consider circumstances *post hoc* and because they adhere to the principle that it is not their duty to exclude evidence in order to punish the police.

Recent Home Office research found ongoing problems with reasonable suspicion. In the three years to November 2004 the percentage of those arrested following a stop remained constant at 13%. In that officers needed reasonable suspicion to stop, this yield was seen as 'ineffective use' (Home Office, 2004a). The ratio of blacks stopped to whites was 6:1 in 2002–03, that of Asians to whites was 3:1; there was also large regional variation. In 2004, ministers declared the levels of disproportionality 'unacceptable' and formed a 'Stop and Search Action Team'. The regional variations suggest uncertainty about reasonable suspicion, since it is implausible that signs that something is amiss will vary systematically by force location; indeed, the Home Office itself cites two extraneous factors – chief officer policies, and the local media – that may interact in drives for the use of street stop tactics. The Action Team aimed to conduct 'practitioner seminars' to discuss with operational officers the factors informing their use of the powers, and emphasised that stop tactics related to 'the decision-making process of operational officers' in which grounds for suspicion were central. Local use of intelligence and variations in the quality of briefings influenced the effectiveness of stop and search practices. Occupational culture was also an influence, and 'long-serving officers who may have pre-set views' were a problem. From 1 April 2005 a statutory requirement to record, monitor and report applied where an officer has 'reasonable grounds, so stops, detains and physically searches'; the requirement also applies to a stop without a search, a vehicle stop, a search under the Criminal Justice and Public Order Act 1994, but not to an officer who 'engages with' a group of witnesses to seek the background to an incident.

The most extensive conflict is routine and everyday, emanating from legal and judicial interpretations favourable to the police more than from lobbying by them; much is achieved by commonality of interest. For their pervasiveness such things are more troubling than the high-profile repression of public protest. As McBarnet (1981) classically demonstrated, 'due process is for crime control'. The right of silence was long considered the most fundamental right of a suspect. During the 1990s police sources maintained their hostility to the right, releasing research in 1993 showing that suspects with five or more convictions were three and a half times more likely to refuse to answer questions ('Crooks and police "use silence ploy"', *Guardian*, 2 December 1993), a fact balanced immediately by the Police Complaints Authority (PCA) noting that over 250 police had exercised the right during PCA investigations in the previous year. Interestingly, when it came to parliamentary debate the Federation, while supporting abolition of the right of silence generally, demanded a change to protect officers from suspect accusations of 'non-verballing'. Unless the new limit on the right was restricted to what happened in recorded interviews, officers could be vulnerable to accusations that they ignored explanations offered by suspects prior to recording, and it would be impractical to record everything from arrest to arrival at the station ('Police attack plan to scrap silence right', *Guardian*, 2 February 1994). It was a pretty instance of playing both sides of the argument, in that PCEA safeguards have had the effect of diverting interrogatory pressure to interactions prior to the stages of the process falling under tight regulation. Meanwhile, it was the government's intention that an inference about guilt could also be drawn by the courts from a suspect's silence when questioned by store detectives and security guards, signalling a further blurring of the private/public policing distinction ('Stores to get "must reply" inquiry right', *Guardian*, 5 March 1994).

The Criminal Justice and Public Order Act 1994 curtailed the right. Courts may draw such inferences as appear proper from: the fact of one's silence where there is failure to mention a fact when questioned under caution before charge that is then relied on in one's defence; the failure, at the time of being charged with an offence, to mention a fact that it would have been reasonable to mention; the failure or refusal to account for 'objects, substances or marks' found on one's person or clothes or otherwise in one's possession; or the failure or refusal following arrest to account for one's presence at a place or about the time the offence is alleged to have been committed.

The European Court of Human Rights (ECtHR) regards inroads into the right very seriously under Art 6, the right to a fair trial (Liberty, 2003). In 2000, an appeal to the Court succeeded in the case of two heroin addicts whose solicitor had advised them that due to withdrawal symptoms they were unfit to answer police questions. The ECtHR found fault with the manner in which the trial judge directed the jury on the issue of the applicants' silence. At their trial the defendants had explained their silence at police interview, and while the judge had drawn the jury's attention to their explanation 'he did so in terms which left the jury at liberty to draw an adverse inference notwithstanding that it might have been satisfied as to the plausibility of the explanation' (*The Times*, 9 May 2000). The move away from the right to silence is a shift from the principle that citizens are innocent until proved guilty. New Labour appeared comfortable with dismantling such fundamental principles, as its 2005 anti-terrorism legislation was based on the Home Secretary being able to detain suspects indefinitely without trial.

There is no doubt that law enforcement by the police has assisted the population in many ways; but there is no gain in ignoring their individual and collective malpractices or in denying their role in protecting things as they are. The police have the power, authority and resources to suppress social conflict, but where the causes of social conflict signal the need for social change they only have the ability to delay the inevitable. When the concept of social change is invoked, the chaotic present is invariably contrasted with the stable past, when the family was strong, the community was solid, and permissiveness had not debased our amusements (Pearson, 1985). However, such constructions of 'social change' cannot be reconciled with history; when the facts are examined, there is an infinite regress of the golden age, and the concerns of the present uncomfortably resemble those of the past. Britain before the Second World War had rehearsed our contemporary laments, against the failings of democracy, the decline of community, the threat from outsiders. Social change was seen as rapid and decisive, and as having happened within a generation. In turn, the preoccupation with social change had been dwelt on in Victorian times, when the term 'hooligan' was coined for the 'new' social problems reflecting sweeping social change. The bottom line on the police and social conflict is stark. Both will always be with us.

Bibliography

ACPO (1990) *The Operational Policing Review*, London: Police Federation

Alderson, J (1979) *Policing Freedom*, Plymouth: Macdonald and Evans

Amey, P, Hale, C and Uglow, S (1996) *Development and Evaluation of a Crime Management Model*, London: Home Office

Audit Commission (1988) *Improving Performance of Fingerprint Service*, London: HMSO

Audit Commission (2003) *About Us*, London: Audit Commission. Available from www.audit-commission.gov.uk

Bancroft, A (2000) 'No interest in land', 4(1) Space and Polit 41–56

Banfield, E (1968) 'Rioting mainly for fun and profit', in Wilson, J (ed), *The Metropolitan Enigma*, Cambridge MA: Harvard University Press

Banton, M (1964) *The Policeman in the Community*, London: Tavistock

Barton, A (2002) *Managing Fragmentation*, Aldershot: Ashgate

Bayley, D and Shearing, C (1996) 'The future of policing', 30(3) Law and Society Review 586–606

Beck, U (1992) *Risk Society*, London: Sage

Beck, U (1994) *Reflexive Modernization*, Cambridge: Polity

Becker, H (1963) *The Outsiders*, Glencoe IL: Free Press

Bennett, T (1987) *An Evaluation of Two Neighbourhood Watch Schemes in London*, Cambridge: Cambridge Institute of Criminology

Bennett, T (1990) *Evaluating Neighbourhood Watch*, Aldershot: Gower

Bennett, T (1991a) 'The effectiveness of a police-initiated fear reducing strategy', (31) British Journal of Criminology 11–14

Bennett, T (1991b) 'Themes and variations in neighbourhood watch', in Evans, D, Fyfe, N and Herbert, D (eds), *Crime, Policing and Place: Essays in Environmental Criminology*, London: Routledge

Benyon, J (1984) 'The riots, perceptions and distortions', in Benyon, J (ed), *Scarman and After*, London: Pergamon

Bittner, E (1974) 'Florence Nightingale in pursuit of Willie Sutton: a theory of the police', in Jacobs, H (ed), *The Potential for Reform of Criminal Justice*, Beverly Hills: Sage

Bittner, E (1980) *The Functions of the Police in Modern Society*, Cambridge MA: Oelgeschlager, Gunn and Hain

Blagg, H, Sampson, A, Pearson, G, Smith, D and Stubbs, P (1988) 'Interagency cooperation: rhetoric and reality', in Hope, T and Shaw, M (eds), *Communities and Crime Reduction*, London: HMSO

Bolton, K and Feagin, JR (2004) *Black in Blue*, London: Routledge

Bonifacio, P (1982) *The Psychological Effects of Police Work*, New York: Plenum

Bottoms, A (1995) 'The philosophy and politics of punishment and sentencing', in Clarkson, C and Morgan, R (eds), *The Politics of Sentencing Reform*, Oxford: Clarendon

Bowes, S (1966) *The Police and Civil Liberties*, London: Lawrence and Wishart

Bowling, B (1999) 'The rise and fall of New York murder', 39(4) British Journal of Criminology 531–54

Bowling, B and Foster, J (2002) Policing and the police', in Maguire, M, Morgan, R and Reiner, R (eds), *The Oxford Handbook of Criminology*, 3rd edn, Oxford: Clarendon, 980–1035

Bowling, B, Phillips, C, Campbell, A and Docking, M (2004) *Policing and Human Rights*, Geneva: UN Research Institute for Social Development

Boyle, K and Hadden, T (1985) *Ireland: a Positive Proposal*, Harmondsworth: Penguin

Braithwaite, J (2001) *Restorative Justice and Responsive Regulation*, Oxford: OUP

Brewer, J, Guelke, A, Hume, I, Moxon-Browne, E and Wilford, R (1988) *The Police, Public Order and the State*, Basingstoke: Macmillan

Bridges, L (1999) 'The Lawrence Inquiry: incompetence, corruption and institutional racism', (26) Journal of Law and Society 298

Brogden, M (1981) '"All police is conning bastards": policing and the problem of consent', in Fryer, B *et al* (eds), *Law, State and Society*, London: Lawrence and Wishart

Brogden, M (1982) *The Police: Autonomy and Consent*, London: Academic

Brown, D (1989) *Detention at the Police Station*, London: Home Office

Brown, D (1997) *The Police Complaints Procedure: a Survey of Complainants' Views*, London: HMSO

Brown, J (1975) 'The social compact of the police service', in Brown, J and Howes, G (eds), *The Police and the Community*, Farnborough: Saxon House

Budd, T and Sims, L (2001) *Antisocial Behaviour and Disorder*, London: Home Office

Bullock, K and Tilley, N (eds) (2003) *Crime Reduction and Problem-oriented Policing*, Cullompton, Devon: Willan

Bunyan, T (1976) *The Political Police in Britain*, London: Julian Friedmann

Bunyan, T (2001) 'Internet surveillance', 33 Socio-Legal Newsletter 1

Burns-Howell, A (1982) 'Policing strategy', unpublished report, Bramshill Police College

Burrows, J and Lewis, H (1988) *Directing Patrol Work*, London : HMSO

Cain, M (1973) *Society and the Policeman's Role*, London: Routledge

Cerny, PG (1990) *The Changing Architecture of Politics*, London: Sage

Chatterton, M (1991), 'Organizational constraints on the uses of information technology in problem focused area policing', paper presented to British Criminology Conference, July

Chibnall, S (1975) 'The police and the press', in Brown, J and Howes, G (eds), *The Police and the Community*, Farnborough: Saxon House

Commission for Racial Equality (1991) *The Point of Order: a Study of Consultative Arrangements under Section 106*, London: CRE

Cotton, J (2004) *Police Complaints and Discipline*, Home Office Statistical Bulletin Issue 04/04, February

Cowell, D and Lea, J (1982) 'Scarman and after' in Cowell, D *et al* (eds), *Policing the Riots*, London: Junction

Crawford, A (1998) *Crime Prevention and Community Safety*, Harlow: Longman

Crawford, A (2000) 'Situational crime prevention, urban governance and trust relations', in von Hirsch, A, Garland, D and Wakefield, A (eds), *Ethical and Social Perspectives on Situational Crime Prevention*, Oxford: Hart

Crawford, A and Jones, M (1996), 'Kirkholt revisited', 35(1) Howard Journal of Criminal Justice 21–39

Critchley, T (1978) *A History of Police in England and Wales*, London: Constable

Cummings, E (1965) 'Police as philosopher, friend and guide', 22(3) Social Problems

Davies, C (1978) 'Crime, police and courts', *New Society*, 23 February

Davies, N (2003) 'Using new tools to attack the roots of crime', *Guardian* features section, 12 July

Dear, G (1975) 'The future development of police organisation', in Brown, J and Howes, G (eds), *The Police and the Community*, Farnborough: Saxon House

de Frend, R and Uglow, S (1985) 'Policing industrial disputes', in Baxter, J and Koffman, L (eds), *Police*, Abingdon: Professional

Department of Justice (2003) *European Law Enforcement Reference Manual*, Dublin: An Garda Siochana

Deutscher, I (1973) *Sentiments and Acts*, Chicago IL: Scott Foresman

Elliott, R and Nicholls, J (1996) *'It's good to talk': Lessons in Public Consultation and Feedback*, London: Home Office

Ericson, R (1994) 'The division of expert knowledge in policing and security', 45 British Journal of Sociology 149–76

Ericson, R and Haggerty, KD (1997) *Policing the Risk Society*, Oxford: Clarendon

Evans, P (1974) *The Police Revolution*, London: Allen and Unwin

Evans, P (1975) 'The police and the public', in Brown, J and Howes, G. (eds), *The Police and the Community*, Farnborough: Saxon House

FFT (1996) *Confined, Constrained and Condemned*, Glastonbury: FFT

Farr, J and Osborn, S (1997) *High Hopes: Concierge Controlled Entry and Similar Schemes for High Risk Blocks*, London: Department of the Environment

Field, S (1982) 'Urban disorders in Britain and America', in Field, S and Southgate, P (eds), *Public Disorder*, London: HMSO

Field, S and Southgate, P (eds) (1982) *Public Disorder*, London: HMSO

Fielding, N (1988) *Joining Forces*, London: Routledge

Fielding, N (1995) *Community Policing*, Oxford: Clarendon

Fielding, N (1999) 'Policing's dark secret: the career paths of ethnic minority officers', 4(1) Sociological Research Online

Fielding, N (2001a) 'Community policing: fighting crime or fighting colleagues', 3(4) International Journal of Police Science and Management 289–302

Fielding, N (2001b) 'The police: social control, the State and democracy', in Amir, M and Einstein, S (eds), *Policing, Security and Democracy:*

Theory and Practice, Huntsville TX: Office of International Criminal Justice, Inc

Fielding, N and Innes, M (2005) 'Reassurance policing, community policing and measuring police performance', Policing and Society, in press

Fielding, N, Innes, M and Fielding, J (2002) *Reassurance Policing and the Visual Environmental Crime Audit in Surrey Police: a Report*, Guildford: University of Surrey Department of Sociology

Fielding, N, Tunstill, J and Conroy, S (1990) *Investigating Child Sexual Abuse*, London: Police Foundation/Policy Studies Institute

Fielding, N, Norris, C, Kemp, C and Fielding, J (1992) 'Black and blue: an analysis of the influence of race on being stopped by the police', 43(2) British Journal of Sociology 207–24

FitzGerald, M, Hough, M, Joseph, I and Qureshi, T (2002), *Policing for London*, Cullompton, Devon: Willan

Foster, J (2002) 'People pieces: the neglected but essential elements of community crime prevention', in Hughes, G and Edwards, A (eds), *Community Crime Prevention*, Cullompton, Devon: Willan, 167–96

Fountain, J (1992) 'The social and economic organisation of cannabis dealers', unpublished doctoral thesis, Guildford: University of Surrey

Garland, D (1996) 'The limits of the sovereign state', 36(4) British Journal of Criminology 445–71

Garland, D (2001) *The Culture of Control*, Oxford: Clarendon

Garland, D and Sparks, R (eds) (2000) *Criminology and Social Theory*, Oxford: OUP

Garside, R (2005) *Penalty Notices for Disorder*, London: Crime and Society Foundation

Giddens, A (1990) *The Consequences of Modernity*, Cambridge: Polity

Gilling, D (1997) *Crime Prevention: Theory, Policy and Politics*, London: UCL Press

Gilling, D (2000) 'Policing, crime prevention and partnerships', in Leishman, F, Loveday, B and Savage, S (eds), *Core Issues in Policing*, Harlow: Longman

Goldstein, H (1960) 'Police discretion not to invoke the criminal process', 69 Yale Law Journal

Goldstein, H (1990) *Problem-oriented Policing*, New York: McGraw Hill

Goold, BJ (2005) *CCTV and Policing: Public Area Surveillance and Police Practices in Britain*, Oxford: OUP

Gordon, D (2001) 'Democratic consolidation and community policing', 11(2) Policing and Society 121–50

Grimshaw, R and Jefferson, T (1987) *Interpreting Policework*, London: Allen and Unwin

Hain, P (ed) (1979) *Policing the Police*, London: Calder

Hall, S *et al* (1978) *Policing the Crisis*, London: Macmillan

Harrington, V (2000) *Under-age drinking*, Research Findings No 125, London: Home Office

Heaton, R (2000) 'The prospects for intelligence-led policing', 9(4) Policing and Society 337–56

Hillery, G (1955) 'Definitions of community', 20(4) Rural Sociology

HMIC (1997a) *Lost Time: Thematic Inspection*, London: Home Office

HMIC (1997b) *Policing with Intelligence*, London: Home Office

HMIC (1998) *Beating Crime*, London: HMSO

HMIC (2002) *PNC Data Quality and Timeliness*, Thematic Review, London: Home Office

HMIC (2004) *Modernising the Police Service*, London: Home Office

Hobbs, D, Hadfield, P, Lister, S and Winlow, S (2003) *Bouncers: Violence and Governance in the Night-time Economy*, Oxford: OUP

Hogarth, John (1982) 'Police accountability', in Donelan, R (ed), *The Maintenance of Order in Society*, Ottawa: Ministry of Supply

Holdaway, S and Barron, A (1997) *Resigners: the Experience of Black and Asian Police Officers*, Basingstoke: Macmillan.

Home Office (1983) 'Manpower, effectiveness and efficiency in the police service', Home Office Circular 114/83

Home Office (1989) *The 1988 British Crime Survey*, London: HMSO

Home Office (1991a) *Report of Independent Working Group of Standing Conference on Crime Prevention* (chair Morgan, J), London: Home Office

Home Office (1991b) *Safer Communities: the Local Delivery of Crime Prevention Through the Partnership Approach*, London: HMSO

Home Office (1993a) *Inquiry into Police Responsibilities and Rewards: Report*, Cm 2280, I-II, London: HMSO

Home Office (1993b) *Review of Core and Ancillary Tasks: Final Report*, London: HMSO

Home Office (1998) *The 1998 British Crime Survey*, Statistical Bulletin 21/98

Home Office (1999) *Criminal Justice Digest 4*, London: Home Office

Home Office (2001) *Neighbourhood Watch: Findings from the 2000 British Crime Survey*, London: Home Office

Home Office (2003a) *Involving the Public: the Role of Police Authorities*, London: Home Office

Home Office (2003b) 'Statistics on race and the criminal justice system', London: Home Office

Home Office (2004a) 'Ethnicity, victimisation and worry about crime', Home Office Findings No 237, London: Home Office

Home Office (2004b) *Retaining Officers in the Police Service*, Findings Bulletin 21, London: Home Office

Home Office (2004c) 'Stop and Search News', London: HMSO, November

Home Office (2004d) *Statistics on Football-related Arrests and Banning Orders*, London: Home Office

Home Office (2005) *Crime and Justice Survey 2005*, London: Home Office

Hough, M (1994) *Anxiety about Crime*, London: Home Office

House of Commons Home Affairs Committee (1998) *Police Disciplinary and Complaints Procedures*, London: HMSO

Independent Police Complaints Commission (2004) 'Draft statutory guidance', December

Innes, M (2003) *Investigating Murder: Detective Work and the Police Response to Criminal Homicide*, Oxford: Clarendon

Innes, M, Fielding, N and Cope, N (2004) '"The Appliance of Science?": the theory and practice of Crime Intelligence Analysis', 45(1) British Journal of Criminology 39–57

Irving, B *et al* (1989) *Neighbourhood Policing*, London: Police Foundation

Institute of Race Relations (1987) *Policing against Black People*, London: Institute of Race Relations

James, A (2003) 'The man with sights on gangland targets', *The Higher*, 31 January

James, Z (2004) 'New travellers, new policing?', unpublished doctoral thesis, Guildford: University of Surrey

Jefferson, T (1990) *The Case Against Paramilitary Policing*, Buckingham: Open University Press

Jefferson, T and Grimshaw, R (1984) *Controlling the Constable*, London: Frederick Muller

Johnston, L (2000), *Policing Britain: Risk, Security and Governance*, Harlow: Longman

Johnston, L (2002) 'Reinventing governance: the case of private policing', in McKenzie, I and Bull, R (eds), *Criminal Justice Research*, Farnborough: Avebury, 135–58

Jones, JM (1980) *Organisational Aspects of Police Behaviour*, Farnborough: Gower

Jones, T and Newburn, T (1996) *Policing and Disaffected Communities*, London: Policy Studies Institute

Jones, T and Newburn, T (1997) *Policing after the Act*, London: Policy Studies Institute

Jones, T and Newburn, T (1998) *Private Security and Public Policing*, Oxford: Clarendon

Jones, T and Newburn, T (2001) *Widening Access: Improving Police Relations with Hard to Reach Groups*, London: Home Office

Jones, T and Newburn, T (2002) 'The transformation of policing? Understanding current trends in policing systems', 42 British Journal of Criminology 129–46

Judge, T (1995) *The Force of Persuasion*, London: Police Federation

Kappeller, V, Sluder, RD and Alpert, P (1994) *Forces of Deviance: Understanding the Dark Side of Policing*, Prospect Heights IL: Waveland

Karmen, A (2000) *New York Murder Mystery: the True Story Behind the Crime Crash of the 1990s*, New York: New York University Press

Kelling, G (1998) 'The evolution of broken windows', in Weatheritt, M (ed), *Zero Tolerance: What Does it Mean and Is It Right for Policing in Britain?* London: Police Foundation, 3–12.

Kerner, O et al (1968) *Report of the National Advisory Commission on Civil Disorders*, Washington, DC: USGPO

King, M and Brearley, N (1996) *Public Order Policing*, Leicester: Perpetuity Press

Kinsey, R and Young, J (1982) 'Police autonomy and the politics of discretion', in Cowell, D et al (eds), *Policing the Riots*, London: Junction

Kleinig, I (1996) *The Ethics of Policing*, Cambridge: CUP

Knopf, T (1970) 'Media myths on violence', 23 Columbia Journalism Review

Koch, B (1998) *The Politics of Crime Prevention*, Aldershot: Ashgate

Komiya, N (1999) 'A cultural study of the low crime rate in Japan', 39(3) British Journal of Criminology 369–90

Lambert, J (1986) *Police Powers and Accountability*, London: Croom Helm

Lea, J and Young, J (1982) 'The riots in Britain 1981', in Cowell, D *et al* (eds), *Policing the Riots*, London: Junction

Leishman, F, Loveday, B and Savage, S (eds) (1996) *Core Issues in Policing*, Harlow: Longman

Liberty (2003) 'The right of silence', www.yourrights.org.uk

Liddle, M and Gelsthorpe, L (1994) *Crime Prevention and Interagency Cooperation*, London: Home Office

Lidstone, K (1984) 'Magistrates, the police and search warrants', 449 Criminal Law Review

Loader, I (1997) 'Private security and the demand for protection in contemporary Britain', 7 Policing and Society 43–62

Loader, I (1999) 'Consumer culture and the commodification of policing and security', 33(2) Sociology 373–92

Loader, I (2000) 'Plural policing and democratic governance', 9(3) Social and Legal Studies 323–45

Loader, I and Mulcahy, A (2003) *Policing and the Condition of England*, Oxford: Clarendon

Loader, I and Sparks, R (2002) 'Contemporary landscapes of crime, order and social control', in Maguire, M, Morgan, R and Reiner, R (eds), *The Oxford Handbook of Criminology*, Oxford: OUP

Loveday, B (1998) 'Waving not drowning: chief constables and the new configuration of accountability in the provinces', 1 International Journal of Police Science and Management 133

Loveday, B (2000) 'Crime at the core?', in Leishman, F, Loveday, B and Savage, S (eds), *Core Issues in Policing*, Harlow: Longman

Lurigio, P and Rosenbaum, D (1994) 'The impact of community policing on police personnel', in Rosenbaum, D (ed), *The Challenge of CP: Testing the Promises*, London: Sage

Lurigio, P and Skogan, W (1994) 'Winning the hearts and minds of police officers: an assessment of staff perceptions of CP in Chicago', 40 Crime and Delinquency 315–30

Lustgarten, L (1986) *The Governance of Police*, London: Sweet & Maxwell

Lustgarten, L (2002) 'The future of stop and search', Criminal Law Review, August, 601–18

McBarnet, D (1981) *Conviction: Law, the State and the Construction of Justice*, Basingstoke: Macmillan

McCabe, S and Wallington, P (1988) *Police, Public Order and Civil Liberties*, London: Routledge

McMullan, J (1987) 'Policing the criminal underworld: state power and decentralised social control in London 1550–1700', in Lowman, J (ed), *Transcarceration*, Aldershot: Gower, 119–38

Maguire, M (2000) 'Policing by risks and targets: some dimensions and implications of intelligence-led social control', 9/4 Policing and Society 315–37

Maguire, M (2003) 'Criminal investigation and crime control', in Newburn, T (ed), *Handbook of Policing*, Cullompton, Devon: Willan

Maguire, M and Corbett, C (1989) 'Patterns and profiles of complaints against police', in Morgan, R and Smith, D (eds), *Coming to Terms with Policing*, London: Routledge

Maguire, M and John, T (1995) *Intelligence, Surveillance and Informants*, London: Home Office

Manning, P (1977) *Police Work*, Cambridge MA: MIT Press

Manning, P (1982) 'Modern police administration', in Donelan, R (ed), *The Maintenance of Order in Society*, Ottawa: Ministry of Supply

Manolias, M and Hyatt-Williams, A (1988) *Stress in the Police Service*, London: Home Office

Manwaring-White, S (1983) *The Policing Revolution*, Brighton: Harvester

Marshall, G (1965) *The Police and Government*, London: Methuen

Marshall, P (1975) 'Urban stress and policing', in Brown, J and Howes, G (eds), *The Police and the Community*, Farnborough: Saxon House

Maslach, C and Jackson, S (1981) 'Burned out cops and their families', in Territo, L and Vetter, H (eds), *Stress and Police Personnel*, Boston: Allyn & Bacon

Melville, N (1999) *The Taming of the Blue: Regulating Police Misconduct in South Africa*, Pretoria: Human Sciences Research Council

Metropolitan Police (2000) *Annual Report*, London: Metropolitan Police

Miller, J, Bland, N and Quinton, P (2002) *The Impact of Stops and Searches on Crime and the Community*, London: Home Office

Mitchell, B (1984) 'The role of the public in criminal detection', Criminal Law Review 459–66

Morgan, J (1988) *Conflict and Order*, Oxford: OUP

Morgan, R and Newburn, T (1997) *The Future of Policing*, Oxford: Clarendon

Moston, S and Stephenson, G (1993) *The Questioning and Interviewing of Suspects Outside the Police Station*, London: HMSO

Muir, W (1977) *Police: Streetcorner Politicians*, Chicago: University of Chicago Press

Murdoch, G (1984) 'Reporting the riots', in Benyon, J (ed) *Scarman and After*, London: Pergamon

Newburn, T (1994) 'Private security industry set to outstrip the police', Social Sciences, Issue 25, Swindon: ESRC

Newburn, T (1995) *Crime and Criminal Justice Policy*, Harlow: Longman

Newburn, T (2003) *Handbook of Policing*, Cullompton, Devon: Willan

Newburn, T and Jones, T (2002) *Consultation by Crime and Disorder Partnerships*, London: Home Office

Norris, C (1995) 'Video charts', 20 Criminal Justice Matters 7–8

Northern Ireland Office (1986) *Commentary on Crime Statistics*, Belfast: Northern Ireland Office

O'Malley, P (1992) 'Risk, power and crime prevention', 21(3) Economy and Society 252–75

Oliver, I (1987) *Police, Government and Accountability*, London: Macmillan

Parker, N (2004) 'Coping strategies and enduring psychological trauma in some "miscarriage of justice" victims', unpublished dissertation, Guildford: University of Surrey

Parsons, T (1952) *The Social System*, London: Tavistock

Paternoster, R, Brame, R, Bachman, R and Sherman, L (1997) 'Do fair procedures matter? The effect of procedural justice on spouse assault', 31(1) Law and Society Review 163–204

Patten, C (1999) *A New Beginning: Policing in Northern Ireland*, London: HMSO

Pattillo, M (1998) 'Sweet mothers and gangbangers: managing crime in a black middle class neighbourhood', 76 Social Forces 747–74

Pearson, G (1985) 'Lawlessness, modernity and social change', 2(3) Theory, Culture and Society

Pike, F (2005) unpublished doctoral thesis, Guildford: University of Surrey

Pilkington, E (1989) 'Private bobbies, public beats', *Guardian*, 8 March

Police Complaints Authority (2000) *Annual Report*, London: PCA

Punch, M (1975) 'Research and the police', in Brown, J and Howes, G (eds), *The Police and the Community*, Farnborough: Saxon House

Punch, M and Naylor, T (1973) 'The police: a social service', *New Society*, 17 May

Reiner, R (1985) *The Politics of the Police*, Brighton: Wheatsheaf

Reiner, R (1992) *Chief Constables: Bobbies, Bosses or Bureaucrats?* Oxford: OUP

Reiner, R (1998) 'Policing protest and disorder in Britain', in Della Porta, D and Reiter, H (eds), *Policing Protest*, Minneapolis: University of Minnesota Press

Reiner, R (2000a) 'Police research', in King, RD and Wincup, E (eds), *Doing Research on Crime and Justice*, Oxford: OUP

Reiner, R (2000b) *The Politics of the Police*, 3rd edn, Oxford: OUP

Reiner, R (2003) 'Policing and the media', in Newburn, T (ed), *Handbook of Policing*, Cullompton, Devon: Willan, 259–81

Rex, J (1981) *Social Conflict*, London: Longman

Reynolds, G and Judge, A (1968) *The Night the Police Went on Strike*, London: Weidenfeld

Rock, P (1973) 'News as eternal recurrence', in Cohen, S and Young, J (eds), *The Manufacture of News*, London: Constable

Rock, P (1981) 'Rioting', *London Review of Books*, 17–30 September

Royal Commission on Criminal Justice (1993) *Final Report*, London: HMSO

Royal Commission on the Police (1962) *Final Report*, London: HMSO

Salisbury, H and Upson, A (2004) *Ethnicity, Victimisation and Worry about Crime*, London: HMSO

Sampson, R and Raudenbush, S (1999) 'Systematic social observation of public spaces', 105(3) American Journal of Sociology 603–51

Sanders, A and Young, R (2000) *Criminal Justice*, London: Butterworths

Savage, S, Charman, S and Cope, S (2000) *Policing and the Power of Persuasion: the Changing Face of the Association of Chief Police Officers*, London: Blackstone Press

Scarman, Lord (1981) *The Brixton Disorders*, London: HMSO

Schwarz, B and Hall, S (1985) 'State and society 1880–1930', in Langan, M and Schwarz, B (eds), *Crises of the British State*, London: Hutchinson

Scraton, R (1982) 'Policing and institutionalised racism on Merseyside', in Cowell, D *et al* (eds), *Policing the Riots*, London: Junction

Shapland, J and Vagg, J (1988) *Policing by the Public*, London: Tavistock

Sharp, D (2005) 'Democracy and policing', 44(1) Howard Journal of Criminal Justice 86–88

Shaw, S (1986) 'Crime prevention', in Harrison, A and Gretton, J (eds), *Crime UK*, Newbury: Policy Journals

Shearing, C (1996) 'Reinventing policing: policing as governance', in Marenin, O (ed), *Changing Police*, New York: Garland

Sherman, L (1992) 'Attacking crime: police and crime control', in Tonry, M and Morris, N (eds), *Modern Policing*, Chicago IL: University of Chicago Press, 159–230

Silver, A (1967) 'The demand for order in civil society', in Bordua, J (ed), *The Police*, New York: Wiley

Simmons, J (2002) *Crime in England and Wales 2001/2*, London: Home Office

Simon, J (1997) 'Governing through crime', in Friedman, L and Fisher, G (eds), *The Crime Conundrum*, Boulder CO: Westview

Singer, L (ed) (2001) *Diary of a Police Officer*, London: Home Office

Skogan, W (1990a) *Disorder and Decline: Crime and Spirals of Decay in American Neighborhoods*, New York: Free Press

Skogan, W (1990b) *The Police and Public in England and Wales*, London: HMSO

Smith, D and Gray, J (1983) *Police and People in London*, London: Policy Studies Institute

Smith, G (1999) 'Double trouble', New Law Journal Practitioner, 1223–224, 6 August

Smith, G (2004) 'Rethinking police complaints', 44(1) British Journal of Criminology 15–33

Southgate, P (1982) 'The disturbances of July 1981 in Handsworth, Birmingham', in Field, S and Southgate, P (eds), *Public Disorder*, London: HMSO

Statewatch (1998) 'Update on Europe', 8(5) SLSA Newsletter 28–29

Statewatch (2003) 'Special Report on Special Branch', September

Steedman, C (1984) *Policing the Victorian Community*, London: Routledge

Tarling, R and Dowds, LA (1997) 'Crime and punishment', in Jowell, R (ed), *British Social Attitudes*, London: Office for National Statistics

Thomas, T (1989) 'A cautionary tale', 7(1) Criminal Justice

Thompson, E (1980) *Writing by Candlelight*, London: Merlin

Tilley, N (2003) 'Community policing, problem-oriented policing and intelligence-led policing', in Newburn, T (ed), *Handbook of Policing*, Cullompton, Devon: Willan

Tonnies, F (1955) *Community and Association*, London: Routledge

Townsend, C (1993) *Making the Peace: Public Order and Public Security in Modern Britain*, Oxford: OUP

Trojanowicz, R (1988) 'Serious threats to the future of policing', 2(1) Footprints

Trojanowicz, R and Moore, M (1988) *The Meaning of Community in Community Policing*, East Lansing: Michigan State University

Troup, E (1928) 'Police administration, local and national', 1(5) Police Journal

Tuck, M (1989) *Drinking and Disorder*, London: HMSO

Tyler, T (1990) *Why People Obey the Law*, New Haven CT: Yale UP

Waddington, D (1996) 'Key issues', in Critcher, C and Waddington, D (eds), *Policing Public Order*, Aldershot: Avebury

Waddington, D, Jones, K and Critcher, C (1989) *Flashpoints*, London: Routledge

Waddington, P (1989) 'Riot control', paper presented to British Criminology Conference, Bristol Polytechnic

Waddington, P (1994) *Liberty and Order: Public Order Policing in a Capital City*, 1994, London: UCL Press

Waddington, P (1999) *Policing Citizens: Authority and Rights*, London: UCL Press

Walker, N (2000) *Policing in a Changing Constitutional Order*, London: Sweet & Maxwell

Walker, R and Ward, R (1994) *English Legal System*, London: Butterworths

Wallbank, T (2004) *UK Public Expenditure on Law Order and Protective Services Development Research Report*, Manchester: Market and Business Development Ltd

Warburton, H, May, T and Hough, M (2005) 'Looking the other way: the impact of reclassifying cannabis on police warnings, arrests and informal action', 42(2) British Journal of Criminology 113–28

Warren, K and Tredinnick, D (1982) *Protecting the Police*, London: Conservative Political Centre

Waters, I and Brown K (2000) 'Police complaints and the complainants' experience', 40(4) British Journal of Criminology 617–38

Weber, M (1968) *Economy and Society*, New York: Bedminster Press

Weitzer, R (1995) *Policing Under Fire: Ethnic Conflict and Police–Community Relations in Northern Ireland*, Albany: State University of New York

Westley, W (1957) 'The nature and control of hostile crowds', 23(1) The Canadian Journal of Economics and Political Science 33–41

Westley, W (1956) 'Secrecy and the police', 34(3) Social Forces 254–57

Westley, W (1953) 'Violence and the police', 59 American Journal of Sociology 34–41

Whitaker, B (1979) *The Police in Society*, London: Methuen

White, J (1983) 'Police and people in London in the 1930s', 11(2) Oral History

Whyte, W (1943) *Street Corner Society*, Chicago IL: University of Chicago Press

Wilson, JQ (1968) *Varieties of Police Behaviour*, Cambridge MA: Harvard UP

Wright, A (2002) *Policing*, Cullompton, Devon: Willan

Young, J (1989) 'Are you young? Are you male? Are you black?', Social Science, Swindon: ESRC

Index |